DEALING WITH DRUGS

ANNAS DIXON

D0939996

BBC BOOKS

Annas Dixon is a social worker
who is currently Training
and Development Coordinator
responsible for the Drug Training
Project of The London Boroughs
Training Committee.

Note: Where case histories are mentioned,
certain details have been changed to protect
people's identities.

This book accompanies the BBC radio series
Dealing with Drugs, first broadcast on
Radio 4 from June 1987. The series was
produced by Christopher Stone and Lynne Jones.

Published to accompany a series of programmes
prepared in consultation with the BBC Educational
Broadcasting Council.

Published by BBC Books, a division of
BBC Enterprises Limited,
Woodlands, 80 Wood Lane, London W12 0TT
First published 1987
© Annas Dixon 1987

ISBN 0 563 21135 0

Typeset in 9/10½ pt Palatino Roman by
Wilmaset Limited, Birkenhead and printed
in England by St Edmundsbury Press,
Bury St Edmunds.
Cover printed by The Malvern Press, London.

CONTENTS

ACKNOWLEDGEMENTS

The material in this book is based primarily on my own experience as a social work practitioner and consultant in dealing with drug problems since the mid-60s. However, I also received valuable assistance from numerous colleagues, agencies and ex-drug takers from different parts of the country. I am extremely grateful to those who were willing to discuss their experiences and methods of working with me and who made helpful suggestions about material they thought should be included in the book.

I owe a particular debt of gratitude to Peter Evans, who read through the book and made valuable comments and suggested possible changes based on his experience as a journalist and broadcaster. Martin Mitcheson (ex-consultant to University College Hospital Drug Clinic, London) made many helpful comments, and I am particularly grateful for his suggestions on Chapter 1 and Appendix 1. The chapter on residential rehabilitation (Chapter 10) owes much to the original ideas and experience of Brian Langley when he was at City Roads (Crisis Intervention) Limited as the first Deputy Director. Vicky Pattinson of the Scottish Drug Training Project made helpful suggestions on the earlier drafts of the chapters on Assessment. Of the many professionals who found time to share their experiences with me I owe special thanks to Geoff Boyd, Robin Dewes, Maralyn Felgate, Kathy McGregor, John Morrison, Anne Stoker and Dennis Yandoli. My thanks are also due to Paul Burlison and the CADET team in Newcastle-upon-Tyne, Rowdy Yates and the Lifeline Project staff in Manchester, and Bob Campbell and staff at Phoenix House in Sheffield.

I am extremely grateful to Russ Hayton, Tricia Kearney and John Strang for commenting on the final draft, to Annie Barlow and Maggi Fielder for assisting with the typing, and to the library and information staff of ISDD for helping to find references.

Finally, I should like to record my personal appreciation and thanks to Christopher Stone, the producer of the *Dealing with Drugs* radio series. His encouragement and support over the past two years have helped me to translate my ideas into reality.

The rapidly changing nature of patterns of drug use and service development makes it difficult to produce information that is not already out-of-date at the time of publication. I have tried to ensure that this will not happen, but the responsibility for any errors, out-of-date or inaccurate information is mine, and not of friends and colleagues who commented on the material and shared their experiences with me.

Annas Dixon

INTRODUCTION

This book is designed to help social workers and other professionals to plan effective work with problem drug takers – that is, those clients whose lives are controlled by their use of psycho-active substances, primarily opioids (and, to a lesser extent, stimulants, minor tranquillisers, sedatives and solvents), and who risk serious harm because of them.

The introductory chapters help in understanding the historical, societal, theoretical and pharmacological aspects of the drug problem. Later chapters provide practical guidelines for assessing the nature of a client's drug problem, examine different methods of intervention, the role of the specialist medical and rehabilitation services, and touch on some other areas of special concern and interest.

The book is based on many years of personal experience working with drug takers and their problems. Many of the chapters are based on teaching notes and exercises developed on multi-disciplinary in-service training courses for social workers and other professional groups in the past ten years. These courses were designed for staff working in different parts of the United Kingdom, many without easy access to specialist drug resources. Over the years, course participants have helped me to identify the specific difficulties and problems that all workers – whether specialist or non-specialist, doctor or social worker – experience when dealing with drug-taking clients. I hope that most of these have been included in this book.

This book should also be of use and offer insights to the families and friends of drug takers. However, I have assumed that most readers will already have some training, experience and skills in casework or counselling techniques. Armed with these, there is no need to learn a separate set of skills to work with drug takers; the principles of acceptance and a non-judgemental attitude which lie at the heart of social work practice are the same for all clients. Of course, as with all client groups (whether mentally ill, delinquent, or whatever) there is a body of specialist knowledge that needs to be integrated with these generic skills and which helps us to understand more fully the drug takers's problems, the difficulties he or she* experiences in trying to overcome them and the specialist resources available. This book is designed to provide most of that specialist information.

Intensive work with drug takers aimed at achieving effective change is a lengthy and skilled business. It should primarily be undertaken by trained and experienced professionals whether they be social workers, probation officers, community psychiatric nurses, general practitioners or ex-addicts. This is not to deny or devalue the invaluable help and support that can be given by self-help groups, families and volunteers. Some current initiatives being developed by these groups are described in later chapters.

Ambivalent attitudes

Most drug takers are highly ambivalent about stopping or even modifying their pattern of drug use. Although they would like to stop using drugs 'one day', they avoid, often for many years, the eventual emptiness of psychological pain they fear will come from abstinence. They are reluctant to run the risk of finding out whether life really could be happier without drugs. This ambivalence towards change is often described as 'poor motivation'. It exhausts the drug taker's family, friends and workers. All need to develop skills that will enable them to stand back from the problem. Only then will they be able to offer the right help at the right time; that is, when the client is finally ready to start playing an active part in his or her own treatment. Most professionals develop these skills from hard experience and from sharing problems with colleagues. Many family members are now receiving invaluable support from self-help organisations like Families Anonymous, so that they can learn to cope with having an addict in the family. Like parents, workers have to learn not to assume too much responsibility for their client and fall into the role of 'saviour', determined to provide an escape route from the world of drugs. We cannot come off drugs for our clients. Drug takers have to want to stop. Working with people who may often behave in self-destructive ways can create major dilemmas for professionals who have been trained to treat and care for vulnerable people.

Although short-term work with clients who are highly motivated to change is sometimes effective, in most instances a worker's efforts will need to be long term, often spread over several years, with few immediate results. Good staff support is essential, as are realistic objectives. If you are going to work with problem drug takers, it is important to believe that clients can stop taking drugs, and that they *can* rebuild their lives. You have to feel that your client is capable of change and that he or she is worth helping. You can then communicate some sense of hope and self-esteem.

If you do not believe that drug takers can be helped then it is doubtful whether you will ever achieve much success. In short, you need to suffer from modified optimism (or enhanced pessimism!) to work with drug takers. It takes patience and an ability to judge when the time is right to encourage change and to offer maximum help. When there is positive change and your client is finally able to develop a drug-free lifestyle, you will both feel that the effort and frustration along the way were undoubtedly justified.

Annas Dixon   *April 1987*

---

*Although I often refer to a drug taker only as 'he' in this book I realise that women are equally affected by drug problems and my comments are intended to apply to them as much as to male drug takers.

CHAPTER ONE

Drugs and the drug problem

The very word 'drug' means different things to different people. For some people, drugs are those substances which are illegal and socially disapproved of, associated with stereotype images of 'junkies' or solvent sniffers and not with everyday substances that ordinary people use. On the other hand, many people increasingly refer to all medicinal preparations as drugs. One useful definition suggests that 'a drug is a substance which, when introduced to the body, alters the structure or function of the organism'. This book is concerned with problems related to the use of *psycho-active drugs*. They act on the brain, altering mood, sensations, consciousness and other psychological and behavioural functions. Put at its simplest, it is about those drugs that alter the way we feel.

Clearly, from this description, we all take drugs every day, the most common being those that are socially and legally allowed. Caffeine-based drinks are a part of our daily routine, both at home and at work. Many people regard the stimulus provided by tea and coffee as essential for them to get through the day. Although there is evidence that people may suffer undesirable effects from drinking too many cups of coffee over a short period of time, it is generally accepted that we are unlikely to suffer any serious harm as a result of the habit.

Paradoxically, those drugs which actually cause the maximum degree of physical harm, including death, in our society are also among those that are legal, freely available with minimal controls and socially acceptable. Alcohol, though causing untold damage physically, socially and psychologically to thousands of people (almost a million in the United Kingdom according to one recent estimate), is regarded as an essential part of life in western society. Despite some restrictions on where and when it is available, and indirect control through taxation, alcohol remains something that most people would not want to see banned, and are prepared to tolerate in the face of the risks. Tobacco, likewise, is responsible for a high proportion of deaths due to lung cancer, heart disease and bronchitis. Attitudes towards smoking *have* changed over the past decade, regulations are increasingly being introduced to restrict smoking in public places and advertising has been controlled. Many regular smokers have reduced their intake to safer limits while others persistently attempt to give up altogether. Despite all this, though, tobacco is still widely used and, again, most people would not want it banned.

If we compare the damage caused by alcohol and cigarettes in society with the recent statistics on deaths related to controlled drugs, the current public concern over illicit drug use seems somewhat hypocritical (*see below*). While cigarette smoking may become an increasingly deviant activity, alcohol consumption continues to increase despite the obvious damage to individuals, families and society.

Comparison of harm	deaths related to alcohol, cigarettes and illicit drugs
Alcohol *1985* (estimated total of all alcohol-related deaths)	40,000 (Royal College of GPs)
Cigarettes *1984*	95,000 (deaths from lung cancer, heart disease and bronchitis)
Controlled drug use (includes drug dependent and non-dependent) *1984*	235 *Note* – nearly half also included alcohol consumption

(*Comparative mortality from drugs of addiction* Action on Alcohol Abuse and BMA Professional Division, 1986.)

At the medicinal level, minor analgesics (pain-killers), such as aspirin, both for pain relief and for their mildly sedative side-effects are widely used. We also take considerable quantities of minor tranquillisers. A large percentage of users find they need to continue using these latter products long after the initial reason for taking them has passed. Indeed, anyone who uses tranquillisers on a daily basis is, in a sense, no different from the heroin addict stabilised on legal methadone prescriptions from the drug clinic. Both lives are controlled by a drug and both people feel unhappy if their supply is curtailed. At one time it was thought that heroin addicts were quite different from other drug users because they experience withdrawal. Now, however, medical evidence suggests that regular consumers of some minor tranquillisers are equally liable to experience unpleasant withdrawal symptoms, which can be relieved by a continuous supply of the same drug.

Barbiturates, once accepted as an essential drug by the medical profession in the treatment of psychiatric disorders, insomnia and anxiety are now regarded as very dangerous drugs. Regular, long-term use of large doses may lead to a state of physical dependence and, consequently, dangerous withdrawal symptoms. The high incidence of accidental and deliberate self-poisoning by barbiturates, as well as their popular misuse (by injection) by young people in the 1970s, led to pressure for their control under the Misuse of Drugs Act. This finally came into effect on 1 January 1985, following the initiative of the educational Campaign on the Use and Restriction of Barbiturates (CURB), set up in the mid-1970s with the aim of reducing the prescribing of these drugs by doctors in the United Kingdom.

The use of drugs such as heroin and cocaine that provoke fear and righteous indignation needs to be seen against a background of a drug orientated society which both depends on drugs to aid social interaction and pleasure, and has also come to want 'a pill for every ill'. It is tempting to take an aspirin to prevent an anticipated tension headache, or a sleeping pill to avoid a sleepless night, rather than look at alternative ways of solving problems.

Attitudes towards drug taking
Societies seem to pass through a series of natural processes in reacting to new substances, and in their consequent acceptance or rejection. A revealing historical example is the reaction in western Europe to the introduction of tobacco and coffee in the sixteenth and seventeenth centuries. Initially these strange substances were thought to be acceptable, even desirable, as therapeutic or medical agents. When the authorities discovered that they were overwhelmingly popular recreationally they tried to restrict their availability. When this failed they taxed them heavily instead. As a general rule almost all great drug crises have occurred when a new drug has been introduced into a society which was neither familiar with it, nor had established social controls over its use, or when existing controls were disrupted or abused by a particular group of individuals. Tobacco and caffeine based products such as tea and coffee are examples of the latter. In this country, and earlier in the United States, the phenomenon of solvent inhalation by teenagers has been greeted with hostility

and fear by adults and the media, despite the fact that the inhalation of ether was not an uncommon recreation among the middle classes in the nineteenth century.

Substances that attract the most disapproval are invariably used in an 'alien' manner – by self-injection, sniffing or, in the case of solvents, inhalation. Generally there is a more tolerant attitude towards substances taken in a socially acceptable way: by mouth (drinking or swallowing tablets) or by smoking. And that in itself may be one of the factors influencing an individual who turns to drugs. For example, it is said that the potential cannabis user is partly conditioned into the habit by the 'normal' and pleasurable experience of tobacco. That means that, having learnt and enjoyed the process of tobacco smoking, a person is more open to the possibility of smoking cannabis. Heroin use became more attractive to young people in the 1980s when they discovered that it could be smoked and did not have to be injected. Of equal importance, perhaps, in influencing reactions to drug users are the stereotyped images portrayed in the media, which enhance the anti-social nature of drug use. In contrast, people who use alcohol are often shown in advertisements as popular and attractive.

Our own personal experience of drug use, whether limited to the conventional use of tea, coffee, alcohol and cigarettes, or widened to include prescribed drugs, is invaluable in dealing with drug problems. It helps us to understand some aspects of dependence, particularly the psychological and social attractions of drugs. Understanding the similarity of experience, being able to appreciate the enjoyment and importance of day-to-day rituals, such as drinking tea or coffee or smoking a cigarette, and the way we feel when unable to 'get another fix' of caffeine or nicotine, helps us to begin to understand something of what goes on in the minds of clients.

It is important to be aware of our own personal attitudes, needs, prejudices and beliefs where our own drug and alcohol use is concerned. They may affect our clients by colouring our attitudes towards them and by influencing our evaluation of their drug use. This self-awareness is not always easy to come by. Some professionals may find it hard to accept that the occasional user of cannabis or solvents may not be at risk physically or psychologically, and indeed that their own regular use of sleeping tablets, alcohol or cigarettes may be more harmful.

Rumour has it that in the late 1970s an area team of social workers dismissed any possibility of minor tranquillisers causing problems for their clients as they themselves had used them regularly or at times of crisis. Being able to acknowledge our own dependence on some substances at particular times of the day or during a crisis is an important step in appreciating our clients' difficulties in controlling their drug use. Conversely, avoiding any discussion of drug use which might threaten us with the need to face our own dependence is likely to prevent clients from recognising the cause of their difficulties. There are parallels here with many other aspects of social work and counselling that invoke a personal response in us and demand an awareness of our own defences, prejudices and vulnerabilities. Marital problems, sexual difficulties, psychiatric illness, physical handicap and death are but a few examples of other areas where our personal and professional interests are likely to overlap, even clash.

Terms of reference

The terms used by professionals and the media to imply that certain types of drug use are unacceptable can be confusing. For example, drug 'abuse' and 'misuse' are both used to indicate a degree of wrongful use with a strong element of social disapproval. It is perhaps less misleading to refer initially to drug 'use' and drug 'takers' and then qualify these terms subsequently depending on their context. Even so, 'use', which is increasingly the expression used to indicate experience of a drug – including infrequent or controlled consumption – may still be equated with 'addiction'. Yet, quite illogically, the excessive use of legal and socially acceptable drugs such as alcohol is equated by many with 'ordinary use'. Terms that are often used to qualify the word 'use' may include: *legal* or *illegal*, *medical* and *non-medical* (misuse is often applied to the latter but this can be misleading because much so-called medical use could also be described as misuse). Likewise, the term 'problem drug taker' is increasingly used to qualify the expression 'drug taker'.

Patterns of drug use: some definitions

Drug takers are often described as 'experimental', 'casual' (recreational, intermittent) or 'regular' (problematic, habitual) users. The term 'experimental user' describes someone who has only used a drug or solvent a few times, usually out of curiosity, but who does not appear to have an established pattern of use. He or she may, or may not, in time become a 'recreational' or 'intermittent' user of the drug, using drugs frequently, but not on a daily basis. Drug use may perhaps be confined to weekends, rarely straying into weekdays. This group is very like the social or recreational users of alcohol. That is, the level of consumption is within limits that provide pleasure and relaxation but do not create problems of dependence or intoxication. These users believe that they can take it or leave it.

If we compare both these groups with the more committed 'problem drug taker' who, by definition, has progressed to frequent use that creates problems of intoxication, medical complications and/or dependence, the majority have few, if any immediately identifiable social, medical or personal problems. Certainly they are less at risk. Perhaps of equal importance, the majority would not see themselves to be in need of help and, to a certain extent, they are right.

However, even experimental and casual users can get into difficulties with mind-altering substances, be it alcohol, cannabis, heroin or amphetamines, especially if they mix different drugs, overdose or develop medical complications from using adulterated substances or dirty needles. The casual user is of course 'flirting with danger' by using substances known to carry a high risk of physical and psychological dependence. Many will stop at either the experimental or casual stage because they recognise their own vulnerability to risk, while others consider the experience enjoyable, but not so attractive that it is worth sacrificing money and time needed for the other priorities in their lives. Many who are able to make those decisions are likely to have a relatively stable family background, friends who do not take drugs, other interests, and some job satisfaction. It is important to recognise that progression from casual drug use to problematic use is not inevitable. The 'escalation' theory suggesting that experimental use of cannabis or heroin automatically leads to eventual drug dependence has never been proved.

What is a drug problem?
Most people are able to use legally prescribed, socially acceptable, and over-the-counter drugs in a responsible way and do not suffer harm as a result. Therefore they do not develop any associated problems. Contrary to general belief the same can be true of people who intermittently use illegal drugs such as cannabis, LSD, and even heroin. Such users are likely to run into financial or legal problems but may not necessarily meet with medical, social, or emotional difficulties. Drug use can only be said to become harmful when an individual's life becomes increasingly or totally drug centred, when the need to obtain regular supplies of the drug takes precedence over social activities including personal relationships, or, to put it simply, drugs are entirely in control of a person's life.

This means that the term 'a drug problem' can be used to describe drug use that creates one or more difficulties for users, but some will experience a wider and more life-threatening range of problems than others. It is these people, whose lives are controlled by drugs, that the specialist services for dealing with drug problems are primarily designed to help, not those whose drug use is of a casual nature and who do not wish or intend to stop.

All this means that the answer to the question 'what is a drug problem?' depends on the definition and values adopted. Many years ago, when I was leading a seminar on drug problems with a group of youth workers, I posed that question. Back came the prompt reply from an experienced youth worker, who chain-smoked throughout the session: 'The use of a drug that I have not used and do not approve of'. Subjective responses of this kind are typical. Drug taking can be a problem because it causes concern to the user, or to other people such as parents, friends, teachers, employers, police or interested bystanders. Their concern may arise either because they have good reason to believe the person's drug use is harmful on the strength of visible evidence of medical and/or social problems, or because they believe that even the occasional use of certain drugs or substances is dangerous.

Although a client's use of a drug may not be defined as 'problematic' by the user or a drug specialist, it may be seen as such by others. Therefore, as workers, we need, particularly where experimental or casual use is concerned, to ask ourselves 'Whose problem is it?' 'Is it the client's or the parents'? Or the worker's?' If the last, then this may be due to the worker's personal beliefs, experiences, values and attitudes which may be built on inadequate information, sensational media reporting and the policy of his or her agency. Many social workers, for example, are surprised to learn that one fix of heroin does not automatically lead to dependence. This means that workers have to rethink their perception of experimental drug use. Ultimately, if effective work is to be carried out to modify or stop a client's drug use, there has to be some agreement between the worker and the client that there is a drug problem requiring attention. There must be some degree of motivation, however minimal, on the part of the user.

Many workers, particularly those dealing with adolescents, are dismayed when they discover that their client's drug use does not appear to be problematic. The client is using drugs intermittently and does not see himself or herself as having a problem. When the worker seeks advice from specialist drugs workers he or she is told something along these lines, 'For the moment it is probably wiser to adopt a low-key response. Don't panic. Wait and see if the usage increases.' This all makes good sense but where does it leave the worker or parent who still feels anxious that things might get worse? There are, of course no easy answers. It is, however, important to recognise that for the majority of youngsters drug use is a passing phase, usually of a recreational nature. The more the worker reacts in an anxious, over-protective and detective-like manner, the more the risk of provoking antagonism, resentment, secretiveness and increased interest in drugs. So it is important for all who come into contact with clients who may be using drugs to recognise that not all drug use is problematic and that, as with alcohol, many users manage to remain in control or to stop voluntarily.

Understanding the drugs
So far as dealing with drug users is concerned, it is really not necessary to have a detailed knowledge of the precise biochemical processes by which psycho-active substances modify the workings of the nervous system. There is no need to worry unduly about the pharmacology of drugs. What is more important is to be able to understand a user's intentions and expectations, to determine the social setting in which the drug is being consumed, and to recognise the *symbolic* function that the drug taking serves for the consumer, especially in relation to other people.

However, any worker should have a broad knowledge of the actions and effects of the different types of drugs commonly used (see Appendix 1), and must be clear about what is meant by such widely used (and abused) terms as 'dependence', 'addiction', 'tolerance' and so on.

Main effects and side effects
Most drugs can produce a range of different effects on the body, according to dosage and frequency of use. They have an intended main effect when prescribed as medicines, and some may be used or recommended for a variety of seemingly different symptoms. The other unwanted but concurrent effects are 'side-effects'. The distinction between main and side-effects depends on the purpose and anticipated use of the drug. An effect that may be considered unnecessary or undesirable in one application may, in fact, be the main or desired effect in another. For example, the sedative effect of anti-depressants may, depending on circumstances, be convenient or inconvenient.

Many of the drugs sought after by 'addicts' are often used primarily for their side-effects rather than their main clinical effects. For example opiate drugs such as heroin are prescribed to treat pain, to produce euphoria, and to alleviate diarrhoea and coughs. In different circumstances these are all likely to be the main desired effect. So in the clinical treatment of severe pain, the pain-reducing properties of opiates, such as morphine, are considered the main effects, and the attendant psychological euphoria and the constipation undesirable side-effects. To the street addict, however, the euphoric properties of morphine are his desired effects. The analgesic and constipating action may be irrelevant or undesired. The pain-reducing effects, by the way, help to explain why many opiate addicts fail to recognise quite serious symptoms of ill-health, such as pneumonia and bronchitis, in the early stages, and may not seek help until the illness is well developed and intensive treatment is required. Addicts also have a habit of interpreting gastric or influenza-type complaints as withdrawal symptoms, and may demand opiates for their relief in the casuality department rather than accept that they have a physical illness.

Terminology
There are a number of medical terms used regularly by workers in the drug field so it is helpful to have a grasp of the basic terminology. This does not include the jargon used by addicts. While it is not necessary to use slang in discussions with clients it is helpful to have an understanding of the meaning of commonly used expressions that describe certain practices, procedures and drugs (included in Appendix 1).

Problem drug taker
This term is the one most recently recommended by an official committee (*Treatment and Rehabilitation Report* of the Advisory Council on the Misuse of Drugs) to describe any person who 'experiences social, psychological, physical or legal problems related to intoxication and/or excessive consumption and/or dependence as a consequence of his own use of drugs or other chemical substances (excluding alcohol and tobacco).' The expression 'problem drug taker' more adequately and comprehensively describes clients with drug related problems than narrower terms such as 'drug dependent'. Indeed, drug takers may not be dependent either physically or psychologically, but still have problems. Some may have problems related to, for example, 'intoxicated behaviour' that is episodic in nature often alternating with relatively drug-free periods.

This term accords with that recommended by the Advisory Committee on Alcoholism to describe clients in difficulties with alcohol – thus 'problem drinker' is preferred to the more narrow and stigmatising term of 'alcoholic'.

Drug dependence

The World Health Organisation recommends the term 'dependence' to describe 'a state arising from repeated administration of a drug on a periodic or continuous basis which gives rise to a strong psychological need to continue taking the drug; it may or may not induce physical dependence – that is the occurrence of physical withdrawal symptoms when the drug is stopped'.

Dependence can thus be divided into two categories – physical and psychological. The latter is common to all types of drug use, while physical dependence is associated with specific groups of drugs, mainly the opioids,* the sedatives and alcohol. Physical dependence is a physiological state of adaptation to a drug normally following the development of tolerance. In a sense, after adapting to its presence, the body comes to depend on the drug for 'normal' functioning. Physical dependence may not be observable until the drug supply is suddenly absent. Then the user develops withdrawal symptoms – a considerable disruption of certain physiological processes until readjustment develops (see the section on withdrawal symptoms on page 20). There may be no overt signs of physical dependence if the level of drug consumption is kept high enough to avoid withdrawal symptoms.

Although physical dependence can develop with the more commonly used drugs such as alcohol and sedatives, it is not a factor in the drug-taking behaviour of the vast majority of regular users. This occurs much more rapidly with many opiate users, especially when they are consuming on a daily basis. It is an integral part of the whole condition which we classify as 'opiate addiction'. However, despite the discomfort caused by withdrawal symptoms, psychological dependence rather than physical dependence is, in the long run, of more significance as the cause of recurring relapse. It is worth remembering, though, that there is considerable overlap between the two aspects of dependence. For example, withdrawal symptoms will cause a person to experience emotional instability, followed by an over-reaction to his or

---

* The term 'opioid' is used to describe both natural 'opiates' (derived from the opium poppy) and synthetic opiates, such as methadone and pethidine. Morphine and heroin (synthesised from morphine) are the two most common opiate derivatives.

her emotional problems, thus increasing the severity of purely physical dependence.

Psychological dependence (also called 'emotional' or 'psychic' dependence) is a more elusive concept and difficult to define with precision. It is extremely important for anyone working with drug users to understand the significance of their psychological dependence in order to be able to plan therapy. In a sense we all have pyschological dependencies on a whole range of things we tend to take for granted. They are essential to us, though, for our emotional well-being and include religion, music, sex, food, cars, money, gardening, sport and close relationships. Some degree of psychological dependence we consider to be harmlessly normal.

Where psychological dependence becomes harmful is when, as with drug use, it controls a person's life and causes physical, psychological or social harm to the individual or to others involved with him or her. This analogy between drug use and other forms of dependence also holds true when the time comes to cope without a familiar support. A sense of loss occurs, the emotional longing that affects people unable to meet their normal dependence needs. This is an experience similar to the drug user's feelings when suffering drug withdrawal. He or she has an overwhelming desire to obtain the drug in order to feel 'normal' again. It is like the sense of loss and emotional hunger that a person experiences after a bereavement or the break-up of a relationship with a loved one. It does not matter whether the object of dependence was essentially good, for the individual as in the case of a personal relationship or bad, as with intensive drug use. This sense of loss, rather than physical dependence, is what causes an inability to tolerate psychological stress.

Addiction

This term has been largely replaced in current literature by 'dependence' although at times the terms are interchangeable. It is also synonymous with drug abuse. Historically, views on the addiction-producing drugs have been largely based on the effects of the opiates which produce tolerance and physical and psychological dependence. But this traditional approach is unsatisfactory because only selected groups of commonly abused drugs seem to fit that model. The word 'addict' is still used to describe the person dependent upon opiate and other illicit drugs – despite official recommendations that the term 'dependent' or 'problem drug taker' be used instead. The term 'drug dependence' was selected by the World Health Organisation for its applicability to all types of drug use. It carries no inference of the degree of risk to public health or need for any particular type of control.

Tolerance
This develops when the response to a given dose of drugs decreases with repeated use. Or, to put it the other way around, in order to achieve the same effect, an increased dose is required. Depending on the intensity and frequency of drug use the body adjusts to the presence of the new substance over a period of time, thus reducing the effect it has. This is why increased dosage may be needed in order to experience the original effect obtained when tolerance was much lower. Tolerance diminishes after a period of abstinence. If heroin users misjudge their level of tolerance when they have been off drugs for a time and take the larger dose that they were once used to, they risk overdose and possible death. For example, when 'ex-addicts' leave prison after protracted confinement, the temptation to use opiates again is so overpowering that many forget their tolerance has decreased and that they are no longer able to take the same amount of drugs they took prior to imprisonment. As a result a number of deaths have occurred among ex-addicts soon after discharge from prison. Opiate drugs such as heroin are capable of producing immense tolerance and some heavy users have been known to take up to ten times the amount that would normally produce death. Other drugs also produce tolerance. A heavy drinker, for example, may be able to consume two or three times the amount of alcohol tolerated by a novice, although a heavy user of sedatives is just as susceptible to death by overdose as a non-tolerant individual.

Cross tolerance
This occurs when an individual, having become tolerant to one drug will show tolerance to others with a similar chemical reaction. For example, a heavy drinker will show reduced response to barbiturates, tranquillisers and anaesthetics as well as to alcohol, and will therefore need larger amounts to induce sleep or, in the case of an anaesthetic, a higher dose to induce unconsciousness.

Withdrawal symptoms (also known as abstinence syndrome)
These are related to the development of tolerance in the body and describe the physical symptoms produced when the body reacts adversely to a reduced amount of a drug. Through tolerance the drug becomes essential to the 'well-being' of the body's cells. After a period of time the body excretes the drug with the result that there is a reduced amount of the drug in

the blood. At this point the body reacts with signs and symptoms indicating its distress. These may include tremor, sweating, aches and pains, stomach cramps and other influenza-type symptoms. In the extreme case of barbiturate withdrawal, epileptic fits may occur with the danger of sudden death if not treated medically (see the section on sedatives, on page 167). Withdrawal symptoms diminish after administration of a drug from the same group, say by giving methadone to an opiate addict and phenobarbitone to a barbiturate addict.

Craving
This is the over-riding urge or compulsion to obtain a drug to appease or assuage a state of emotional hunger and sometimes physical discomfort (which may be psychologically induced).

Pharmacological effects of drugs
There are essentially two main groups of psychoactive drugs, stimulants and depressants – or 'uppers' and 'downers' to use the slang. Depressants can be further sub-divided into smaller groupings such as opiates and sedatives. The third distinctive group, those which alter perception, is made up of the hallucinogenic drugs, although this group overlaps with the others since some stimulants have hallucinogenic effects while cannabis shows some sedative properties similar to alcohol.

Depressants reduce the activity of the central nervous system. When a depressant drug is used the rate at which messages are transmitted down nerves and across nerve endings is slowed down so that the individual's thinking becomes slower and increasingly uncoordinated. However, these effects are by no means straightforward. A depressant drug may, paradoxically, produce apparent stimulation: alcohol, for example, by reducing the activity of parts of the brain which dampen certain kinds of behaviour may result in an apparent increase in uninhibited behaviour.

Stimulants include the amphetamines, caffeine and cocaine. In general they increase the activity of the brain. The slang term 'speed' is often applied to amphetamines. These have an opposite effect to depressants and may sometimes be used to counteract the depressant effects of some sedative drugs. A combination of the disinhibiting effect of small doses of sedatives (alcohol or barbiturates) and the stimulating effect of amphetamines or cocaine can thus produce a particularly euphoriant effect as in the combination drug formerly marketed as *Drinamyl* – a mixture of dexamphetamine and amylobarbitone. This cocktail effect explains why drug users sometimes combine drugs with apparently different actions.

21

The hallucinogenic drugs include substances such as LSD and mescalin. Cannabis is loosely related to this group, having also some depressant properties. Some solvent and alcohol users also have hallucinogenic experiences, but both these drugs are primarily depressants. Hallucinogens may produce perceptual distortion in time, colour, sound the vision, while providing experiences that most of us are unfamiliar with in our normal life. These drugs are unlikely to cause any major degree of dependence.

Methods of administering drugs

The most common methods of administration are by swallow-ing or smoking. Some illicit drugs (heroin, cocaine, ampheta-mine sulphate) used in a powder form may be sniffed. Inhalation and intravenous injection are the routes with the most rapid effect as the drug reaches the brain and the central nervous system most quickly. Other methods take slightly longer. Drugs are absorbed into the body in these ways:

By mouth	Absorbed through the stomach and/or small bowel.
Sniffed or chewed	Absorbed through the lining of the nose or cheek (intra-nasal/buccal).
Smoked and/or inhaled	Absorbed through the lungs.
Injected	Beneath the skin (subcutaneously) – 'skin-popped';
	Into the muscles (intra-muscular);
	Into a vein (intravenous) – 'mainlining'.

Injection is often referred to as 'fixing', sometimes as 'shooting up'. Sniffing may be referred to as 'snorting'. A 'script' is slang for a prescription. The apparatus to enable someone to 'fix' – a syringe – may sometimes be referred to as 'a set of works'.

More detailed information about the pharmacological action and effects of the different groups of drugs can be found in Appendix 1. This chapter has looked at drugs in relation to the drug problem, stressing the need for workers to be aware of their own attitudes in defining the nature of drug use, and the need to place illicit drug use against a broader perspective of all psycho-active drugs used in our society. The next chapter continues with the theme of the 'drug problem' but concen-trates on drug takers themselves.

CHAPTER TWO

Drug takers past and present: the changing nature of the drug problem

Part 1   The past

Background to the current drug problem

Drug dependence is not a new problem. Drug use, in its widest sense has been part of the British way of life for centuries. The nineteenth century saw the widespread consumption of laudenum – a tincture of opium in alcohol – and chlorodine, both freely available on sale in chemists' and grocers' shops. For a working-class family cheap opium was an alternative to paying for the services of a doctor, when treatment for pain was needed. It was primarily used for medicinal, not recreational purposes, contrary to the way it was perceived by Coleridge and De Quincey and popularly portrayed by Conan Doyle's Sherlock Holmes. By the middle of the century, aided by the invention of the hyperdermic syringe, morphine use had become a fashionable middle-class pursuit.

Prior to the Second World War addiction to morphine and heroin was comparatively rare. Opiate-based medicines were no longer freely available over the counter, while morphine and cocaine were only available on a doctor's prescription after the passing of the 1920 Dangerous Drugs Act. Morphine and heroin addiction was confined chiefly to people with access to drugs for professional reasons, or as a result of prolonged treatment for a medical condition, referred to as 'therapeutic addicts'. The majority were middle-aged or older, middle-class, employed, and were not suspected of supplying drugs to others. After the war the number of addicts known to the Home Office remained relatively stable (approximately 400–500 annually).

Towards the end of the 1950s, however, things began to change. Although non-therapeutic male heroin addicts were still greatly outnumbered by therapeutic or professional addicts, their numbers increased by 80 per cent in the period from 1953 to 1959. Whereas in 1958 the proportion of therapeutic to non-therapeutic addicts was five to one, by 1965 the ratio had completely reversed. Non-therapeutic users now outnumbered the rest five to one, a total of 1,000 known addicts.

These statistics dramatically revealed a changing pattern of age and type of addict. These newer, younger, non-therapeutic addicts were obtaining prescriptions for heroin and cocaine from a small number of private and NHS general practitioners in central London, and selling excess supplies to others, thus leading to a rapid increase in drug use. Meanwhile other groups of young people were indulging in amphetamine based tablets to stay awake and get high. Cannabis was becoming increasingly available and fashionable and LSD was emerging.

In an attempt to control the increase in drug taking, the 1965 Brain Committee produced extensive proposals to limit the numbers of doctors authorised to prescribe heroin and cocaine to addicts, and recommended the setting up of specialist treatment centres. The proposals led to the 1967 Dangerous Drugs Act which required addicts wanting treatment to attend a treatment centre. Doctors working in the treatment centres had to be licensed by the Home Office to prescribe heroin and cocaine, and they were required to notify* the Home Office formally of any person they suspected or could confirm was addicted to dangerous drugs.

Although GPs were banned from prescribing heroin and cocaine to addicts, they were still able to prescribe heroin for treating cancer or heart attack patients.

Despite the moderate success of the new drug clinics in limiting the spread of addiction, by 1969 illicit Chinese heroin was entering the country and was sought after by addicts wishing to supplement their prescriptions and by those who wanted to avoid the formal controls of the clinic system. This coincided with clinic staff moving towards a policy of prescribing smaller amounts of opioids, increasingly in the form of liquid methadone, to encourage the addicts to give up injecting.

1971 Misuse of Drugs Act
This Act consolidated the various bits of legislation developed during the 1960s to form the basis of the present controls,

---

* 'Notification' – sometimes wrongly referred to as 'registration' (see Appendix 2).

including the 1967 Dangerous Drugs Act. A core feature of the Act was to create a system of scheduling 'controlled' drugs which classified substances into Class A, B or C, and laid down a hierarchy of controls for each group. Thus, while Class A drugs include heroin and others thought to carry the highest risk, and therefore the highest penalties for possession and supply, Class C drugs carry lower penalties. (See also Appendices 1 and 2.)

The Act also established the Advisory Council on the Misuse of Drugs as a multi-disciplinary body with the task of keeping the misuse of drugs in the United Kingdom under review and of advising Ministers on measures to deal with the social problems caused by misuse.

Patterns of drug taking in the 1970s

An immediate effect of the 1971 Act was to reduce the availability of prescribed amphetamine and hypnotic sedatives such as *Mandrax*. Later supplies of illicitly manufactured amphetamine sulphate became available on the street and it continues to be a popular drug in most parts of the country for those preferring stimulants.

By the mid-1970s drug clinics had tightened up their prescribing policies, and very few were willing to prescribe injectable drugs to new patients. (See Chapter 9 on Medical and Psychiatric Services.) The reduction of prescribed opiates appeared to some observers to have three main effects:

1 Increased availability of illicit heroin from Iran and Pakistan.
2 Drug takers seeking to persuade GPs to prescribe drugs with effects similar to heroin, such as *Diconal* (dipipanone) and methadone. By the late 1970s, more official notifications of new addicts were received from GPs than from clinics.
3 Increased use of sedatives, especially barbiturates, and latterly benzodiazepines (such as *Valium* and *Mogadon*).

Barbiturate misuse reached epidemic proportions in London during the mid-1970s, as illustrated by chaotic overdosing by 'multiple drug takers' who tended to be young, homeless and at risk. The death rate was higher with this group than with the more stable opiate addict and, indeed, deaths in the latter group were often likely to be associated with barbiturate use, not the prime maintenance opiate. The barbiturate problem in London led to the setting up in 1978 of a unique crisis intervention centre staffed by nurses and social workers with medical support.

While teenage opiate use was comparatively rare, solvent inhalation was becoming increasingly popular amongst adolescents.

Part 2   The present

Trends

By the beginning of the 1980s barbiturate prescribing had decreased dramatically because of campaigns to educate doctors and because of the introduction of 'safer' drugs such as *Valium*. Opiates, though, had become increasingly popular, and socially more widely acceptable. The number of opiate addicts known to the Home Office started to increase alarmingly by 20 per cent per annum, while the age of initiation went down. By the end of 1984 the number of new addicts notified to the Home Office during the year was approximately 7,400, with a notable increase amongst those under twenty. These figures only relate to notified addicts. Researchers estimate that a more accurate figure of problem drug takers would be five times the offical statistics.

At another level, a different kind of drug problem has been recognised. The user of minor tranquillisers such as *Valium*, is likely to be respectable and female, though from all age and social groups. Many users have sought help for psychological and physical dependence. The growth of self-help groups such as 'Tranx' has illustrated the lack of adequate resources available through the drug clinics or GPs to deal with these problems.

The 1982 report *Treatment and Rehabilitation* by the Advisory Council on the Misuse of Drugs looked at the problems affecting treatment and rehabilitation services in the United Kingdom and recommended possible responses to the changing patterns of drug use. It advocated new definitions, such as problem drug takers, that would provide a more comprehensive appreciation of the nature of addiction. The report also pointed to the lack of specialist facilities in different parts of the country and recommended that money should be made available to help finance new initiatives. The underlying theme of the document is that a framework should be established which will facilitate the development of a range of services to help those with drug problems, and which will be flexible enough to respond effectively to changing situations and local needs.

The report was accepted by the government which has now allocated financial help to assist in the development of specialist drug services. Unfortunately, most of the funding is only for a period of three years and many projects are likely to find themselves without continuous financial support in the near future. Meanwhile, heroin use has continued to spread to many parts of the United Kingdom, to small towns and cities, while other forms of drug use continue to flourish.

Who are the drug takers?

The short answer must be that it is anyone who has access to drugs, although it is easier to be more specific with some drugs than others. With the minor tranquillisers, for example, users are predominantly adults from their early twenties to the elderly, with more women users than men. Solvents have always been primarily used by youngsters in their early to mid-teens, a few continuing into their twenties. Cases of older adults using solvents have been reported, but are rare. Most research suggests that this activity is more common amongst boys than girls, but there are regional variations. The cannabis smoker is most likely to be someone aged between fifteen and forty-five years, the majority perhaps being in their late teens, twenties or thirties. The users of other illicit drugs, mainly the opiates, cocaine and amphetamines are usually in their mid-teens to mid-thirties, with some variation according to fashion and availability. The male:female ratio of illicit problem drug takers is approximately two to one indicating a gradual increase in women users from a fairly steady level of three to one in the mid-1970s.

Just why adolescent use has spread so widely in the past few years is difficult to say. There is clearly no one reason. Factors such as increased availability of cheaper illicit heroin, newer, more acceptable ways of taking the drug by smoking instead of injecting, wholesale adolescent unemployment – all these have been suggested. Certainly, diminished employment opportunities have created a sense of hopelessness in a whole generation, and drugs can go some way towards countering it, at least in the short term. But not all the new recruits to heroin use are necessarily jobless.

What kind of background do drugs users come from?

Drug problems are found right across the social scale. Those experiencing major drug problems, whether due to alcohol, opiates or tranquillisers come from the highest and lowliest families in the land. Anyone is at risk who consumes these substances and allows them to control their life. The more widely available and acceptable opiate use becomes, the more people will risk becoming dependent. On the other hand reduced availability leads to decreased con sumption and a consequent reduction in problematic drug use.

Drug use can occur in stable as well as unstable families – in 'abnormal' and 'normal' individuals. John Strang, a consultant psychiatrist who specialises in drug dependence, has suggested that as heroin, '. . . becomes more widespread in a population the people using it are likely to become more normal (statistically and in other senses) than the abnormal population who presented originally. When a city with a couple of million inhabitants has only one or two dozen heroin users then this group will probably be deviant and abnormal in many ways; but as this behaviour becomes more widespread the abnormal characteristics will become less noticeable. By the time there are several hundred thousand drug takers in such a city their characteristics would be much more similar to the non-using population.' (*Health and Social Service Journal*, 11 October 1984).

Is there a 'typical addict'?
Many drug takers are quite disillusioned, and others quite relieved, when they are thrown together in a drug-free treatment setting only to find that like everyone else in the place they enjoy taking drugs, but that without drugs many have little in common, save perhaps some similar reasons for taking drugs and some similarity in behaviour patterns associated with a drug taking lifestyle. It is the typical drug taker's lifestyle that leads people to assume that all users have similar personalities and respond in similar ways to drugs. For example, the popular image of an addict is someone who is incapable of work, always on the verge of withdrawals, and who wander around in a semi-stoned state. For a few, this picture may be accurate. Yet many users hold down a job, support a family and regularly make their mortgage payments. They are stabilised, either with the help of a prescription of methadone or regular illicit supplies of heroin.

Many of the adjectives commonly used to describe problem drug takers relate to living a life of deceit and an unwillingness to make a total commitment to change. Workers will often describe addicts as 'unreliable', 'manipulative', 'seductive', 'deceitful', 'unmotivated', and 'lazy', coupled with an inability to assume responsibility for themselves or others. A few may have possessed some of these traits before they embarked on a career of drug use, but the majority probably did not. They acquired them because of the illicit nature of the habit and because drugs took precedence in their life over other activities, including personal relationships.

What happens when someone becomes a regular, committed drug taker?

There are a number of common behaviour patterns that can develop in long term regular users who have become dependent, particularly on the opiate drugs. Only one may apply to certain individuals, while others have several. The way in which people respond to dependence will vary according to the way they use drugs; their personality; their financial circumstances; support from family and friends; and the actual effect of drugs on the individual. The following characteristics *may* be indicators that drug use is beginning to dominate a person's life:

– He or she becomes more detached from everyday life, more selfish and secretive, with less interest in personal and/or sexual relationships.
– There is difficulty in assuming responsibility for his or her own life, or the lives of others who may be dependent financially, physically or emotionally.
– There is a loss of interest in eating. Money goes on drugs rather than food. Self-neglect may lead to loss of weight, malnutrition and illnesses.
– He or she has difficulty in time-keeping, getting to work or to classes. Opiate use may cause a person to oversleep. If he or she has not got enough drugs to see him or her through the day, time may have to be spent obtaining supplies to avoid withdrawals occurring while at work. There may be great difficulty keeping appointments; time is not important, especially if the user is unemployed.
– He or she is unable to continue with education, or regular employment. Where for years the drug use may have been under control, and the job as important as, if not more important than, the drug, as drugs take precedence in life the job ceases to be so important.
– The individual becomes edgy, argumentative, difficult to live with.
– Cash-flow problems create inevitable financial difficulties such as non-payment of rent, mortgage and other bills. Users borrow money to buy drugs and get into debt with drug dealers.
– Cash-flow problems can lead to drug related crime: drug dealing; theft; fraud; forging prescriptions.

Even wealthy drug takers with private incomes are at risk, as the money runs out or family members take steps to restrict access to funds. As with the wealthy problem drinker, it just takes longer to experience social damage but it can still

29

happen. When it does and the user happens to belong to a famous family or the entertainment business he or she often finds himself or herself pilloried in the press for setting a bad example or letting down the family. The higher your position, the further you have to fall.

By the time a worker sees a client with a drug problem, it is likely that there will be one or more related problems that have contributed to the user's decision to ask, however reluctantly, for help. A number of users will still be in work or managing to continue with their education, but probably only just. Regular employment provides not only a routine and self-respect but also a regular source of cash for drugs. It is preferable to the alternatives – the dole, prostitution, or crime. Fear of losing a regular income may have forced users to ask for help before everything gets totally out of control.

It can be difficult for the non-user of drugs to understand why someone, however intelligent (and many drug takers are above average intelligence), can allow themselves to deteriorate so much that they risk losing their friends, family relationships, job and self-respect. They are like fast car drivers who believe that accidents will never happen to them. Or, if they do, they somehow persuade themselves that they will know when danger is around and will be able to stop in time. Some manage to, but many do not, and they eventually end up having to receive help, usually after they have failed to give up drugs on their own. It is extremely difficult to tolerate the sudden emptiness that occurs when drug taking stops, along with the after-effects of physical and psychological dependences that come from over-reliance on chemical support, especially when the drug has served to mask underlying emotional problems. Few long-term users are able to handle detoxification successfully alone; most need support and encouragement from someone who believes that people can give up drugs and rebuild their life.

What are the prospects for the problem drug taker?

Despite the fact that heroin users risk death many times as they seek to obtain a better 'high', most do not die prematurely. Although their mortality rate is estimated to be sixteen times higher than that of the normal population most deaths do not appear to be related to the long-term effects of opiates, but more to sudden overdose or accidents. People do not then necessarily die from illicit drug use, any more than from drinking or smoking every day. However, the risk of a premature death increases depending on how and what a person uses. The same applies to solvent sniffers. There have been casualties over the past ten years from solvent inhalation. But most of these have been due to sudden overdose or accidents rather than the long-term effects of sniffing as such.

Some people suddenly decide to stop using drugs. Their reasons are somewhat difficult to identify, but they range from fear of imprisonment to sudden boredom with the lifestyle; from lack of excitement with a once thrilling drug to the restrictions imposed by illicit drug use. Sometimes a relationship with a non-user provides an incentive to change, or occasionally a job materialises to provide meaning to life. Those who suddenly decide to stop using drugs without professional help do not necessarily have an easy time, but some do manage to stay off with support from family and friends and by avoiding other drug takers and dealers. It is impossible to give an accurate or even crude estimate of the proportion in this category because they will never be known to the authorities, even if they have attended a treatment centre and dropped out of treatment. There are no effective follow-up procedures for assessing reasons for people disappearing from treatment. Many change addresses; a number are unwilling to have any contact with clinic staff, either because of a poor relationship or because they do not wish to be reminded of the past. Many clients attending treatment centres do stop drug use after several years. Change does not happen overnight. It is a process that depends on the client reaching a point when he or she is committed to trying to give up drugs and willing to look at some of the factors that may be linked to his or her continued drug use. Many clients attending drug agencies move in and out of treatment over a period of years, while a few manage to overcome their pysical dependence in a matter of weeks or months with little risk of relapsing. This group is more likely to include people with a short drug history, few drug related problems, and with good friends who do not use drugs, or solid job opportunities.

Whose responsibility is it?
Until the late 1960s dealing with drug addicts was thought to be the responsibility of the medical profession. But now things have changed. Is it the government which is responsible for coping with the problem drug taker of the 1980s? The DHSS or the Home Office? The drug clinics and other specialist drug agencies? Or is it really the responsibility of the primary care agencies, such as health and social services and the client's family? One way or another, it is now the responsibility of everyone. The 1982 report, *Treatment and Rehabilita-*

31

tion by the Advisory Council on the Misuse of Drugs, in its recommendations about services for drug takers, says:

'. . . for some individuals a medical response will predominate and other disciplines will make their contribution. For others a social work repsonse provided by personal social services, a probation officer, or a non-statutory agency worker will be more appropriate. For yet other individuals, an educational and counselling approach provided by teachers or health education staff will be best. No single discipline or service can claim overall expertise or excellence in helping drug misusers with their problems. The need for the various disciplines and services to recognise each other's skills and contributions and to improve collaboration becomes paramount.'

No one agency has all the expertise. It is a shared responsibility, locally and nationally. In some instances, particularly where the request for a prescription has to be considered, a specialist drug agency with a prescribing role, a drug clinic or one of the newer community drug teams can and should be considered. Unless there is already another worker such as a probation officer on the case, the client's drug related social and personal problems should ideally be dealt with by the clinic staff. But if no such facility exists, responsibility may be shouldered by a social worker, community psychiatric nurse or probation officer in collaboration with the client's GP.

We are all responsible

The diagram opposite illustrates the shared responsibility between different agencies, both at the level of central government departments and at a local level though interagency co-operation and the work of District Drug Advisory Committees. This concept of a shared community responsibility and response is explored further in Chapter 16 'Developing a community response'.

Ultimately, responsibility also rests with the problem drug taker himself or herself to take an active part in treatment. No one can come off drugs for a drug taker. They have to want to change. So it is, in effect, a shared responsibility between client and worker. To enable clients to take some personal responsibility for changing their situation, workers in a specialist or generic setting should ensure that the services offered are attractive and easily accessible, and designed with sufficient flexibility to meet a range of needs. In order to assess those needs adequately it helps to have an understanding of the reasons why people might centre their life around drugs.

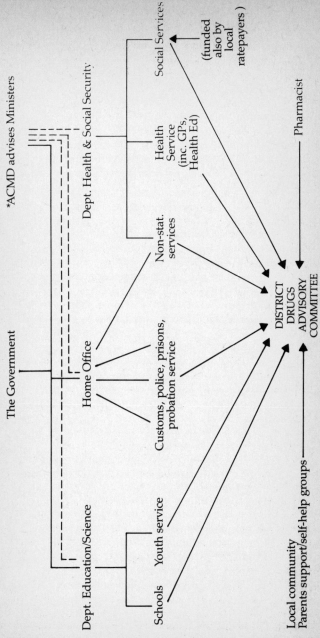

The Government

*ACMD advises Ministers

Dept. Education/Science   Home Office   Dept. Health & Social Security

Schools   Youth service   Customs, police, prisons, probation service   Non-stat. services   Health Service (inc. GPs, Health Ed)   Social Services

(funded also by local ratepayers)

Pharmacist

Local community
Parents support/self-help groups

DISTRICT DRUGS ADVISORY COMMITTEE

* Advisory Council on the Misuse of Drugs.

CHAPTER THREE

Why people take drugs

Many theoretical models have been developed to explain drug use. Only by understanding some of these approaches, and by understanding clients better can a worker design, or hope to design, the most appropriate approach to treatment.

The reasons for people – whether adolescents or adults – starting to use drugs are not necessarily the same as those that cause them to continue using drugs on a long-term basis. However, what can be said as a general rule is that drug related behaviour results from the interaction between the drug, personality, and the environment.

Reasons for starting to use drugs

Curiosity This is a key factor for most adolescents whether the drug be cannabis, alcohol, opiates, or solvents. Most young people would rate curiosity value very highly. It forms part of the well-documented desire among adolescents to try new experiences.

Availability Obviously no-one can use drugs legally or illegally unless they are available: legally, over the counter from the chemist, or on prescription from the general practitioner, for perhaps insomnia or anxiety: and illegally with illicit sales from black-market dealers in cannabis, cocaine or heroin. Legislation and control measures can reduce availability and access, but they do not automatically solve the problem.

Peer group pressures Most, if not all, initial non-medical use of drugs such as cannabis, amphetamines or heroin is likely to be as a result of contact with a friend or peer group member and seen solely as a recreational activity.

Pleasure The pleasure factor in drug taking is often overlooked. Yet it is probably rated most highly by young people and adults who are encouraged to try drugs because they have been with friends who appear to be receiving pleasure, fun, or happiness from the activity.

Fashion There are undoubtedly fashions in drug taking. While in the 1970s glue-sniffing seems to have caught on as a fashion or craze amongst adolescents, in the 1980s heroin and cocaine are the fashionable substances.

A desire to alter the way you feel It is perhaps a basic human need to want to alter the way we feel. Drug use is one way of doing this by changing a mood or providing a sense of 'high'. There are many other ways of trying to reach this state without resorting to drugs, including physical and spiritual exercise, sex, travel and the arts. Drug users will often describe the sensations they feel as 'peak experiences', which the American psychologist, Abraham Maslow, considers necessary to human happiness. Some drug users will describe heroin as a very 'seductive' drug and it may be precisely this elevated state of consciousness that they are referring to.

Self-medication/receiving drugs on prescription Many adults dependent on minor tranquillisers started because of bereavement or stress. Some theorists have suggested that opiate addicts may have taken drugs initially as a form of self-medication, to stop them feeling depressed, help them to relax, remove tension and anxiety, and so on. This may be true for a few who have been using for a long time but would be unlikely to apply to initial use. Of course, earlier generations of British addicts – described as 'therapeutic addicts' – were introduced to opiates by doctors.

Boredom Young drug takers often give boredom as a reason. This, if true, may apply more to the person who has difficulty in deriving any benefits from formal or social education, or to the unemployed youngster who has little idea how to use his time.

Other reasons for starting Some young people will also be tempted to experiment with drugs in order to rebel and challenge parental authority, or because they wish to indulge in a secret activity that adults disapprove of. Undoubtedly, the desire to experiment, experience instant excitement and happiness, pleasure, friendship, and status are more likely to be the primary factors prompting someone to start using drugs. Once started, other factors may encourage the user to continue, provided that he or she finds the experience positive and rewarding.

Reasons for continuing to use drugs on a long-term basis
This is a more controversial area. Some of the primary social factors already discussed will continue to apply. However, sociological theories alone do not adequately explain long-term use. Or, at least, they often fail to convince the worker

faced regularly with clients whose psychological needs seem to be totally invested in drug use. It may well be that social and cultural factors are influential in introducing a person to drug use, but that another set of perhaps predominantly psychological factors becomes more relevant as long-term regular use sets in. Some of the theories that have influenced the treatment responses of practitioners over the years are:

1 Sociological

The theories of 'anomie' and 'alienation', developed originally by Durkheim and Merton respectively, to apply to deviance in the wider sense, seem to fit certain patterns of drug dependence. The addict coming from a socially deprived area, who feels himself denied access to employment and to excitement in the legitimate sense, may seek escape in less acceptable ways. Drug use is not, of course, the inevitable option. Delinquency and criminality are the more obvious choices although, for some, drug use and crime may be inter-related. This theory has its attractions. It does seem to fit the drug scene with its 'alternative' prestige and values for alienated young people, especially the unemployed and those from deprived backgrounds.

Another sociological theory that has been applied to addiction is that of 'labelling'. The idea is that the largely punitive reaction by society to drug use has amplified it by labelling drug users as a 'deviant' group, thereby making them more deviant and detached from society in the process. As a result, society reacts still more punitively so that the deviance is amplified yet further, to the extent that the drug user ends up willingly adopting the label and status of addict and acting out a stereotypical role. Although the theory does not account for the initial rise of drug use it does help to explain epidemics, as well as the over-reaction and self-labelling that happens with some clients who are not so heavily involved in drug use as they would wish others to believe.

2 The family

The family is the starting point for anyone's social and psychological development and is inevitably one of the most important influences on a person's role, security, expectations and values. A substantial proportion of clients seem to come from homes where there appear to be strained parental relationships or where the parents have separated. However, many users have had a secure, 'normal' upbringing. One could not argue consistently in favour of family difficulties as a major determinant of drug problems. Divorce and marital separation are common features of today's society, and therefore an experience likely to be shared by many children who do not become addicts.

The addict may be among those who never adjust to the lack of security occasioned by loss or family break-up, failing to develop a healthy coping mechanism. In their 1970s study on heroin addiction, Salmon and Salmon look closely at this relationship between the addict and his or her family.

'Often the addict is drawn as an immature person with an unstable family environment. As far as specific actors are concerned, the father is pictured frequently as a shadowy figure, absent or detached, and sometimes harsh or punitive. The relationship of the mother to the addict is highlighted in much of the literature and is held to be of critical importance. She is the dominant force in the family and the addict is described as dominated and attached to the mother.'

Certainly, a significant number of problem drug takers known to specialist agencies do seem to have a history of family breakdown, emotional deprivation, weak parental figures or unresolved feelings of rejection or anger about family relationships. Their numbers, however, seem to be proportionately lower when drug use affects a broader section of the community and becomes an activity adopted by people who do not have any significant history of social or emotional deprivation.

3 Psychological theories

Many current treatment approaches, whether in-patient, in a therapeutic community or out-patient counselling, are based on the notion that psychological problems are the underlying cause of drug dependence. There is little hard evidence to suggest that these methods of treatment are any more successful than others. Although the ideal treatment for many problem drug takers may well be intensive therapy, in reality the majority avoid any confrontation with their real feelings. They prefer to blot them out with a regular supply of opiates or tranquillisers. It is important to remember that many of these psychotherapeutic approaches are primarily suitable for clients believed to suffer from marked personality difficulties or psychiatric illness. Therefore some, but not necessarily all, problem drug takers need intensive therapy.

Freud described addiction as 'A substitute for a lack of sexual satisfaction', and added that 'whenever normal sex life cannot be re-established, the patient will relapse'. Freud was not, incidentally, alone in suggesting that drugs are a substitute for sex. Other researchers have also suggested that opiates, especially when injected, are a sexual surrogate providing relief over unresolved sexual conflicts such as latent homosexuality. On balance, though, the connection is not really proven. Although many addicts acknowledge that injecting heroin produces a 'flash' or 'buzz' similar to orgasm, and report that increased involvement in drug use has coincided with a reduced interest in sex, this does not necessarily mean that addicts have more sexual problems than the general population, especially as heroin tends to decrease libido.

The personality traits that are said to 'cause' addiction are extensive. Popular candidates include underlying depression, immaturity, inadequacy, inability to cope with anger or hostility, low self-esteem, anti-authority attitudes, inability to form or maintain lasting relationships and many others. While some clients do appear to have had one or more of these traits prior to drug use, many others do not but may have developed them as a result of long-term drug taking.

Some personality theorists have been attracted to the concept of the 'addictive personality', and are convinced that it is possible to apply this model to all drug problems. It is clearly an attractive idea, but a somewhat simplistic approach. Research studies and personal experience of working with drug takers suggest that there is rarely one specific factor, but rather a range of factors.

4 *Addiction as an illness or a disease*
Doctors in the late nineteenth century described addiction as a disease, 'morphinomania', that should be treated by the medical profession. This perception of addicts as 'patients' rather than criminals, as in the United States, may have had its advantages on humanitarian grounds but it reinforced the idea for many years that the appropriate treatment response was a medical one directed at treating the symptoms of withdrawal – the origin of the so-called British system.

This disease concept of addiction is an integral part of the philosophy of Narcotics Anonymous, supported by advocates of the Minnesota model. The addict is seen as someone who has an illness over which he has no control unless he makes a commitment to become totally abstinent from both drugs and alcohol. Acceptance by the addict that he is a chemically dependent personality is seen as an important part of treatment. While this concept is clearly a quite attractive explanation to many addicts it has been strongly criticised by medical and social work specialists in the statutory and non-statutory drugs field. Many have struggled over the past twenty years to get rid of notions of addicts as 'sick' people who by implication cannot work and are unable to assume responsibility for themselves.

5 Psychiatric illness

Very occasionally it does seem that a client is suffering from an identifiable form of psychiatric illness such as depression or schizophrenia. However, this does not necessarily mean that mental illness has caused the drug taking, even though the use of opiates or amphetamines may well be linked to a desire to control unpleasant symptoms. Some drug taking, particularly the use of amphetamines, can actually cause short-term psychotic episodes. Some people may be more predisposed to these experiences than others, but a degree of paranoia is generally associated with long-term use of stimulants.

A multi-factorial approach

Most comprehensive reviews on both sides of the Atlantic suggest that the aetiology of drug use is multi-factorial, that people become dependent on drugs because of a whole web of inter-related reasons, different in each case. Both social and psychological factors seem to have something to offer as explanations of problematic behaviour. The initial contact with drug taking frequently occurs during adolescence when there are enormous social and emotional pressures for a youngster to cope with. A much smaller number of people start as adults in their twenties or thirties. It should be stressed that the habit-forming process may take several years. For many individuals drugs only start to become a serious problem when they are in their twenties – perhaps when they have intensified their drug use following the breakdown of a relationship, difficulties at work or a bereavement.

Most research on the causes of drug taking is based on selected groups of clients, usually in institutions, who are not necessarily representative of the wider drug using population. Sometimes they provided the researcher with an opportunity to prove a particular hypothesis, idea or prejudice. Even those who treat problem drug takers are not free from the disturbing effects of subjectivity. Here is what one researcher, X. Winick, said on this often overlooked issue.

'The behaviour of clinicians suggests that not all viewpoints about aetiology are held in equal esteem. Some clinicians view one set of aetiological factors as so predominant that treatment approaches aimed at amelioration of other hypothetical factors are virtually excluded from consideration. In many instances, the treatment recommended for a given individual can be predicted better from the history of the clinician than from the history of the drug dependent patient.' The same criticism can be made of social workers and members of other caring professions.

The enormous diversity of explanations that have come out of research studies suggests that drug takers, including those who become dependent, are no different from the rest of us. They are all unique individuals who happen to share one common experience – they like taking drugs. Some people may well have had problems before their drug use, but others will have developed problems as a result of their drug taking. A veritable chicken and egg. It is difficult to know which came first. Perhaps the reflections of one young man with an IQ of 140 and ten 'O' level GCEs demonstrate the relative 'normality' of drug use, and the need to ask clients why they think they need to continue taking drugs. I had been discussing with him the popular reasons why people were said to take drugs, and we agreed that social and emotional deprivation hardly seemed to apply to him.

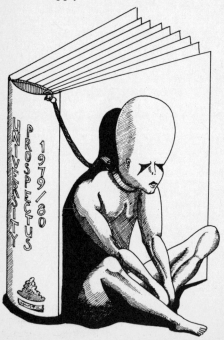

'There is no heavier burden than a great potential.'

Next session, he returned and presented me with the cartoon shown opposite which he felt summed up the reason why he had continued to take heroin. He'd always been the clever one in the family, his parents were both teachers and had hoped he would go to university. Although he recognised the need to look at some aspects of his relationship with his mother, he also felt the cartoon symbolised his personal dilemma regarding his intelligence. He had always been told he had 'a great potential', which felt like an enormous burden. He suspected that the only way out of drug use was to finally 'realise his potential' – which, as he demonstrated, he could manage without difficulty when he finally went to a highly structured drug rehabilitation house!

Having touched briefly on some of the key issues to be considered when trying to understand drug takers, we shall now look at ways of assessing the drug problem, and at the intervention process.

CHAPTER FOUR

Assessing the problem

Non-drug specialists tend to believe that people working in drug agencies share a common approach and philosophy when planning treatment for drug users. Some even suspect that there is one 'correct' approach. Nothing could be further from the truth. Some social workers and clinicians are strongly in favour of short-term prescribing for opioid addicts, while others are strongly opposed to this practice, and would advocate instead a non-prescribing policy with intensive counselling and practical social work intervention. Some workers feel that to spend time trying to work in a psycho-therapeutic way while a client is still consuming regular supplies of drugs that protect him from stress is a waste of time and that only practical medical and social work help is appropriate until the client is drug-free. Which approach is right? Both and neither because *no one way* is correct – different approaches suit different people. In the end what matters most is the relationship that the worker and the agency form with the client, together with the worker's ability to tolerate the client's ambivalence about giving up drugs and accepting help over a period of years. The experience of many workers also suggests that it is better to avoid applying a particular approach too rigidly as this is likely to invite failure.

Nevertheless, as with all specialist areas of work, there are key points to be considered when planning work with drug users. This chapter concentrates on some of the factors that need to be taken into account in the initial assessment process. The following chapter will look at the process of completing a full assessment.

The role of assessment
Assessment is only one stage, though an important one, in the overall process of treatment and rehabilitation. Recognising that, while many clients require all stages of help, others will

not need or accept the more intensive forms of intervention such as psychotherapy. The stages, in full, are as follows:

1 initial contact

2 initial assessment (may be part of 1)

3 full assessment of psycho-social-medical history and presenting problems

4 analysis of problem with client

5 planning short and long-term goals

6 establishing a relationship (already started at 1–3)

7 implementing long-term help, eg casework, counselling, family work, group work, etc.

8 controlling the drug use leading to eventual detoxification

9 preparation for rehabilitation

10 drug-free rehabilitation programme

11 post drug-free period, eg supportive counselling and/or alternatives to drug use, casework, psychotherapy, self-help group, working as an ex-addict staff member.

Some clients manage to pass through all these stages without slipping back or relapsing. Many, though, get so far and then relapse, or decide to discontinue with formal help, or are unable to continue with the worker's treatment plan because of a prison sentence. The majority of problem drug takers make several attempts at becoming totally drug-free over a period of years. During that time they are likely to receive help from several workers and often a variety of agencies.

In an ideal world it is clearly desirable for the same worker to be involved with a client from start to finish, assuming that a good working relationship has been established. Many problem drug takers have difficulty in sustaining long-term relationships. Even if they are good at forming relationships, the majority find it hard to trust those in authority. This is understandable when the illegal nature of their drug taking activities is taken into account. Therefore, if a reasonable degree of trust and empathy can be established during the early stages by a worker who is able to offer consistent long-term help, there is a possibility that this relationship can serve as an effective base for intervention.

Initial contact
Clients will be at different stages of drug use when they first

attend for help. Some will be very unsure about the sort of help they want. They may just feel the need for contact with a friendly adult who can provide them with some sense of security and support when their drug use seems to be getting out of control. Some may want to start thinking about ways of getting out of the mess they are in, although they may not be ready to acknowledge that their problems are related to drug abuse. Some clients may have had sufficient experience of the drug scene and the rehabilitation alternatives available to feel that they are at last ready to contemplate seriously moving on to a residential rehabilitation project. Most clients are likely to need the worker to explain to them the services that are available and to help them decide whether they should be referred on to a specialist project or continue seeing the worker on a regular basis. Many will be best helped initially by the worker alone, and may not need the help of any other agency. At a later stage, a drug-free client may need information and advice about the possibility of entering a rehabilitation house. Initially, most clients are extremely reluctant to consider moving on to an institution without first trying to give up drugs while still living in the community.

Some may still be fairly committed to drug taking and put over very confused messages to the worker because they believe that all social workers want to hear clients express a desire to 'kick' the habit. This may be bewildering and frustrating for someone who perceives their role to be one of helping people to stop their drug use. This may well be the long-term goal for both client and worker but it is unlikely to happen immediately. Occasional exceptions occur when a client comes for help having managed to stop drug use on his own, but is experiencing difficulties at an emotional and/or social level that he fears may force him to relapse.

As with all clients, the first interview is extremely important, for drug users often expect to be rejected as undesirable by professionals if they confess to the sort of lifestyle they have been leading. In truth, many do have unfortunate experiences of agencies and staff who are unwilling to work with drug takers. They often feel rejected by the caring professions. Whether these feelings are real or imaginary they result in fear, and in a lack of empathy and understanding that can drive a destructive wedge between drug user and worker. The client must be accepted as a person with problems who has a right to the best possible help. Some clients expect workers to have disapproving and naïve feelings about drug taking, so it is important from the outset to adopt a non-judgemental attitude; suppress any facial response, for example, that might signify unease or disapproval.

Assessment

The assessment process can be divided into two stages, initial and full assessment. Some agencies, such as those who simply provide advice and information, may be primarily concerned at the initial stage, while drug problem teams and specialist drug agencies may be more involved with the full assessment. Assessment, like initial contact, is a critical time for establishing the trusting relationship that will stand worker and client in good stead in the longer term. Therefore, assessment is best carried out by the worker who is likely to be able to continue working with the client, thereby maximising the rapport established at this stage when often very intimate and sensitive personal experiences may be disclosed.

Initial assessment

Initial assessment includes the process of deciding, with the client, whether there is indeed a drug problem that ought to be tackled. Some workers are particularly well placed to carry out the initial assessment, either because the client is already in contact with them formally or informally, or because they are trusted sufficiently for the user to feel able to confide in them about his drug use. These workers may be youth and community workers, play leaders, volunteers, teachers, residential social workers, youth counsellors, intermediate treatment staff, and many others. Likewise, staff in social services, the probation service and health service may find, in the course of working with clients, that some of the difficulties that arise relate to drug use. The majority of professional workers should be able to make an initial assessment of the client's drug use and, later, a fuller assessment with a view to acting as the key worker themselves. That is unless they decide to refer the client on to a specialist agency for full assessment and treatment.

Start an initial assessment by making a list of the client's problems as he sees them, remembering that even apparently unmotivated clients will have some reason for coming to the agency, unsure though they may be of the sort of help they want. They may be unsure because they do not know what is available. They may not understand what use some forms of help might be to them. Coming to talk to a perfect stranger, for example, about their problems might be an alien concept and not part of their culture. The worker should make his own initial assessment of the client's problems so that both can develop a dialogue around each other's perception of the situation.

One of the first questions for the worker to check out is where the drug problem really exists. That is, is the client's use of drugs creating problems for him, or is he seeing you because his habit is upsetting others? You then need to know:

1 Whether or not the drug use is affecting his daily life physically, socially and/or emotionally;

2 Whether or not there are signs of actual physical or psychological dependence, such as withdrawal symptoms;

3 Whether or not – irrespective of the presence of the latter – there are signs of physical complications such as overdosing or intoxicated behaviour, abscesses or hepatitis.

The areas for discussion then might include:

– What drugs are currently being used and how? For example, is the heroin currently being smoked or injected?
– How many different types of drugs is he using? Only one or several? How discriminating is the client about what he uses and how he uses it? The use of several drugs may demonstrate a lack of cash to enable use of the preferred drug, or it may indicate someone whose approach to drug taking is rather chaotic. He will take anything as long as it has some effect on the way he feels.
– How often is he using drugs? Daily? Several times a day? Weekends? Several times a week, or only on a few occasions? If the last, is he seeing you because of his own concern about the consequences or because, say, his parents are concerned?
– How long has he been using drugs? Weeks; months; years? If using regularly, approximately how long on that basis?

You are trying to obtain a picture of the pattern of drug use before you assess the most appropriate form of intervention.

Begin to assess whether or not there are any related problems, whether or not drug use is beginning to affect the client's lifestyle and to what extent the drug taking has taken control of his life. Areas for discussion may include current employment, school attendance, court cases, accommodation, any close family or friends, financial difficulties. It may be wise at this stage to enquire about just one or two areas. Some clients will be very relieved to have found someone to talk to about the mess they are in, while others may be extremely wary and only be prepared to disclose the barest information until they feel able to trust or are clearer about the sort of help available. Even at the initial stage of assessment some clients may benefit more from seeing a worker for two or three short interviews, perhaps on an informal or drop-in basis, giving them time to decide whether or not they really do want help.

Discussion about drug related problems can include:

– Any close family, partner, or friends? Are they supportive? Do they know about the drug use? Have these relationships deteriorated with increased drug use? Is the fact that others don't know or suspect part of the reason for seeking help, in an attempt to give up drugs before they find out?

– Employment. If the drug user is still working is time-keeping or attendance affected? Does the employer know or suspect? If unemployed, is that a factor influencing drug use?

– If at school or in further or higher education, is attendance regular or has it been affected by drug use? Again, did these problems exist before drug taking became a habit?

– Accommodation. Has he anywhere permanent to live? If so, is he able to pay rent or mortgage? If not, how long has he been without stable accommodation?

– Crime. Any current court case pending? If so, is he hoping for a sympathetic report from you or someone else so that he will not get sent to prison? Any current probation order, deferred or suspended sentence? Are the offences drug related?

– Medical problems. Any withdrawal symptoms? Overdoses? Medical complications such as hepatitis, abscesses, paranoid episodes (if using cocaine or amphetamines)?

– Financial problems. Any outstanding debts, fines, money owed to drug dealers, etc? How is he supporting the drug habit – savings, earnings, dealing (selling drugs), prostitution, borrowing from family, friends?

– What state is he in at interview? Is he calm, relaxed, friendly, anxious, suspicious, stoned, detached, irritable, sleepy, in withdrawals, reluctant to give much information? Do you think he's giving a fairly accurate picture of his drug problem or has it been exaggerated for effect and to ensure that he gets a prescription? Clients are unlikely to be completely truthful about their drug use during the early stage of contact with new workers. A lot depends on what they think you want to hear and on whether they are trying to impress you, or to reduce your enthusiasm to help them give up drugs. This may not be what they want to do – yet. People may deliberately over-estimate or under-estimate the frequency and amounts of their drug use. Current knowledge of street drug prices can help you to assess the accuracy of drug taking information. Asking how much money people are spending on drugs daily or weekly can give some indication of how accurate a client's estimates of drug quantities taken really are.

Finally, when discussing the problems as you both see them, it is important to discuss just what the client wants in the way of help, and what he thinks is the solution to his predicament. Bear in mind that many clients do not know what 'help' means or may involve, and even when you explain it, they may still hope that someone will be able to do something to them so that they can regain some control of their lives. That is clearly wishful thinking. You need to indicate plainly that ultimately any real change can only be achieved by the client – not by others. Any help offered can only be successful if a drug user accepts that the way ahead is of necessity going to be difficult, not just giving up drugs but staying off them. To do so means dealing with the social and emotional troubles that beset him, being prepared to work on some of the problems he may have had around the time he got hooked. Otherwise relapse is inevitable. It is difficult for new clients to understand emotionally – at the gut level – just what all this entails, even though they may appear to understand intellectually.

Checklist to help decide whether client's drug use is problematic:

1 Which drugs is he using?

2 How long for, and how often?

3 Any medical problems?

4 Any legal problems?

5 Financial problems?

6 Is drug use affecting personal, social relationships?

7 Any previous help received for drug problem?

8 Any social problems?

9 Any emotional problems?

If the answer to questions 3 to 9 is 'yes' for one or more questions, then a more detailed, full assessment may be required to enable the worker to make an informed decision about the most appropriate type of intervention. Before I go on to look at that process, I want to outline some possible courses of action open to workers when they ask themselves the question at the end of the initial assessment, 'Is there a drug problem?'

Answer:

1 **Yes** – drug use is affecting a client's life, definite evidence of problem drug use. *Further action required*.

2 **No** – drug use is experimental or casual. Client appears to be in control, able to maintain personal and social relationships and work or educational commitments. *Further action probably unnecessary at present*.

3 **No** – but could develop into difficulties. *May require some counselling to prevent problems*.

4 **No** – but has other social/emotional problems. *Could benefit from other forms of help, e.g. counselling, casework, welfare rights, child guidance, general psychiatric, youth work*.

5 **No** – but parents could benefit from support. *See Chapter 13 on a family affair*.

Many clients experience feelings of rejection if they have been passed on to other agencies when the first agency has preferred not to deal with their case, only to find that the new agency did not welcome their presence either, or was operating a waiting list and was unable to offer them an appointment for several weeks – by which time their initial motivation had weakened. If you are considering referring someone on to another agency, say the local drug clinic, then check first on whether he or she can be seen that week and, secondly, on the current prescribing policy. If there are likely to be difficulties in obtaining immediate help – for example, for a prescription or in-patient detoxification – then consider providing interim support and dealing with any immediate practical problems of a social nature yourself, until the other agency is ready to help. This encourages clients to remain interested in treatment. There may well be no alternative or additional source of help in those areas where specialist resources are non-existent or where, unfortunately, they have a limited role or a bad reputation amongst the drug using community. Bear in mind, though, that if a client is referred on to either a drug clinic or the general practitioner he will have to be formally notified to the Home Office as a suspected or confirmed addict (see Appendix 2).

The next stage of assessment includes taking a more detailed personal and social history of the client to help decide on the most appropriate form of intervention. Many social workers and other caring professionals will be familiar with this process. However, if you are not experienced or trained in this technique and feel you would have difficulty in asking clients such personal questions about their life, this might be the moment to refer on to another worker. If your agency would not normally undertake long-term casework or counselling with clients then referral to a specialist drug agency or social work agency would also be desirable. The next chapter explores the process of completing a full assessment.

CHAPTER FIVE

Completing a full assessment

Every worker has his or her own method of making a detailed assessment. It helps to compile a background history of the person's childhood, family history, education, delinquency, employment, general lifestyle in terms of friendship and relationship patterns and their drug taking history in chronological order, as it relates to the rest of their life. This can be done in one long interview or over several sessions. The process in itself assists in the establishment of a relationship between you and client, while helping the worker to build up a background picture of the person's current situation and problems. Both parties begin to see the relationship between drug taking and the client's life as a whole, whereas previously it might have been more convenient to see drug taking as a separate issue.

Look at those periods of the client's life when he was actually drug-free and stable. Many drug users will have had periods – some brief, some lasting a year or more – when they stopped using drugs, often without the involvement of any professional agency. A worker should examine the reasons why it was possible for the client to cease drug use then, but not now. What events or misfortunes caused him to resume drug use, such as the break up of a relationship, death of a parent, loss of job? By discussing these related factors, a client will find it easier to recognise how his drug use may stem from other emotional and practical areas of his life that he had not previously thought relevant. All aspects of a client's life should be taken into account, remembering that there is strong evidence to suggest that there are many reasons why someone uses drugs. It could be a mixture of pleasurable, social, cultural and emotional cues. With this information you will be better equipped to suggest to your client how his drug use relates to him as a person. It is not just something that has become a problem because he can no longer afford supplies or obtain a prescription.

You need to try to understand what a client gains from drug use. Do not undervalue the enjoyment that it provides. This enjoyment may be one of the factors that has prevented a client from being able to make any real commitment to stop drug use. It explains some of the ambivalence he has towards help. Acknowledge to the client, however young, that to want to alter the way he feels is normal.

Drug users often transmit mixed messages. They express an intellectual and rational reason for changing but without any real emotional desire to do so. This becomes more evident as the worker later attempts to encourage the client to follow through his good intentions. Such ambivalence towards change is not at all unique to drug takers. Most of us have some personal experience of knowing what we ought to do and making all the right noises about 'doing something about ourselves' when a change is desirable in, say, a job or a self-destructive behaviour pattern. It can, however, be extremely difficult, as we all know, to make a genuine commitment to change when the process includes facing up to some unwelcome self-knowledge and emotional pain.

A psycho-social assessment

It is not easy to complete a full psycho-social assessment. Much depends on the interviewer being able to create a relaxed atmosphere of trust and confidentiality, asking questions in a manner that is non-judgemental, friendly and sensitive. The client must also understand why detailed questions are being asked of him about his life. He must be told why you need to talk about, say, his relationship with his parents, and convinced that you are not being just plain nosy or inquisitive. So explain that, having identified the existence of a drug problem, it cannot just be alleviated by a simple prescription or detoxification. Explain, too, that there may be a relationship between your client's early and present life history, and his current drug use, and that you need to explore all this to ensure that the most appropriate form of intervention is offered.

Checklist for completing full assessment

family history	personal relationships
childhood and adolescence	accommodation
education	drug history
employment	medical/psychiatric history
delinquency, crime	contact with other agencies.

If the client asks for drug maintenance or detoxification, then a physical examination will be required, together with urine analysis and investigations for hepatitis and liver damage. This is normally completed by a clinician if the client is attending a drug clinic. If not, there may be an interested general practitioner who will complete that part of the assessment. If the client is not asking for a prescription, then there may be no need to involve a doctor unless there seem to be other medical complications. So far as the practicalities of taking a detailed assessment are concerned, you will find it helpful to run through most of the following questionnaire items.

Family history
Parental background: was the client brought up by both parents all or part of the time; one parent and/or grandparents? If not, was he adopted, fostered or brought up in a children's home(s)? Were the parents happy together? Are they currently separated or divorced, dead or retired? Which parent did the client get on with best? What is his current relationship with his parents? Do they know about his drug use? Is there any regular contact with the parents – if so, what kind – supportive/hostile? Does the client still live with them? (If so, there may be a need for some family interviews or therapy at some stage.) How dependent is the client upon them – have they helped out financially regarding drug use, e.g. provided money for drugs or paid off fines? Is there any family history of psychiatric disturbance, drug or alcohol problems, or apparent social problems, e.g. poverty, unemployment, homelessness, criminality – if so, how did this affect the client? How many brothers and sisters does he have? Who did he get on with best? What are they doing now? Is any of them using drugs or alcohol heavily?

You are trying to explore whether there are any factors in the family relationships, particularly that between the client and his parents, that suggest difficulties that might be causally related to drug use, particularly those of early deprivation and weak or absent father figures. Excessive use of alcohol or drugs can also be a significant factor, suggesting early conditioning and an acceptance of substances being used to cope with stress.

Personal history: childhood and adolescence
Was he a happy, contented child or were there difficulties, eg tantrums, nightmares, bedwetting? Was he a normal, healthy baby/child or was he regarded as 'difficult'? Does the client look back on childhood as good or bad? Was he aware of any

53

family problems or tensions? Were there any parental separations, including lengthy periods in hospital? Did he make friends easily during childhood and adolescence? Was he part of a group or gang or did he tend to have just one or two close friends? What sort of problems did he experience during adolescence? How did he and his parents cope? Were there any family pressures, tensions or changes in family structure at that time, eg divorce, remarriage, new child born into the family?

All these factors have been known to bring extra tension and insecurity to the life of an adolescent undergoing the uneasy transition to adulthood. Drug use, providing as it does, extra confidence and removing stress, can become an important crutch, an escape from learning to cope with distressing feelings.

Education

Drug users are often described as highly intelligent. This is a bit of a myth. Although many are of average or above average intelligence, there are likely to be many who are below average. Educational assessment focuses on whether a client had any problems associated with school, whether he achieved his potential or whether he under-achieved. If so, why? Was he under parental pressure to do well and did he 'rebel' by not passing exams or by not staying on at school to take higher exams? Is the under-achievement related to drug use? Had he already started using drugs to an extent that it interfered with performance and interest in academic achievement? It is useful to note the type of school attended (comprehensive, secondary modern, public, grammar, etc.), and any exams passed (CSE, 'O', 'A' levels). Had he been expected to pass? It is also worth discussing favourite subjects. This may be useful material to consider when thinking about developing alternatives to drug use, future training interests and so on. Other features concerning education include attendance, truancy, and relationships with other pupils and teachers.

Record also any further or higher education, and any professional training courses (full/part-time, technical college, polytechnic, university, etc.) embarked on and completed. For those currently on a course, how are they coping with their studies? Is their attempt to continue on the course realistic at this stage? If not, will they need help in negotiating some time off to sort out their drug problem so they can apply themselves to their studies once their life is more stable?

Employment

Lack of employment or a satisfying job is often said to be a key factor in problematic drug use. By the time most drug users present for help they have usually had a variety of jobs. Many will have been unemployed for some time or worked only on a casual or seasonal basis. Some may never have worked at all. It is helpful to note down the client's employment history since leaving school, including apprenticeships, and Youth Training Schemes. Note down approximately how many jobs he has had. What did he think was the best job he ever had, and why? Was this because of the money? Was it the most interesting, satisfying, most responsible? Why did he leave? What sort of work would he like to do in the future?

Delinquency or criminal history

A significant number of problem drug takers are in trouble with the law before starting drug use. Many inevitably run the risk of prosecution and imprisonment once involved in illicit drug use and dealing. So, for some, drug use is an additional part of a criminal lifestyle, perhaps part of a sub-cultural or recreational activity. For many others, though, the illicit aspect of their habit is an extra risk that might finally push them to seek or accept help. Again, it is helpful to take a chronological history of delinquent offences and penalties, noting whether or not they were drug related. Even when a client has had a delinquent career before drug use, you often find, after dependence has developed, that most offences are drug related, usually a means of financing drug use. Note whether the offences were committed in a group or alone. If the latter, this may say something about an individual's level of desperation or risk-taking. Is he currently on probation? If so, will he allow you to discuss his problems with his probation officer? If he is on a deferred or suspended sentence, or if there is a court case pending, is his interest in obtaining help provoked by the need for a sympathetic court report? Unfortunately, many drug users suffer from a short-lived bout of motivation to change. It quickly subsides once the risk of imprisonment has passed. However, a high percentage of drug takers would probably avoid help far longer were it not for the law initiating a crisis in their drug career.

Personal relationships

To some extent, this part of your assessment interview is a continuation of the section on adolescence, moving into the area of sexual relationships; close friendships; preferred sexual identity (heterosexual, bisexual, homosexual); present and past stable relationships; and marriage. Try to obtain information about the approximate age of first sexual intercourse and dates of significant relationships, such as those leading to the birth of children or pregnancies started. If pregnancy resulted in termination, how did the client cope afterwards? Was she depressed? Did she receive any support or counselling? If the client has a current relationship, is it satisfactory? Or is drug use causing the client or partner (who may also be using drugs) to lose interest in sex? If so, is this because injecting provides greater satisfaction? There is no evidence, by the way, to suggest that drug takers have more sexual problems than other people. Most rediscover their interest once drug use ceases, particularly self-injection. Some clients, though, will have had problems related to sexuality and performance prior to drug taking. In some cases this may need attention at a later stage. When talking about sex you are unlikely to get someone to confide in you until they feel able to trust you and see it as a relevant subject that they want to talk about.

It is also helpful to assess the client's ability to make and maintain long-standing friendships with either sex. Does he have any close friends who are not drug takers or who, even though they have lost regular contact because of the client's lifestyle, would be willing to resume the friendship if the client were to give up drugs? These human supports are invaluable in assisting the longer-term rehabilitation process. If the client has no really close friends, why not? Is it because of his drug use, or because he has never found it easy to maintain a friendship? Does that suggest the need for long-term work on establishing social relationships?

Accommodation
Information about accommodation is important. It helps to identify problems that may need urgent attention if a drug user is to establish any degree of stability, and face some of his or her emotional stresses. You therefore need to obtain a picture of present living conditions. Is the client living alone, with a partner, or parents, or sharing with others? Is he living in a hostel, own home (house, flat, bedsit, squat, etc.), and is he paying rent or a mortgage? If so, is he in arrears of payment?

If he has housing problems, check whether this has happened recently because of the drug taking, or whether there is a long history of housing difficulties. If the latter, was this due to problems outside his control or of his own making? Does homelessness seem to be part of his adopted life-style, drifting from squats to hostels to the street? Or has he failed to pay rent and/or been evicted because of rows and/or drugs?

Clearly, if a client has a record of settled accommodation, that immediately removes an important practical problem from the discussion (unless, that is, he decides to move elsewhere in order to remain drug free). If there is no accommodation readily available you will need to assess just how much energy you should put into offering help in this area. Is supportive hostel accommodation preferable to a flat or bed-sit, especially with the more chaotic clients accustomed to homelessness or unstable living arrangements? With the latter, a period of residential rehabilitation may be necessary before the drug user can develop skills in maintaining permanent accommodation. Finally, enquire whether he is living with others who are using drugs on a regular basis and perhaps receiving treatment. You may not get an honest answer to this question early on, but make sure that the client realises that, if he is serious about giving up the habit, then he is doomed to failure if he continues to live with others who are still drug users.

Drug history

There is a lot to be said for asking more detailed questions about drug use later rather than earlier in the history taking interview. It demonstrates that you are primarily interested in the client as a person, and only secondly as a drug taker. Full assessment of a client's drug taking should include a chronological history of drug use from start to present. Clearly some of the present drug use will have been described during the initial assessment, but it is important to recap on that because sometimes the original version may be modified once the client has begun to trust the agency and worker. You get a fuller picture once a client is willing to provide a relatively honest version of his activities.

Initial questions to ask can include: when did you first start smoking cigarettes, drinking alcohol or taking a drug for non-medical reasons? Was it taken for enjoyment? The substances the client used may include minor tranquillisers, or over-the-counter medicines obtained from the family medicine chest, so don't just ask about illicit drugs. For example, one 14-year-old girl once confided that her first introduction to the attractive side-effects of some over-the-counter medicines was from her father. She was having difficulty sleeping at about 12 years, so he suggested she took one of his own anti-histamine tablets to help her sleep. She later began to buy large quantities of these for herself when, after social work intervention, she had 'given up' the use of barbiturates and tranquillisers obtained from illicit sources. She developed a major drug and alcohol problem instead, from mixing red wine and anti-histamines.

For the majority of youngsters the first illicit drug is likely to be cannabis. Increasingly, however, many will have smoked or snorted heroin first. You may find that you get the best account by leading a client through his drug taking career year by year, gathering a picture of the periods of drug use (type of drug, frequency, methods of use, etc.) and noting any drug-free periods. At this stage of the interview some clients are likely to start making connections between their personal and work history, and their drug use, perhaps for the first time. This is not the moment to produce some deeply significant interpretation about the meaning of their drug use (they may disappear, never to be seen again). But it clearly helps if clients have any understanding at all of the 'meaning' of their drug taking beyond the idea of pure enjoyment, which may still be an important factor.

Some agencies ask clients to complete a questionnaire or check list about their drug use. Though it may be a useful way of getting people to recall their drug taking history, this method is no substitute for a sensitive interview.

In the initial stages of assessment you may be able to do no more than establish contact and start suggesting ways in which the client might change his situation. Clients who are ambivalent about accepting help may only see a worker on a few occasions, then disappear or only maintain contact in a minimal way. Later, they may reappear, asking to see the same worker when their problems are becoming more pressing and they are becoming aware of the need to do something about themselves. They may well be returning because the worker was sympathetic, but realistic in his or her attitude towards them, apparently able to get some definition and structure in their relationship so that the client felt he knew where he stood. For many it will not be until they can see some over-riding reason to stop taking drugs that they will seriously consider abandoning what can be seen as a love – hate relationship with these powerful substances. It is difficult to give up something that seems reliably to offer short term happiness. Assessment completed, the next step is to decide precisely what sort of help you might best offer. It is time to plan your intervention.

CHAPTER SIX

Planning intervention

Any method of intervention has to take into account any previous experience clients may have of help, their expectations, their degree of motivation to change, their potential for using different types of help, and the nature of any personal and social problems discovered during assessment. A few clients may be highly motivated to change and be convinced of the need to do something about themselves. Many others, though, are, in the early stages of contact, better served by a supportive counselling or casework approach that allows time for a therapeutic relationship to develop and for the client to test out the worker and the agency, to see whether it is worth taking a risk and putting faith in the professionals.

Analysis of problems that need to be tackled
Discuss with the client those problems that you feel need to be addressed. Ask your client to tell you what he thinks are his main problems, and try to establish whether the assessment interviews have helped to identify or throw light on difficulties that he might previously not have considered important. Focus initially on those problems that have developed as a result of the drug taking, rather than concentrating on any detailed analysis of issues that appear to have preceded drug use. Although these may well be areas that will eventually need some attention to ensure long term change, clients are not usually receptive to hearing a detailed assessment of their predisposition to drug use. Most new clients are likely to see their physical dependence as the main problem, and may express some concern about a few practical problems such as debts or a court case.

If, as the key worker, you feel very strongly that a client is refusing to face up to emotional or interpersonal difficulties that, if left unresolved, will continue to cause relapse, you may say something like, 'I think we need to concentrate on getting your drug use under control and deal with some of these practical problems initially. However, I think as you begin to rely less on the drug you may find you have some problems of anxiety (or anger, personal confidence, loneliness, depression, etc.). From what you have told me, I think this may be one of the reasons why you have found it so difficult to cope without drugs.' At this stage, even if clients refuse to accept that there are any psychological or social reasons for their drug use, make it clear that you do not think that all their troubles will be over once they have been through a relatively painless detoxification.

It can be difficult at this stage to sort out which clients are being totally honest with you and which ones are simply saying what they know you want to hear. Some drug takers, especially those with years of experience of doctors, social workers and probation officers excel at playing the 'good client' role. 'I want to find out why I'm using drugs', 'I need to sort my head out', 'I've tried giving up before but I never really accepted that my use of drugs might be something to do with some psychological problem or my relationship with my father', and so on. Even if someone does make these noises and sounds genuine he may well not be willing or able in practice to look in any depth at his feelings. It is very tempting to want to offer intensive counselling or psychotherapy sessions when clients make such apparently well motivated and insightful comments. They may be genuine, but while they continue to consume drugs, even on prescription, they are incapable of understanding your interpretations.

Setting goals and identifying priorities

When the client and worker have come to some agreement over the problems that need to be tackled, they can begin to identify realistic short-term goals, as well as ones for the intermediate and the long term. If it is possible to achieve some success, however minor, for the client early on, he will gain confidence and self-esteem and be more inclined to consider longer-term strategies. Some workers find it helps themselves and their clients to sketch out a framework or plan of action related to identifiable short-term and longer-term goals. This is designed to take into account the client's own circumstances and assessment of priorities. Such a plan may help the client to take a more active part in treatment, encouraging him to adopt a positive attitude towards the whole therapeutic process. These goals or objectives can be reviewed periodically and revised in the light of progress.

Remember that, although a drug-free lifestyle is invariably the ultimate long-term goal for the majority, when it comes to deciding on other issues, different people have different priorities in their immediate goals. Detoxification, for example, may be a short-term goal for some, but an intermediate or long-term goal for others. The priority attached to improving family relationships depends on whether a drug user is still living at home and on the nature of current relationships. Likewise, accommodation and financial problems may require both short-term and long-term attention according to the severity of the problems. There are no hard and fast rules. Try to help clients to accept that complex difficulties take time to resolve, especially if there are heavy debts or major housing problems, or if personal and social relationships are involved. In these circumstances it helps to set quite modest short-term goals in order to boost confidence.

Identifying priorities
Some problems require immediate attention, particularly medical, legal and social difficulties.

Medical problems
Medical problems, such as abscesses, must be treated straight away. These are caused by injecting ground-up tablets such as barbiturates, *DF118* and *Diconal*, or by using unsterile injecting techniques (such as tap water to dissolve drugs), or by using dirty needles or syringes. Some doctors prefer to ensure that clients who have been injecting have been screened for hepatitis B and HIV, sometimes called the 'AIDS virus'. While many clients are understandably apprehensive about the latter investigations, many welcome an opportunity to talk about their fears. Some (but not all) prefer to know the worst, especially if they have a partner and children. Advice and counselling to help people reduce some of the health risks is worth trying. For example, encouraging someone to avoid injecting or using dirty injection equipment (which includes sharing their best mate's needles) will reduce their chances of contracting AIDS, hepatitis B and abscesses (see Appendix 4).

If you are unhappy about a drug taker's general state of health, have him checked over by a doctor to ensure that his drug use is not concealing a physical illness. Poor health and physique are quite likely to be due to lack of proper diet. Remember the advice of two experienced doctors in the field, 'There are few drug takers who do not benefit from vitamin supplements and a good meal' (Banks and Waller). Amphetamine users often go for days without eating properly.

They are likely to suffer vitamin deficiencies. Medical problems associated with withdrawal vary according to the drugs
consumed. For example, if the withdrawals are due to
barbiturate use, then immediate medical attention is necessary
to prevent convulsions. In the case of opiates, doctors are less
inclined to offer immediate relief, because the dangers are
fewer. Some, however, may be willing to provide a day's
supply of medication. (See also Chapter 9 on Medical and
Psychiatric Services.)

Legal problems

A large percentage of opiate users come forward for help
following an arrest in the hope that a sympathetic doctor or
social worker will tell the court that they are 'receiving
treatment', thereby eliciting a minimal sentence. A probation
officer may already be involved either because he has been
asked for a social enquiry report to assist the court's decision,
or because he has known the client for some time and may
even be his current supervising officer. Try to persuade your
client that it is in his interest for you to discuss his case with
the probation officer. If time allows, arrange for a meeting
between all three of you.

If there is a risk of imprisonment, then the client may want a
fairly rapid detoxification, knowing that the alternatives may
either be imprisonment or, if the court is willing to consider a
residential alternative, a period in a drug rehabilitation
community such as Phoenix House. If a client has no solicitor
he may need help in finding one who is prepared to take his
case on, preferably someone with a declared interest in drug
problems. The organisation, 'Release', keeps a list of solicitors
from all over the United Kingdom who are willing to help drug
takers.

Unfortunately, many clients are poorly motivated to do
something about their drug problem once the court case is
over; some even regard a probation order as a 'soft option'.
They are unlikely to keep to a treatment programme that
includes regular attendance and, say, a reducing prescription
of methadone mixture. Some experienced probation officers
and drug specialists are reluctant to embark on an ambitious
programme if the court case seems to be the only motivating
factor, particularly if it seems not to have provoked a
sufficiently alarming crisis to spur the client on to make
significant changes. Once the outcome of the court case is
known, the worker can assess how committed the client is to
continuing with treatment. If a deferred sentence is given it
may serve as a useful framework in which to move towards

more realistic goals in the three to six months before returning to court.

Social problems

The most urgent of these are likely to be money and housing, usually because all available cash has been spent on drugs. There are often unpaid rent or mortgage commitments, arrears on gas, electricity, telephone, hire purchase payments, etc. While some workers will be accustomed to helping clients sort out the most urgent debts, others may need to find appropriate staff or an agency who can advise them on these matters. For many clients these are long-term problems, but in the short-term try to see if anything can be done immediately with the help of the appropriate agencies such as Social Security, Citizens Advice Bureau, and Social Services if children are involved. Wherever it is possible, encourage clients to take some responsibility for doing this themselves, rather than allowing them to depend on you to sort out the mess. If someone is too ill or emotionally disturbed at the time to do this you may have to set the wheels in motion, leaving the client to deal with them when he is more stable.

In some larger cities, accommodation may be an urgent problem needing both short-term and longer-term solutions. Few parts of the country have short-term accommodation designed to meet the specific needs of drug takers. In London, ROMA, a residential rehabilitation hostel for notified addicts, probably still offers the best option for addicts who are receiving a regular prescription from a clinic or their general practitioner, and who are willing to use staff support to work towards a drug-free lifestyle.

For some, the immediate need may be people to whom they can turn for help in dealing with their drug problem. They may have become estranged from close family and friends and have no real contact with anyone who does not take drugs. They may see contact with a sympathetic worker as a major step forward in helping them to develop confidence in their ability to make friends. Many long-term drug takers have very low self-esteem, regarding themselves as failures whom no-one would want as a friend. Longer term goals may need to be an improved self-image and developing greater confidence in social situations.

Unemployment is a common problem for many drug takers, especially for those who have never had any significant work experience. They may have begun dealing in drugs as an alternative 'career'. No longer is it possible to suggest that a client scans the local papers, signs on at the Job Centre, or takes any job he can obtain in order to get some routine into his life, let alone income, self-respect, and social outlets. In some parts of the country there may still be opportunities to do that, particularly if clients have some relevant training and previous work experience to recommend them to an employer, but even then the chances will be few. If a drug user can find some form of employment at an early stage this can make a major contribution towards facing any longer-term difficulties that he may have when he is finally drug-free, such as coping with lack of personal confidence, loneliness, and the need to rebuild a social life away from drug using contacts. If employment prospects are non-existent you need to get your client to contemplate educational needs, retraining schemes, voluntary work and, perhaps, attendance at a suitable day centre. This does not necessarily have to be a centre that specialises in drug takers, but it should be orientated towards the problems of the unemployed or the mentally ill or, if appropriate, people on a probation order. Unfortunately, starting a new job as soon as detoxification is completed can be too much for the newly drug free person to handle.

When trying to determine priorities, you need to decide whether to concentrate initially on practical issues before focusing on drug related emotional and personality problems. This is not easy. Although you may be trained to deal with both social and emotional problems, you will probably have a personal preference for dealing with one or the other. Usually, emotional problems are more attractive on the grounds that one can waste a lot of effort dealing with the practical difficulties of clients who really need to resolve some of their underlying emotional problems before they can make use of the practical help. To put it another way, there is no point in sorting out a client's external world until he has dealt with his own internal world. However, many would argue the opposite: that you should not try to sort out emotional troubles until major practical problems of, for example, housing and finance have been dealt with. Both arguments have some validity. However, with clients who have major drug related social problems some practical help is essential if they are to concentrate on dealing with their drug taking. If experience suggests that a client is incapable of using practical and financial help constructively then he is equally unlikely to be able to cope with intensive counselling. He may benefit from a stay in a residential setting where more intensive support is available. (See also Chapter 8 on Achieving Longer-Term goals.)

Dealing with the actual drug taking

Some of your clients who do not have social, legal or financial problems needing immediate attention, and who have maintained a degree of stability in their lives, should regard detoxification as their immediate short-term goal. In the longer term they need to develop self-confidence, secure suitable employment or training, and evolve interests, personal strengths and insights to help maintain a drug-free lifestyle.

However, there will be some who are not ready to commit themselves immediately to a detoxification programme. Before they do, they may need, in the short term, to control their drug use and limit any medical complications. This can be tackled in various ways. One may be to look at the three key indicators of drug problems already discussed in earlier chapters: excessive consumption, intoxication, and dependence. Initially, by tackling the way someone uses drugs, you can help to achieve greater stability so that the user can approach a supervised detoxification with a greater chance of success.

Reducing excessive consumption

Consuming large quantities of drugs invariably leads to drug takers becoming 'out of control'. They may become extremely intoxicated and 'punch drunk', behaving in a threatening and abusive manner before passing out. If using amphetamines, they become increasingly paranoid, sometimes psychotic as their contact with reality becomes more and more distorted, and as such they present a major management problem. If a client has a pattern of behaviour that might be more stable if his drug consumption were reduced, then try to see if he can be encouraged to monitor his drug use by keeping a record or diary of drugs used, noting frequency of use. In this way, according to the City Roads 'Drug Resource Pack',

'. . . it may be possible for the client to grasp the advantage of more controlled drug use – i.e. fewer overdoses, saving money and avoiding arrest as well as to understand the significance of periods of excessive consumption'.

Preventing intoxication

If your client has problems related to intoxication try to persuade him to reduce simultaneously the quantity and range of drugs used, particularly those with a sedative or hypnotic effect. These can be lethal if used to excess with alcohol and other psycho-active substances. Intoxicated drug behaviour is often indicative of a person who lives from one drug crisis to another. This type of client needs to look at the sorts of crises that push him into an escapist state of intoxication and to accept that other responses to crises are preferable to overdosing.

As the City Roads 'Drug Resource Pack' puts it, 'If a client can identify the sorts of crises which lead to use then it is possible for the worker to mobilise other support or therapeutic mechanisms for the client to use. Encouragment to visit the office, make use of telephone counselling services, being readily available to meet the client and the use of other agencies may be presented as alternative methods of coping once the behaviour has been recognised. It is of course very important to positively reinforce avoidance of intoxication. If the client has to learn new behaviours these must be encouraged and rewarded'.

Dealing with dependence

If a person's drug use is relatively stable and he wants to deal with his dependence, you need to spend some time preparing him for life without drugs. What will he be giving up? How much is the client's current identity (dealer, junkie, deviant, sick, etc.) tied up in drug use? What is going to be put in its place? You need also to discuss how important is the support the user gets from drugs; where emotional support will come from without drugs; and what personal needs drugs satisfy that will go unsatisfied in future. Clients needs to be aware of the importance of these issues before embarking on a detoxification programme. It is usually easier to achieve this the second time round with someone who has tried at least once and relapsed. As drug use becomes more stable and daily intake decreases (perhaps with the help of a short-term stabilising prescription), users become aware of their emotional feelings and needs. At that point they may be more open to looking at the anxieties and fears they experience without the support of anaesthetising chemicals.

One of the advantages of being able to work with someone for a few weeks or months prior to supervising them through either an out-patient or in-patient detoxification is the opportunity to develop a relationship of trust. You can help clients anticipate some of the emotional problems that will arise as drugs cease to have any effect. Clients' fears about giving up drugs can be explored. They should be encouraged to weigh the reasons for continuing to use against the reasons why they want to give up. In this way, they feel that they are making a decision for themselves, not just to please relatives, or the worker. Otherwise most clients will initially view their forthcoming abstinence through rose-tinted spectacles, unprepared for the crash when their emotional support has gone. A planned approach to abstinence will not guarantee success but it will help clients approach it with some awareness of the inevitable after-effects that must be overcome if they are ever to be in control of their drug use.

Choosing the method of intervention

Individual casework and counselling
The most common method is likely to be some form of individual casework which includes a strong element of counselling coupled with help in dealing with practical problems. Individual casework is usually carried out with a set of tasks and goals agreed between client and worker, either on a contractual basis (ie within a set number of weeks or months), or in a more open-ended style. The strategy you choose will depend on your preferred method of working, your theoretical orientation, and previous experience of working with similar clients, rather than any generally agreed 'correct' approach. The most important factor is the relationship established between client and worker; if that is distant or hostile then any counselling technique is doomed to failure.

Group therapy
Although the use of therapeutic groups has long been an accepted way of working with recovering addicts in drug rehabilitation houses and in specialist hospital in-patient units, until fairly recently it has not been used in most out-patient or social work settings. In the past, many workers were reluctant to set up therapeutic groups while clients were still using drugs because they tended to use the time reminiscing about their past drug taking activities and exchanging current information. Given that people were trying to give up drugs, such group sessions were counter-productive. Clients were likely to crave drugs more. Indeed, they were at their most vulnerable on the day the group met and almost inevitably relapsed or increased their drug use. Unless the majority of group members really wanted to effect real change in their lives, they could be held back by the others. Nowadays things are rather different. No longer is it the norm to obtain a generous prescription of injectable drugs. The ethos of treatment is no longer social control, but change. Over the past few years some clinics, probation offices and other specialist settings have started to develop group work as an

integral part of their service, sometimes as part of the initial contract agreeing to offer a prescription.

The group needs to have a defined set of objectives. The group leader(s) should preferably have some training and experience of group work techniques. It can be helpful to have two leaders of equal status. However, there must be agreement between the two on aims and technique, based on a relationship of reasonable trust and respect. There are distinct advantages in groups having two workers. They can compare notes after sessions, pool their insights and discuss possible interpretations, and offer the group members a choice of roles for the leaders, traditionally that of two parents. For those clients with a history of family problems this is particularly beneficial. The two group leaders can mirror well established behaviour patterns laid down at an early age when for example clients may have been played off between parents or, in order to get their own way, have perfected the art of splitting their parents by themselves playing one off against the other. This kind of behaviour is inevitably repeated in a group where it is used to try to drive a wedge between the leaders.

Participation in a therapeutic group helps to prepare clients for some of the more daunting aspects of joining a drug rehabilitation community, especially the 'concept' houses where confrontational groups are an integral part of the programme. It can also enable people to learn from each others' experiences: how for example, to cope with craving, with reducing their prescriptions, and handling relapse. Group sessions help clients to understand some of the reasons why they became regular drug users, to see how common these are and to share the problematic experience of becoming drug-free.

Clients allocated to a group need to have at least a minimal degree of motivation. Some need to recognise that somehow there must be a degree of control of their lives and their drug use. Others of a more active nature will want to bring about some real change in their lifestyle. It may be wiser to place those who are seeking to exert control in one group, and those who are more actively seeking change in a second group. Some clients will adjust quite happily to a group setting. Others will be more apprehensive and perhaps fare better initially with a period of individual counselling. Some may benefit from both. Deciding whether to offer group work may have as much to do with the economic use of your time as any therapeutic goals. Being able to see seven or eight people simultaneously in an hour and a half is clearly more cost-effective than seeing them all individually for an hour at a time. This may have its attractions for drug clinics with waiting lists, especially those dealing with clients who are best offered help at the time they are most motivated, rather than three months later when motivation may have weakened or disappeared.

Family work (see also Chapter 13 – A family affair)
During the full assessment you will have gained some idea of how actively the client has been involved with members of his family, and whether there appear to be any relationship difficulties that need to be resolved if the client is to become drug-free. Many clients are reluctant to allow family members to have contact with their worker. If so do not rush into examining family problems before the client is willing to recognise the possible value of doing so. Many drug users automatically suspect that the worker will form an alliance with their spouse or parents and that they will end up feeling totally isolated and 'got at'. Sometimes an over-zealous therapist, who practises family therapy techniques to the exclusion of individual methods, can alienate the very person who most needs to feel understood by insisting that the whole family meet together too early in the treatment. Never fail to recognise the client's need to be treated as an individual in his own right.

Contact with relatives is most likely to be of a 'one-off' nature, or a series of brief interviews helping them to understand the problems of stopping drug use. But spouses themselves may need positive help in coping with their addicted partners, emotional support and/or help with related social or emotional problems, especially if the family finances have been used on illicit drugs. The partner should be seen by a second worker either in the same team or agency, or in a different agency, such as the local social services area team. If the couple have young children a social worker may already have been allocated to the family. If the couple are experiencing difficulties in their relationship, having trouble in communicating their feelings to each other, they may be further helped by regular or occasional conjoint meetings where angry and hurt feelings can be ventilated. Clients may need persuading of their partner's own need for support and their wish to be more actively involved in treatment.

Once a client has learnt to value regular support and counselling from a trusted worker, the partner may feel jealous and excluded, perhaps believing that the worker is not hearing the whole story. Those partners who have struggled to maintain a respectable image to the outside world of friends and family, and have found themselves very few, if any, close friends they can confide in, should be offered help and recognition of their own needs. Some partners will telephone the worker, ostensibly to 'find out whether he is really coming for treatment' but really hoping to talk about themselves. This can create difficulties for workers who have had trouble persuading clients that their discussions are confidential. At the same time they recognise the partner's resentment at being excluded. Tell the partner that it is not possible to discuss the details of the treatment but suggest that he or she should tell the drug user how much they wish to be more involved with helping him. After all, the partner is the person most affected by any changes that may occur. They could ask the client if they could accompany him to meet the worker at the next appointment. There is no one 'correct' way in which to deal with this situation. The worker can certainly help things by indicating to the client at an early stage, perhaps when analysing the problems, that it may be beneficial to include their partner in the treatment process.

Working with couples who are both drug takers
When a couple are dependent on drugs, both should work towards becoming drug-free at the same time. Otherwise the one attempting it alone will have great difficulty in remaining abstinent for long in the regular company of a drug using partner. It can cause the break-up of the relationship. For some, this may need to happen if either or both partners are to be able to stop drug use, and more often it is the partner who is trying to change who is the one who brings it to an end. The most appropriate methods of work to use when working with couples may be determined as much by agency policy and your own preferences as by any objective criteria.

You should begin by assessing each partner individually in the usual manner. Then discuss with them, first separately and then together, the common problems that need to be addressed, especially those affecting their personal and sexual life, and the effect that coming off drugs may have on the relationship. While they may need each other more after they have relinquished their drug use, they may, paradoxically, find it hard to cope with a close relationhip when no longer leaning on chemical support. Sex is likely to be fairly intermittent or non-existent because of drug induced, diminished sexual drive. This may be one reason for one or both partners seeking help. Conversely it may also be a reason for avoiding becoming drug-free. Some drug takers prefer to avoid the responsibility of a close relationship. To invite a return to intimacy may be extremely threatening, particularly for clients whose experience suggests that people let you down, and that drugs are in the end definitely more reliable.

It is advisable for each partner to be seen by separate workers. If you see them both separately it may be difficult for each to tolerate the worker knowing things about their partner that they may not know. If there are two workers, consider introducing conjoint sessions, either regularly or on every alternate or third individual session. If both partners have a high degree of ambivalence about talking openly in front of each other and have a lot of personal problems they should spend time with their own worker until they are ready for conjoint sessions. If this is not the case and you judge their needs to be adjusting to a relationship without drugs and helping with practical problems, you may be able to see the couple together throughout the treatment. If you are responsible for prescribing, it is advisable to treat them as a couple, preferably stabilising them on the same amount, and then reducing their prescriptions at similar intervals. They can still see separate workers for therapeutic purposes.

This chapter has examined many of the key issues that need to be considered after the full assessment has been completed. As many clients are now expected to embark on a detoxification regime at an early stage of treatment, and therefore have to see physical withdrawal from drugs as a short-term or intermediate-term goal, the next chapter looks at this process before going on to look at the long-term therapeutic relationship which may take some months or longer to develop.

CHAPTER SEVEN

Planning detoxification

Drug specialists and ex-users frequently remark that it is easy for someone to stop taking drugs physically but ten times more difficult to do so psychologically. However true that may be, physically ceasing to take drugs remains an experience that many users dread and will avoid at all costs, either because they have had previous bad experiences or have extremely low tolerance to any form of psychic or physical pain. Unpleasant experiences may stem from a sudden onset of withdrawal symptoms when supplies ran out, rather than from the effects of a supervised detoxification regime.

Detoxification is more successful if clients are reasonably motivated to stop using drugs and have had some previous experience of trying to give up. They are then more likely to accept that the main obstacle to success is the difficulty of coping not with physical pain, but with the longer-term psychological and social problems. The experience can thus be approached in a more realistic manner, recognising that in some ways the problems are just beginning once physical detoxification is completed.

If the detoxification process is managed and supervised carefully, most drug users are unlikely to suffer unduly. At worst withdrawal symptoms are no more taxing than a bad dose of influenza, fairly mild for some, though very uncomfortable for others. Much depends on clients' attitudes, the amount of drugs they have been taking, the support available and the rate of the detoxification programme, whether it is managed rapidly, over, say, a ten-day period, or designed to take several weeks or months. Highly motivated clients with an immediate goal in sight, such as admission to a drug-free community, can reduce very quickly. Some prefer to do so with minimal chemical support, knowing that once they have got through the first few days they will start to feel better, with the worst of the withdrawal symptoms now behind them.

Remember that, while detoxification without drugs ('cold turkey') or with minimal medication from some drugs, including the opioids, is not life threatening, detoxification from others, notably the barbiturates, benzodiazepines and alcohol can be dangerous. It should not be attempted without medical supervision. If there is the slightest doubt, seek expert help before beginning detoxification on a self-help basis (see also Chapter 1 on Drugs and the Drug Problem and Appendix 1, page 164).

Some clients ask for immediate help with detoxification. Others prefer a period of stabilisation (short- or long-term maintenance) before reducing. The latter option has become increasingly unavailable in most parts of the United Kingdom but some clinics and doctors may be prepared to offer an initial period of stabilisation before expecting the client to detoxify. If short-term maintenance is considered most clients who are on opioid drugs will only be offered methadone mixture, not injectable heroin or methadone, as recommended in the *Guidelines of Good Practice in the Treatment of Drug Misuse* (DHSS 1984): 'The drug of choice for prescriptions is oral methadone mixture DTF (1 mgm/ml). There are no clinical guidelines for heroin or other opioids being prescribed unless the patient shows an allergic reaction or other intolerable side-effects of methadone'.

The *Guidelines* also state that a medically supervised detox-ification is more likely to be successful, 'when doctor and patient have got to know each other, and a basic contract about the regime has been mutually agreed. Doctor and patient must therefore be in clear agreement about the need to reduce the drug dose and about the time-scale of the regime. In general it is best to respond to a patient's own determination and time-scale to withdraw from drugs, rather than the doctor imposing a too speedy or protracted regime. If a patient is eager to come off drugs quickly or abruptly, it may be better to support this clinically so as to reinforce motivation. If, however, the patient finds speedy withdrawal too stressful, the doctor can adjust the regime to be more gradual. Very long, protracted withdrawal schedules – for opioids, in excess of six months – are too close to a self-perpetuating maintenance type schedule, and are to be avoided. All regimes should keep in the forefront a clear management strategy of eventual drug abstinence.'

When clients are preparing for detoxification some clearly have a variety of options available, while others have very few, depending on the part of the country in which they live and whether or not they have private financial means. The following list describes most of the currently available ways by which someone can detoxify:

– admission to a specialist in-patient unit in hospital, either for a specific period of physical detoxification or for several months to include participation in a longer-term therapeutic programme. (This is a scarce resource.)

– admission to a general medical or psychiatric ward. Some drug clinics have access to one or two beds, usually on the understanding that only one problem drug taker is admitted to a ward at a time to avoid management problems.

– supervision by the patient's general practitioner who may or may not know the patient well.

– an out-patient supervised reduction at the local drug clinic.

– in a crisis intervention unit.

– at home with the support of a community psychiatric nurse or a member of a local community drug problem team in liaison with the general practitioner.

– at home, without methadone. Self-help with support from family, friends or professional worker.

– admission to a private clinic for up to six weeks. These are expensive, but a number have an assisted places scheme for which there is usually a waiting list.

The most common resource is likely to be the patient's general practitioner working in liaison with another member of the primary health or social care team such as a community psychiatric nurse, social worker or probation officer, and preferably with support from the regional drug problem team. Clients who have a multiplicity of problems, those who are fairly chaotic, and those who have already tried and failed to stop several times on an out-patient basis may benefit from admission to a specialist in-patient unit. Unfortunately they may then have to wait several months before a vacancy occurs. A small number of private clinics take people with chemical dependence problems for up to six to eight weeks for both detoxification and individual and group counselling. The programme (based on the 'Minnesota method') introduces people to Narcotics Anonymous and encourages continued attendance at NA meetings after discharge. As with any in-patient facility in the National Health Service, the programme is unlikely to be the end of treatment. Ultimate success for the majority is likely to depend on the client receiving continued support from professionals and family, with attendance at NA meetings to consolidate the residential treatment.

Clients in full-time employment may not be able, or willing, to enter a hospital or drug-free community, unless their employer knows about their drug problem. Most are reluctant to jeopardise their job or career. With regular counselling and support they should be able to succeed by slowly cutting down their prescription of methadone as an out-patient, provided that any emotional problems masked by drug use do not threaten an early relapse. Ironically, while a client may have been motivated to stop using drugs because he was spending his earnings on the habit, once off drugs he has again to be highly motivated not to buy drugs with his spare cash. Luckily, most clients are likely to have a backlog of debts to pay so this need not be a problem. If this is not so, then encourage your client to put the surplus cash to good use by improving the home, buying new clothes and picking up old interests.

The first attempt to come off drugs on a reducing prescription may be successful. For many clients, however, the first attempt is a 'trial run' followed by several others. If a client has never made a conscious attempt to detoxify before he may have a limited understanding of the emotional problems this can generate. People are often unwilling to acknowledge the gap which ceasing to take drugs leaves in their life, to recognise the need to find some purpose for their existence and to try to cope without an emotional crutch. Your assessment should have given some indication of the importance of drugs in a person's life but some factors may not become apparent to either client or worker until drugs are removed. The first attempt may be a learning experience that can stand clients in good stead when they next try to stop. The second or third time round they will perhaps be more prepared to avail themselves of any support and advice available. Try to help the client to handle relapse by seeing it as part of the process of stopping drug use. It is a way of identifying the difficulties they need to give greater attention to the next time. (See also Chapter 8 on Achieving longer-term goals.)

If someone tries to come off without seeing the worker for regular support or while still living with drug users he is very likely to relapse. Indeed, it could be said that he is setting himself up to fail. Without motivation and the ability to organise his life he simply lacks enough commitment to treatment.

Opinions differ as to whether it is preferable to wait until a client is highly motivated to come off drugs before putting him on a detoxification programme, or whether he should be encouraged to accept a reducing prescription even if he is poorly motivated and would prefer a period of maintenance methadone. Rather than start someone on a reducing programme that he cannot handle, some agencies have tried developing a flexible approach, recognising the inevitable ambivalence of the new client who feels forced to attend, perhaps because of a court case or angry spouse. Instead of automatically completing a structured full assessment and initiating a reducing prescription, they offer more informal sessions on certain days when clients can drop in and talk about their situation. Slowly they can thus be helped to decide what they want to do. This approach does have some merit in giving people much needed time and space to talk to an objective listener, to obtain advice in dealing with practical problems, to get a clearer idea of treatment options available and to ponder the implications of becoming drug free. It also means clients have a chance to establish a therapeutic relationship as a sound basis for support during the detoxification phase. in this way they approach detoxification with a greater degree of motivation.

Attendance at Narcotics Anonymous as part of the detoxification programme

Branches of Narcotics Anonymous (NA) are being established all over the country, particularly in the London area, some meeting in NHS drug clinics. Following a programme based on the original 'ten steps' of Alcoholics Anonymous, members are encouraged to view themselves as chemically dependent. They learn to appreciate the need to avoid using not only their preferred drug but also other chemical substances, such as alcohol and tranquillisers, with abuse potential. Members are encouraged to adopt the philosophy of living 'a day at a time' and to acknowledge the power of a force greater than themselves, which for the spiritually inclined may be God, and for others may be the Group itself.

Some workers encourage clients to attend NA meetings while embarking on either a self-help detoxification or a supervised detoxification. This enables the drug user to reduce while obtaining support from others in a similar situation. This can increase confidence in the possibility of succeeding. Some may reject the advice of the worker to attend because it is all too demanding or threatening. Or they do not like to see themselves mirrored in the face of other NA members, preferring to avoid the reality of their own situation.

Suzanne

At thirty, Suzanne had been married for six years and had settled in London because of her husband's work. She referred herself for help to her local drug clinic after she had been smoking heroin regularly for two years. Although she was not currently employed, she had a good record of work in a variety of semi-skilled jobs. She was concerned about the effects her drug use was having on her marriage which had deteriorated over the past year. She was spending more and more money on heroin, had lost weight, had frequent rows with her husband about her drug use, had lost all interest in sex and was becoming increasingly depressed.

On assessment Suzanne was co-operative and friendly. Although she did not appear to have any significant emotional or social problems she had obviously had difficulty in settling in London. Both she and her husband came from Wales. Suzanne was one of a large close-knit family and missed her parents badly. Her worker felt this might be something that Suzanne would need to look at carefully if she were to give up taking heroin. She was offered a reducing prescription to cover a three month period, of 40 mgm methadone mixture on the understanding that she would collect her drugs daily from a local chemist and attend the clinic weekly for supportive counselling sessions with her key worker, one of the clinic social workers.

After the first month of treatment she had made considerable improvement. She had stopped buying illicit drugs. There were no signs of stress. She had found a part-time job and had started to eat a more balanced diet. The worker described her as positively 'glowing'. However, towards the end of the second month, it was clear that, as a result of her apparent rapid movement, she had decided that there was no need to discuss any other substantial issues such as what the future might be like without drugs. The worker realised that she was on a 'pink cloud' and somewhat confused. Surely, argued Suzanne, the problem as far as she was concerned was heroin. Her personal circumstances and needs were not relevant. She assumed that the only other problem was where she had settled. If she and her husband had not moved to London away from her family she would not have developed a heroin problem. The worker realised that if he tried to point out that there were, in his opinion, some other questions that needed to be addressed, Suzanne would simply refuse to listen. However, he felt it necessary to say to her that her marital problems and use of free time would not automatically disappear once she stopped her medication. He encouraged her to go to Narcotics Anonymous, suggesting that it was a good time for her to see how others experienced the difficulties of coming off drugs. She was reluctant to do so, through a mixture of pride and guilt. Moreover, she did not want to hear others say how difficult coming off drugs could be.

By the third month she was using other drugs and had started to miss her regular appointments. By the end of the fourth month she was again using heroin regularly and had dropped out of treatment. She felt depressed, disillusioned and guilty at letting down her worker. Eventually, three months later, she returned for help. She was again put on a reducing prescription, and again did well initially but still refused to go to NA. This time the worker put more pressure on her to look at the reasons for her drug use and this time she was more ready to do so. There was no 'pink cloud' to colour her judgement. She continued to dabble intermittently, using small amounts of heroin, until she eventually assumed more control and stopped altogether. After she had stopped using for three months she and her husband moved back to Wales, so that she could be nearer her family. He would continue to work partly in London until he could transfer his work elsewhere.

On her second attempt at a detox, Suzanne was more realistic, discussing some of the conflicts she had about living in London, and the fact that she did not have a satisfying career like her husband. She admitted that she needed to do something about her work rather than flit from one job to another. She seemed to have difficulty allowing herself to develop as an individual. She lacked self-esteem, preferring to avoid conflict by taking heroin. She recognised that she had to look at some of her own needs. What did she want out of life? Was she going to have children? If not, she needed to find some other way of obtaining personal fulfilment. She chose, in the end, to give up drugs to save her marriage. The couple compromised, so that Suzanne was able to return to her native Wales. Her ability to stay drug-free from now on will depend on her ability to make use of the counselling she received and whether she, in reality, feels more 'at home' and sure of herself back in her original environment. It is also vital of course that her husband copes with the change in his routine and living arrangements.

Self-help detox

Many opiate drug users do not want a medically supervised detoxification. Many know from experience that they can cut down themselves, either by slowly taking a smaller amount each day or just stopping altogether and 'sweating it out' at home with the help of minor analgesics and family or friends. Many have difficulty in finally stopping all drugs, persuading themselves that they are virtually drug-free when they have managed to stop taking their preferred drug, usually the one they believe they will have most difficulty in stopping. Some may be tempted to replace their original drug of choice with minor tranqullisers, sedatives, over-the-counter medicines or alcohol.

Clients who have managed to stop using opiates on their own may need help in finally giving up other drugs that they regard as less important. For example:

Mark

When Mark decided after four years of regular use that it was time he tried to stop (primarily because the police were becoming too interested in his activities), he and a close friend who had a similar drug habit decided to come off drugs together by virtually cutting out all opiates and taking minor painkillers to overcome the worst of the withdrawals. They achieved this without too much difficulty. Some weeks later, in response to family pressure, Mark agreed to see a worker to prevent a relapse and to see if he could sort out his life. He claimed during the initial interviews that he was just taking some tranquillisers prescribed by his GP to help him sleep, and that otherwise he was virtually off all drugs.

After several sessions, during which he expressed some interest in going to a drug-free rehabilitation community, he admitted that he was using amphetamine sulphate, but sought to reassure the worker that he was not dependent, that he could 'take it or leave it'. His worker reminded him of the need to be totally drug-free if he wanted to go to the drug rehabilitation house and suggested that he might find it helpful to monitor his drug use in the coming week by keeping a daily record of consumption. At the next weekly session Mark reported that he had kept a diary, more out of curiosity than anything, and was embarrassed to find that he had genuinely under-estimated his daily consumption of different drugs. He felt that he had been fooling himself into believing that, as he had managed to finish with heroin, he had no need to worry about taking other drugs. He was particularly concerned about his use of amphetamine which he only took because, like opiates, this could be injected. This made him realise that he was still dependent on injecting and on the idea of taking drugs to help him through the day. He saw that he still had some way to go if he was to be able to describe himself as 'drug-free'.

At the end of the session Mark decided that his first goal would be to try to cut out amphetamine, in the hope that this would stop him injecting. He also determined to reduce his consumption of tranquillisers in the day-time, which he may have been using partly to counteract the effects of the amphetamine, and partly to be able to take 'something'. He also realised that finally stopping drugs completely might mean confronting some unwelcome feelings about himself and his family. He could not avoid indefinitely looking at the gaps left by his drug taking career. He decided that perhaps a drug rehabilitation house might help him both to sort himself out and to find some alternatives to drug use. Otherwise drugs would again be controlling his life.

These two studies illustrate different ways of detoxifying from drugs. The methods you and your client choose will depend on a variety of factors, not least, how this aspect of treatment fits in with an overall treatment plan. You may be able to help them concentrate on achieving some longer-term goals, while getting used to coping with being 'straight' or drug-free.

CHAPTER EIGHT

Achieving longer-term goals

Developing a therapeutic relationship

The need to establish a relationship of trust and confidentiality when working with drug users cannot be over-estimated. It is an essential part of the therapeutic process, common to all social work practice. You should regard it as the most important skill the worker has to acquire. Most workers learn to establish a relationship with clients through experience and trial and error. If you have no training or experience in interpersonal skills and wish to learn how to counsel drug users, your starting point should be a broader training in counselling and/or casework skills. (Full or part-time and evening courses may be available locally.) These can be adapted to the problems of drug users. The key skills needed are generic, similar to those employed with mentally ill or child care cases, and are not specific to work with opioid, amphetamine or solvent users.

During the early stages of establishing a relationship, the client's ambivalence towards accepting help and trusting the worker needs to be recognised, along with his inevitable mixed motivation. Some workers find it difficult to tolerate what often appear to be minimal rewards at this stage. However, you have to accept that ambivalence and fear on the part of the client are normal. Dealing with these is an essential part of the process of the therapeutic relationship. Drug users, especially those dependent on a daily supply of illicit substances, survive by living a lie from day to day, hoping that there will always be enough drugs for tomorrow and that they will not fall ill. They therefore find it difficult to trust anyone, including other drug takers. A worker has to understand the world of a client. That does not mean appearing to be an active part of it or condoning it. Equally, it does not mean making facial expressions of shock and disapproval that will only serve to reinforce the client's belief that professionals 'don't understand about drugs', thereby reducing the chance of developing trust and empathy.

Getting across the message that you are interested both in helping clients with their drug problem and in getting to know the person behind the problem is of key importance. Many problem drug takers have a very low sense of self-esteem, contrary to the external image they may present. They may not believe they are worth helping, or can be helped. In the early stages of contact they can enjoy talking to someone in confidence about themselves, someone who believes that they are capable of change and who is interested in them as a person. While clients need to feel that you have something to offer that will help them sort out their difficulties, they also need to feel that you understand the attraction of drugs and how they can fill a gap of loneliness, lack of confidence, emptiness and emotional pain. They need to feel that you recognise that they are taking a big leap into the unknown by trying to assume some responsibility for their problems. Make it clear that you see how difficult it is for them to envisage a life without drugs.

Opinions vary as to the degree of in-depth work that can and should be attempted with drug takers while they are still using drugs. Opioids, sedatives and tranquillisers enable the client to block off any unpleasant feelings. Heroin, particularly, seems to provide a symbolic glass wall between the user and the external stresses, irritations and pressures of everyday life including the demands of personal relationships. It is therefore unlikely that any in-depth counselling or psychotherapy will be of much benefit until the user has become drug-free and made some commitment to overcoming his drug related problems, and even then the progress will be slow. The dilemma for the worker with a preference for in-depth work is clear. If you rush into interpretative work too early with clients for whom personal therapy is thought to be necessary they may not return for further appointments. You may, quite simply, be banging your head against a brick wall, wasting your own time and energy. The client is being asked to look at feelings that he is not used to experiencing or recognising, and is certainly not ready to explore.

When working with clients who are extremely vulnerable with a high degree of emotional disturbance, it is even more questionable whether therapy that includes interpretative work can be achieved satisfactorily on an out-patient or non-residential basis. Such clients can sometimes be referred to an in-patient unit, either a drug unit or sometimes even a psychotherapy unit. If the client is drug-free referral can be made to a suitable drug rehabilitation house offering individual and group therapeutic treatment. In a residential setting it is easier for clients to work on personal areas of their life in the company of peers who have had similar experiences and where support is available should painful insights occur that would have provoked a drug crisis in the world outside.

While most social workers would accept that client dependence on the worker is inevitable, some are more wary of establishing a relationship with drug taking clients that risks creating another sort of dependence problem. They see the helping relationship being offered as an alternative to drugs, thus causing some clients to become too reliant on the worker. In fact many clients say that their worker is the 'only friend' they have, sometimes to flatter and gain approval, but more often because it is true. At the same time many clients are afraid of becoming over-dependent on their worker because it awakens experiences of loss or rejection by family or other professionals. When they find themselves becoming dependent they may become anxious that the worker is going to leave (especially during the holiday season, even if they have been told it is only for two weeks) and test out the relationship by taking extra drugs. Some dependence on the part of clients, whether mentally ill, delinquent, elderly or problem drug takers is inevitable. This dependence needs to be recognised by the worker, and perhaps discussed with the client at some stage, as part of the process of learning to cope with relationships without drugs and learning to trust others. Both worker and client also need to recognise that close relationships or friendships usually have an element of interdependence. It may be necessary tactfully to clarify the nature of the client–worker relationship, to help clients accept that, although you may be a friendly professional whom they can confide in, this is not quite the same as a friendship between two people who offer each other mutual care and companionship.

When the client becomes more self-reliant, the worker may reduce the frequency of sessions, from say weekly to fortnightly, then perhaps monthly. You could introduce clients to a support group or Narcotics Anonymous that will provide an opportunity for developing outside interests, thus increasing confidence in coping in the long term without the help of the worker. Recognising the problem of worker dependence is crucial when staff leave an agency. Clients need to be prepared for this eventuality and helped to accept that they have not 'done something' to drive the worker away. Ideally it helps if the new worker can be introduced to the client by the departing worker to ensure smooth handover. Unfortunately, employment practices sometimes make it difficult for this to happen. Anyone assuming responsibility for a previous worker's clients, particularly when the worker had the affection and respect of clients, needs to be sensitive to the clients' feelings.

Achieving longer term goals

Staff in specialist drug agencies often talk about the need to encourage clients to accept responsibility for themselves. Clients often make workers feel that they should be taking responsibility for them or that they should be finding a doctor who will do this by giving them the drugs that they claim are essential for their well-being. For example, when they are out of control, overdosing, physically sick, suffering from self-neglect or withdrawals, some clients may imply that it is not their fault or responsibility, thus playing on the worker's natural feelings of responsibility and humanitarian wish to care for people, reinforced by the unpleasant fear that someone might die if something is not done. (See also Chapter 15 on Some Common Problems).

When discussing issues around unemployment, workers should avoid getting caught up in such discussions as, 'If only I could find something else to do with my life as an alternative to taking drugs: if only I could be an artist, brain surgeon, musician, social worker . . .'. Such yearnings are often little more than a diversionary trap for a worker anxious to provide alternatives. The alternative is admittedly not necessarily exciting. At times it may well be dreary and depressing; quite simply, life itself is the alternative, learning to cope with the highs and lows of everyday life without the artificial support of drugs. That in itself is a frightening prospect for many who have forgotten what so called 'normality' is and may not even be sure of what it involves.

One of the frustrations of long-term work with this group is the feeling of 'sitting it out'. For long periods it may feel as if nothing much is happening for the client. There may be little the worker can do except 'be around' to maintain the relationship, giving positive reinforcement when there seems to be some attempt at progress.

Crisis

Invariably, at some stage a crisis will occur. When it does, you can capitalise on it because the client will then be more motivated to see the need for change. The temptation to want to help people to avoid crises may well be strong, but in some instances they may be the only occasions when any real growth takes place. A crisis may take several forms: an overdose, the loss of a relationship or a court case resulting in a remand in custody. Some of the most notable changes have occurred with clients I have known and 'sat it out' with for years until they finally reached a major crisis, culminating in admission to a psychiatric unit or to a general hospital, or to a crisis intervention unit. They had finally reached 'rock bottom' because they could no longer avoid the consequences of their self-destructive behaviour. At this point they were at their most vulnerable and so were willing to consider alternatives to drug use. The role of the worker is to encourage clients to put into practice some of their good intentions, helping them to take advantage of the opportunity for growth created by events. Motivation, which may have been virtually non-existent, may suddenly re-appear and enable the client to be more responsive to professional intervention. When a client has been putting off decisions about finally giving up drugs, a crisis may be all that is required to give the push towards making some creative changes.

Carol

Carol is a good example of someone who reached crisis point. She was in her early thirties and had used heroin and other drugs on and off since her late teens. In her mid-twenties her small daughter was run over and killed when she ran into the road while her mother was talking to friends. Carol went from crisis to crisis, frequently over-dosing by supplementing her methadone with sedatives and alcohol. After a period of comparative stability she slowly began to reduce her prescription and talk vaguely about finally stopping drug use.

After a particularly disastrous relationship broke up, she suddenly went into an acute anxiety state and had to be admitted to the local psychiatric unit. After 24 hours' admission she told the staff and her clinic worker that she wanted to transfer to a methadone detoxification regime, and would not listen to any advice to the contrary. She came off her drugs without too much discomfort physically, but emotionally she was overwhelmed with a sense of grief and guilt about her daughter's death which she had never allowed herself to experience before. She used the counselling sessions with her clinic worker to face the pain of the past and to begin to make some tentative plans for the future. She decided to make a clean break from the area and accepted the offer of a place in a supportive hostel. When last heard of she had a rewarding job, a stable relationship and had been drug-free for 5 years.

Post-detoxification

Clearly, the process of coming off drugs need not be too difficult – the problem is staying off drugs. Some clients feel quite depressed after their initial feelings of achievement on completing a successful detoxification. With some drug users this may be due to physiological factors. Amphetamine users, for example, invariably feel tired and depressed after coming down from existing on artificial adrenaline. For many clients, though, depression is likely to derive from a sense of loss when they decide to give up the drug that once brought pleasure and escape. In addition they lose the lifestyle and friends that went with drug taking. Inevitably, like the end of a love affair, however painful it may have been, when it is over there is invariably nothing else to fill the immediate gap. It becomes easier to remember the good times and forget the bad. It is important for the worker to recognise this phase as one of 'mourning' for a part of life that has had to be relinquished. With the regrets comes an ambivalence that could threaten a relapse. Clients need to be helped to recognise this as a natural process, not as a sign that the detox has failed. Some feel anger and resentment that they have had to stop, while their friends or acquaintances are still able to enjoy the use of the same drugs, apparently remaining in control.

One of the frustrating aspects at this stage is the strong likelihood that many clients will suddenly decide that they are no longer in need of support following completion of their physical detoxification programme. They stop attending counselling sessions designed to deal with the emotional difficulties disguised by drugs. Some may attend once or twice and then telephone to say that they have decided that they do not want to see the worker again, that they must do the rest on their own. While some, particularly those without major drug related problems, will be able to turn their back on the old life and resist temptation, others will inevitably relapse and perhaps make contact again.

Some will ask to see their worker when they have found out that it is difficult to cope alone without having someone to talk to who understands why they still feel they need to use drugs. They need the worker to support their attempt to avoid relapse. When they resume contact some will say that they are now prepared to accept that they need to look at the emotional aspects of giving up drugs that they had previously avoided recognising. They may then be more committed to enter into another phase of help, perhaps on a more psychotherapeutic basis when their reactions to painful insight may be less likely to lead to drug use.

Workers must be able to adopt a long-term perspective when working with problem drug takers. Some will make as many as six, ten, fifteen or even twenty attempts at stopping before they finally manage to take control of their drug use. During that time they will perhaps, but not necessarily, have had intermittent drug-free periods when they have made several steps forward.

Relapse

During these drug-free periods you can work with the client to identify the factors and situations that seem to trigger off a relapse back into drug taking. The relapsing nature of problem drug use has already been referred to several times. Most people are liable to return to behaviours that include an element of pleasure or escape; therefore relapse is not unique to drug users, it is part of normal behaviour. It is important for a worker to be aware of his own likely responses when clients resume drug use. Evident disappointment may only increase the sense of hopelessness and guilt that they feel because they have wasted the worker's time – let you down. Unfortunately, some clients try giving up drugs more to please the worker, or their relatives, than themselves. They have to do it because *they* want to.

It is important to help clients accept that although relapse may be inevitable in the early stages it may be possible for them to learn to anticipate a relapse and to develop ways of coping with the event. As Rowdy Yates of the Lifeline project has suggested, for most drug takers relapse is not a sudden occurrence. It generally follows a slip or a lapse; perhaps the isolated use of a drug with friends to see if they can enjoy it without becoming 'addicted'. While a few people may be able to handle that one 'slip' others will continue to have 'lapses' so that the frequency of use builds up to the extent that drugs and not the individual are once again 'in control'. Some users, having tried again just once will tell themselves, 'It's no good, I can't cope without drugs'.

There are any number of reasons why relapse occurs. But it is hardly ever accidental. Some common factors include:

– the inability to find alternatives – a job, new friends
– trying to achieve too much, too soon. Some try to be perfect at work and at home, and in caring for their children. (See also Chapter 14 on Pregnancy and Child Care.)
– working too hard with little time for a social life
– unresolved anger or hurt towards relatives or friends
– isolation, shyness, and spending too much time alone. Some people manage to maintain a large number of acquaintances but avoid developing close friendships – friends 'let you down if you get too close'

– mixing with current drug takers
– the use of alcohol or prescribed psycho–active drugs, perhaps for depression

Some specialist workers in Britain are becoming interested in developing relapse prevention techniques (RP), especially since most heroin addicts can no longer expect a maintenance supply of drugs. These techniques were originally developed by G. Alan Martlatt and colleagues in the United States. Briefly, RP is 'a self-management program designed to enhance the maintenance stage of the habit-change process . . . RP procedures can be applied in the form of specific maintenance program to prevent relapse or as a more global program of lifestyle change'.

Peter visited a social worker who had been developing her skills on relapse prevention techniques:

'He had used amphetamines regularly for twelve years. He was a successful sales representative, who had managed to cease taking drugs completely several times on his own, but he always relapsed after six to eight weeks. He and the worker identified several key factors that seemed to precipitate a relapse: availability, contact with drug using friends, low self-esteem, alcohol use and losing his temper. They began by looking at the first two factors, availability and friends. Peter decided that easy availability was perhaps not the real issue – he had to choose to make himself unavailable. In relation to that his drug taking "friends" were really only acquaintances, whom he didn't bother associating with unless he wanted to use drugs. At times he planned a relapse by, for example, deliberately engineering a row with his wife, which he would then use as an excuse for going in search of amphetamine sulphate. At a later session he was pleased to be able to recount a recent argument when, instead of resorting to drug or alcohol use, he had gone for a long walk to cool off, returning later to discuss their differences more rationally.'

Maintaining a drug-free lifestyle
Maintaining change is a continuous process that has to become part of a new way of coping with life's pressures, with boredom, stress and frustration. Many ex-drug users (recovering addicts) need longer-term support with personal counselling or group psychotherapy. Those who have unresolved emotional difficulties may find continued professional help essential to enable them to avoid relapse. For some, NA may provide the support they need. Like its sister organisa-

tion, Alcoholics Anonymous, it has a highly structured and spiritual format that suits some people but not others.

Coping with alcohol

Recovering addicts have to cope with society's socially approved (and most dangerous) drug, alcohol. Do they attempt to become a controlled drinker, do they use alcohol as a substitute or do they opt for total abstinence? Even if they drank only occasionally while using opioids or their preferred drug, most are tempted to seek support from alcohol during recovery. Many find themselves tempted to drink in much the same way as they took drugs, to blot out stress and gain confidence in facing new social situations. This invariably means getting drunk. The situation is often unwittingly encouraged by well intentioned relatives and friends who fail to grasp that the person is at risk of just exchanging one problem for another.

Professionals and friends often find it extremely difficult to accept that the recovering addict cannot become a social drinker immediately. Workers have to help clients recognise that alcohol may be a problem in the short term, while for some abstinence may be the only answer if they are going to regain control of their life.

Many recovering addicts have embraced the NA philosophy of total abstinence because they found that they transferred their dependency needs to alcohol, despite many attempts at being a controlled drinker. Some attend NA meetings for several years until they have rebuilt their personal and social life and no longer feel in need of the continued support of other drug users.

Becoming a professional in the drug field

Many drug takers express a genuine interest while in treatment in helping others with similar problems to their own. The majority eventually decide after several years of drugs and social workers that it is not for them. But many clients do acquire considerable skills in counselling and group work techniques through participating in intensive therapeutic community programmes. They also have a unique understanding of the client's situation which can never be quite equalled by even the most experienced professional.

If someone is seriously going to attempt to join the ranks of the professionals, he should wait until he can cope with the pressures of everyday life. Most drug agencies prefer ex-users to have had at least a year out of treatment and to be able to demonstrate that in that time they have held down a job, however unskilled, away from the drugs field, or that they have completed some further education or done some voluntary work. They need to be able to prove to themselves and future employers that they are not going to want to experience being an addict at second hand, by working with people with similar problems. If they have not been able to establish another life for themselves in the community they will have an unhealthy reliance on work and colleagues, depending on the latter for their personal and social life.

There are advantages and disadvantages for ex-users to consider when thinking of opting for a career in the drugs field. Being a stable ex-user is not the only acceptable qualification. The usual qualities looked for when selecting staff are of equal importance. The emotional pressures of dealing with other people's problems day after day should not be under-estimated. Some people may benefit from trying themselves out as a volunteer on, say, a telephone drug line to see how they handle the pressures.

Other advantages that ex-users have include:

– being able to empathise with other drug takers and to have an automatic understanding of their experiences
– the fact that drug takers have trust in the worker when they realise that he or she is an ex-user. They assume (not always correctly) that the worker has used the same drugs as they did and therefore understands
– being able, almost intuitively, to confront the client when he is lying. As one experienced worker who is a recovering addict said, 'You are able to blow people's cover. It is much easier when you know they are telling lies and indulging in games playing.'

However, some apparent advantages can also be disadvantages:

– clients can be wary of ex-users who are good at confrontation
– workers can get carried away by their over-enthusiasm and be too confrontative. This is not helpful for all clients
– there is a danger of over-identification. It is tempting to see someone else's behaviour as a reflection of the ex-user's own past
– some can be over-committed to one particular treatment approach: 'What worked for me is the only right approach.'

Those ex-users who lack formal qualifications may have difficulty in coping with some practical situations. For example, having to attend court with clients, to visit prison or hospitals can be difficult because of the memories that come flooding back. Most ex-users who decide to return to the drugs field as workers realise that it will not be easy. They need regular support and supervision from seniors and opportunities for developing professional skills. Having a drug-related criminal record will not necessarily bar someone from being considered for a position in a social work or drug agency. Most employing authorities, statutory or non-statutory, require people to declare any criminal record. Most employers interested in having ex-users on their staff realise that such applicants are likely to have had some brush with the law, and to have served a probation order or even a prison sentence. Most will be more interested in looking at how the person dealt with that experience, rather than automatically rejecting him or her, unless the offence was related to assault or offences against adults or children.

Any ex-user contemplating a career in social work or counselling would be well advised to try eventually to undertake a formal professional training. It helps to avoid some of the possible professional problems listed earlier, and to use their personal experiences objectively, to stand back and look at theory and practice and have an opportunity for intensive supervised practical experience. It also provides much greater flexibility and security when it comes to future employment. Those who have managed to complete their training as a counsellor, therapist or social worker have a great sense of achievement and will be able to work in a wide variety of settings. They can also demonstrate that they have finally 'made it' in more ways than one.

Most of the 'stages of intervention' described in Chapter 4 have now been discussed. Those that remain relate to the use of outside agencies, and although some clients may not actually need to be referred elsewhere, it is important to be familiar with the role of the specialist drug services. The next two chapters describe the range of medical, psychiatric and residential rehabilitation facilities currently available in the United Kingdom. It is important to note that there are now many other specialist facilities, such as community drug teams and advice and counselling centres (see Chapter 16) which are able to see problem drug takers themselves, to support other professionals, or to help identify the most appropriate specialist resources.

CHAPTER NINE

Medical and psychiatric services

The past twenty years or so have seen a marked change in attitudes towards the treatment of drug problems. And this is reflected in corresponding changes in professional practice. Until the late 1960s drug problems were almost exclusively the province of the medical profession. It was widely assumed that doctors, and doctors alone, possessed the expertise necessary to understand and cope with these particular clients. But, encouragingly, the drug taker has become increasingly 'demedicalised'. Instead of doctors taking sole responsibility, the trend has been towards a multidisciplinary style of intervention. Now the medical profession has been joined by social workers, psychologists and nurses, not to mention secretaries, all forming part of an integrated team. Only the GP for the most part remains, by the very nature of his job, in relative isolation and concentrating primarily on the medical aspects of care.

The term 'multidisciplinary team' can be applied at two levels. First, and most commonly, it is the group of staff based in a specific unit such as a hospital or clinic. Secondly, though, there is a tendency for professionals to link up on a community-wide basis. Each member of the team in this sort of structure will work for a different agency in the community but will still identify with a symbolic team that shares responsibility for a given group of clients.

Whatever the structure – institution or community-centred – there are two main approaches to the multidisciplinary effort. It is worthwhile bearing in mind these two quite different models, which can be called the 'key-worker' and the 'expertise' models.

In the *key-worker* approach everyone in the team, irrespective of his or her background discipline is responsible for the personal management of a group of clients. This involves seeking help and advice from other team members when specialised knowledge is required or when particular problems crop up, but for the most part the key-worker model means a blurring of staff roles and greater flexibility on the part of each team member. Even decisions on such matters as prescribing policy are shared by all team members which must, in this case, include a doctor.

The *expertise* model – the more traditional approach – has a team working together, often, but not always, in the same building, each doing his or her duties strictly according to discipline. The means that the doctor is chiefly responsible for the clinical assessment and management of the patient (any consultation with non-medical members of the team being optional on the doctor's part). Social workers in this set-up may be more or less confined to dealing with the practicalities of the client's life and working with the client's family.

With both models, however democratic the organisation may be, the person leading the team, and with ultimate professional responsibility, is always a consultant psychiatrist. This is not always so in other countries. In the United States and Canada, for example, the leader of a methadone clinic may well be a social worker, a psychologist or a recovered addict.

While the doctor's role may have diminished over the past twenty years, it is important to recognise that doctors still have a part to play because of their specific training and skills and also because of their unique treatment and referral duties as family physicians. Areas requiring special attention from doctors include; physical complications, drug therapy, overdose, emotional and psychiatric problems, and possibly referral on to specialist medical or psychiatric services. The doctor most likely to be involved initially is the client's general practitioner. Many drug users, however, particularly those in some big cities who have no permanent address, are unlikely to have a concerned GP, although they may perhaps have a temporary arrangement with a doctor in order to obtain prescriptions for drugs that have only added further to their problems.

Primary health care – the role of the general practitioner
In the 1960s a small number of mainly private, 'specialist' GPs were identified with the indiscriminate prescribing of heroin and cocaine. Although their right to prescribe these drugs to addicts was withdrawn under the 1967 Dangerous Drugs Act (and *Diconal* since 1984), GPs can still prescribe methadone and other drugs popular with drug users, such as the amphetamines and methylphenodate. All these drugs are

subject to the controls of the 1971 Misuse of Drugs Act so that irresponsible prescribing is likely to attract the attention of the Home Office. Most doctors are reluctant to prescribe, particularly to someone with whom they have had no previous contact. However, an increasing number of GPs are prepared to prescribe methadone to addicts either on a short-term detoxification basis or to assist stabilisation. Where possible, they are encouraged to seek advice and support from the local drug clinic. They may also assist in supporting individual clients seen initially by the regional or district drug problem team, particularly when the client lives a long way from the specialist centre. A specially prepared set of guidelines for GPs and other doctors was published by the DHSS in 1984 to assist in treating drug misuse (see Appendix 3).

It is often difficult to decide when it is appropriate to involve the GP with drug users on psychiatric grounds, especially if the social worker has been responsible for the overall casework with the client. Generally, the client is not just someone who is unhappy and having difficulties with 'coping with life' but rather a person who is quite clearly clinically depressed, possibly suicidal, over-anxious and/or presenting clear signs of formal psychiatric illness, particularly if he or she has a history of psychiatric treatment. In such circumstances, it may be helpful to refer to the GP for advice or medication to treat, for example, a severe depressive episode, if it is felt that the client will use this responsibly. If the psychiatric symptoms are so serious that the client needs in-patient care, the GP's help is needed to refer the client to hospital for admission.

Other conditions that would require treatment by the GP include acute drug taking pathology (problems arising from physical dependence), renal or liver damage (including hepatitis), and other infections caused by dirty needles. It is also important to encourage clients to learn when to use GP services for more generalised physical complaints and not to leave them until a more serious condition such as pneumonia has developed. This is a very real danger when a client has avoided contact with his doctor or has been black-listed from the surgery because of attempts to obtain drugs.

The problems of drug users take time to unravel and time is a commodity that many GPs simply do not have. Consultations are often limited to a mere five to ten minutes per patient, so it is not surprising that drug users tend to see GPs as sources of supply rather than as clinicians who are there to help them kick the habit. The GP perhaps best placed to help is the one in a group practice at a health centre. He can then either refer people on to hospital or see if additional community support can be given by a member of the health care team such as the community psychiatric nurse (sometimes attached to a GP practice), health visitor or social worker. Some practices may have counsellors attached to them whose help might be appropriately enlisted – especially, perhaps, with the non-opiate user who is looking to drugs such as tranquillisers and sedatives to relieve anxiety and stress. Where the doctor has time and a special personal interest, he may wish to undertake the counselling himself or to liaise closely with another worker for this purpose.

If social workers or probation officers find they are seeing an increasing number of clients with drug problems, they might profitably contact those local GPs who are known to be concerned about young people (though not of course those known to be willing to prescribe generously). Drug users are invariably known to a variety of helping agencies in an area, unknown to each other, so the development of closer complementary working relationships between professionals is likely to be more effective in the long run for both clients and staff. Clients (by the way) often do not like this sort of arrangement. They prefer to keep all professional groups apart.

Secondary health care – casualty department, general and psychiatric hospitals

General hospital accident and emergency (casualty) departments are often well acquainted with local drug users who get into difficulties and who tend to fall into three groups:

1 Those who are using opioids and have gone into withdrawals because they have either run out of money to buy drugs or have had to go without their regular clinic supply may attend casualty departments for emergency help. They may very occasionally be given a small amount of oral methadone to treat the withdrawals, at the discretion of the casualty officer and depending on the policy of that department.

2 The second group of attenders at casualty are the overdose clients, both accidental and deliberate. These patients often create enormous problems for the casualty staff in their management, not to mention the feelings of frustration at seeing the same people return time and time again.

3 The third group of attenders are those with medical complications arising from their drug use such as abscesses caused by injecting adulterated drugs or using unsterile

methods. Because of their reluctance to use GPs appropriately they tend to end up in the casualty department instead.

Drug users in Groups 2 and 3 above may need to be admitted to a general medical ward or occasionally to a psychiatric unit. In the London area casualty staff (and other professionals) may refer overdose patients to City Roads, the short-stay crisis intervention centre where they will be able to stay for a maximum period of three weeks for assessment and detox-ification – and possibly be referred on to long-term rehabilita-tion. It is important for social workers in regular contact with drug users to work at developing closer links with the staff in hospital accident and emergency departments. This will improve discharge liaison and enable the staff to be more effective in persuading patients to accept further help.

Admission to psychiatric units may be of limited value for drug users. Many clients find the whole experience disturbing and endeavour to discharge themselves as soon as possible. Admission may occur because of suicidal behaviour, acute depression and/or drug related psychotic behaviour. Any of these causes may justify compulsory admission. However, bear in mind that drug dependence alone is not a justifiable reason for admission under the 1983 Mental Health Act. Once a client is over the immediate crisis it is probably wiser to arrange community-based support as soon as possible in a drug-free environment. The acute admission ward in psychiatric hospitals is primarily for people with major mental illness requiring medication with psycho-active drugs and is therefore hardly appropriate to the needs of drug users, who need to be dissuaded from using these very substances. Unless a psychiatric hospital has a unit specialising in, say, alcoholism, therapeutic community techniques, or behaviour therapy, there will usually be little opportunity for therapy. So the admission is more likely to be a short-term remedy offering relief to the family or the anxious social worker rather than the drug taker.

With any emergency admission, contact with the family is important, if it can be provided. This offers background support and enables the drug user to leave hospital sooner than he or she might otherwise have done.

Drug dependence treatment centres
Special centres, commonly known as 'drug clinics', were originally set up to respond to the problems of the heroin and cocaine addict that emerged in the mid 1960s. When they opened in 1968 it was possible, for a few years at least, for

95

addicts to receive a maintenance prescription of heroin or methadone in injectable form, but it is unlikely nowadays that any new patient would be prescribed such drugs. Since the late 1970s the general policy has been to prescribe, to new patients only, methadone in mixture or linctus form. Many clinics are now prepared to prescribe only on the same basis to ex-patients returning for treatment, often to the dismay of the drug users who may have hoped that they would be entitled to receive their old prescription of injectable substances after a spell in one of Her Majesty's prisons.

Prescribing policies have changed as staff have better understood the problems of treating drug dependence. But as prescribing policies have changed, so too have patterns of drug use and the range of licit and illicit substances misused. Although treatment centres were primarily set up to deal with the opiate user they have come under considerable attack for being unwilling or unable to provide an effective service for the multi-drug or non-opiate user who is not suitable for maintenance treatment. Some clinics, if they have sufficient staff, offer the alternative of support and counselling to these clients. The clients themselves, however, are often reluctant to attend if they cannot obtain a prescription. The sorts of services appropriate for this group will be discussed later, but I want to look first at provisions for the opioid user.

Although it has always been assumed that special clinics were supposed to offer treatment that included a prescription of opiate drugs it is difficult to find any real evidence to support that belief. The Brain Committee was set up in the 1960s to discuss the need for special treatment centres, possibly attached to psychiatric departments, that had both in-patient and out-patient facilities. On the subject of prescribing, the Committee's report argued that 'It would be the duty of the doctors at the treatment centres to determine a course of treatment and, if thought necessary, to provide the addict with drugs.' So, according to the Brain recommendations, it is left to the discretion of the consultants in charge of drug centres to decide on their own prescribing policy. In so far as they were taking over responsibility for treatment from general practitioners, the majority of clinicians were in favour of encouraging addicts to attend their centres with the offer of continued maintenance, and in doing so perhaps satisfying their clients' drug needs sufficiently to discourage the development of a black market. Not everyone agreed with this approach, and a few clinicians, particularly outside the London area, were reluctant to adopt this strategy and pursued instead a non-prescribing policy which offered immediate detoxification and psychotherapeutic help. This mixed approach to interpreting the role of the centres continues today. In general the current picture seems to be that in London and at a number of provincial clinics there is likely to be a treatment service that includes the offer of an oral methadone prescription for a limited period of, say, three to six months to those patients who appear to have become physically dependent on opiates, and to have been using them for a minimum period of, say, six to twelve months.

The majority of drug takers who are regularly injecting opiate drugs come to a clinic for help because they can no longer support an illegal drug habit and they want a prescription. Some are also interested in doing something about their drug use and welcome the opportunity to talk to someone about their problems. The major concerns of the new patient are of being unable to carry on supporting his illicit drug habit and of getting sick. Many will also attend because they have run up against the law in their drug use, and hope that the clinics will be prepared to submit a report indicating that they are trying to give up drugs. When clients attend for the first time they have usually been using heroin or a similar preparation regularly for six months to two years or so. They may well have been casually using a variety of other drugs for five or more years. There are, then, various reasons why people decide to attend, but the reasons why they do not offer themselves for treatment are equally varied. Many will have put off the event for a long time, unwilling to acknowledge their dependence and overcome their reluctance to accept medical and social work help. Some may also fear the possible implications of notification to the Home Office. Attending a clinic also imposes certain restrictions if one is given a prescription, such as collecting the prescription on a daily basis, and there is also, perhaps, a certain unwelcome pressure to acknowledge that drug use is not as pleasurable as it might originally have seemed.

Most clinics expect people to attend several times for a full assessment before they are offered a prescription. This may take two or three weeks, depending on the clinic's waiting list and its prescribing policy. The assessment includes an in-depth interview with one or more professional staff members to complete a psycho-social case history (depending on the teamwork model adopted by the consultant) and a medical examination and urine analysis to check the accuracy of the patient's account of his drug intake. In some clinics the final case assessment and decision about treatment method (including the prescription) is decided by the whole team. This avoids some of the difficulties inherent in a doctor working alone. It also ensures that the patient realises that the decisions about drugs are taken by the whole team and that it is not possible to persuade the doctor unilaterally to take a separate – and to the user favourable – decision.

In theory there are several strategies available for future management and treatment. Some clinics will consider them all while others will be fairly restricted depending on their staffing, their preference for developing non-medical treatment approaches, and in-patient facilities. Alternatives for future management and treatment are:

– no prescription but out-patient counselling, casework or psychotherapy
– a maintenance prescription of oral methadone to assist stabilisation together with support, counselling, casework or psychotherapy
– a short-term reduction prescription of oral methadone over one to three months with support as above
– initial in-patient/out-patient assessment of drug taking for approximately seventy-two hours followed by out-patient detoxification with community based support from either drug clinic or family GP and/or community psychiatric nurse with family support
– detoxification in either a general hospital or psychiatric ward if a bed is obtainable, or admission to a special drug unit followed by a programme of rehabilitation in the unit or elsewhere, or out-patient support
– immediate referral to a drug rehabilitation house such as Phoenix House.

The first approach would probably be offered to those who are not sufficiently physically dependent to justify prescribing opioids or whose problems mainly concerned non-opiate drugs. The majority of patients would, if given the choice, want the second, third, or fourth treatments strategy. Those who are anxious to come off drugs and have had previous experience of trying to succeed in the community may well opt for treatment in an institutional setting, recognising that they need intensive help to learn to live without drugs.

All patients who are confirmed to be addicts, whether or not they receive a prescription, have to be notified to the Home Office. They remain on the notification list (which is the basis for Britain's official statistics on addiction) until they come off drugs or stop attending. This is the system that is referred to, incorrectly, as being 'registered'. There is no register as such which ensures that, once a person has acquired a prescription, he is guaranteed one for life. The usual system adopted in the United Kingdom is to ensure that patients receive their drugs on a daily basis and involves the co-operation of the local pharmacist. Patients collect their drugs for the day at a chemist's near to their home or employment and are responsible for them while they are in their possession. If they are searched by the police for drugs they will not be arrested for possession of those substances to which they are legally entitled. They will, though, risk prosecution in the normal way if found in possession of any substances obtained illegally.

The degree of contact with clients, as well as the method of working adopted by clinics, varies considerably according to the philosophy and orientation of the consultant psychiatrist and team members. With some, attendance is minimal – restricted to a routine medical check on the patient's drug needs sometimes with little active contact with non-medical staff. Other clinics though have an intensive treatment policy that offers casework and psychotherapeutic help on an individual and group basis.

Attitudes among clinicians and social workers vary as to the value of psychotherapy, particularly for the addict who is committed to staying on drugs for as long as possible. In cases of this kind, what seems to be more important is that the addict has the opportunity to form a relationship with a member of staff whom he feels able to trust and with whom he can share his problems. This may not immediately lead to a radical change in his drug taking habits but it will provide him with the necessary trust and support when a crisis occurs that makes him question his drug use. The worker has to be content with adopting a long-term perspective, setting minimal goals with the patient while the latter attempts to stabilise on an oral prescription and to stop injecting illicit heroin.

Many clients will slowly be reducing their prescriptions while attending as out-patients while others may choose to come into hospital. Withdrawal in a general hospital ward under the supervision of experienced nursing staff, with support from the primary worker involved in the patient's therapy, can be an affective method of helping someone to come off drugs with the minimum of physical discomfort. It also provides an opportunity to talk over anxieties and fears concerning the psychological need to take drugs and face the unknown. For this reason many addicts would choose to go into hospital provided they could do so with the continued support of a staff member whom they knew. They prefer not to risk relapsing while withdrawing as an out-patient because of lack of emotional support. Unfortunately, many, once they have technically come off drugs, avoid returning for counselling and support and attempt to cope on their own. Although some are successful, particularly if they already have a job and a stable relationship with a partner who does not use drugs, many will relapse because they have not learnt sufficient coping skills to manage without drugs.

Clinics cannot exist in isolation. They are part of a range of services. Their strength is that they should have specialist resources designed to deal with the physical aspects of dependence. Except in a minority of cases, most provide an out-patient service only and have difficulty in obtaining beds for detoxification. Clinics are part of the initial process of help. They assess and clarify a person's drug problems and prepare him for what may well be several years of help. This help may involve the clinic staff working closely with the patient's probation officer, local authority social worker or health visitor. It may also mean referring on the person to long-term drug-free rehabilitation, thus ultimately ending any intensive contact with the clinic. Single parents with young children have particular problems if they wish to enter a rehabilitation house because there are, as yet, few permanent facilities for children, although arrangments can be made for them to visit at weekends. If there seems to be no other way in which such parents can come off drugs successfully, and there is no suitable relation or friend who can look after the children, they may have to be taken into care. Most people try to avoid this last option. The fear of not getting their children back will deter most parents from placing their children in the care of the local authority.

Effectiveness of clinics

Who then is best helped by the clinics? Clearly, the regularly injecting opiate user who is likely to 'qualify' for a prescription is the most suitable referral. The non-opiate user who is psychologically dependent on amphetamines, barbiturates or minor tranquillisers may be offered counselling but is likely to reject this if he believes that drugs are the answer to his needs. While some clinics will attempt to offer social work help and counselling and perhaps a reduction by means of phenobarbitone for the barbiturate addict (rarely successful on an out-patient basis without strict supervision), others may restrict their clientele to opiate addicts. So, before sending a client along to the local clinic it is important for referrers to check on its policy so as not to waste the time of both client and clinic. It is also important to ascertain the clinic's current prescribing policy so that the client has realistic expectations.

Youngsters misusing solvents and those who happen to be using drugs (legal and illegal) on a casual basis should rarely be referred to drug clinics which serve a predominantly opioid clientele. These clients are likely to be better helped by a non-drug specialist agency or by a social worker who has already been able to establish a relationship with them. Referral to a drug clinic will only be another form of 'labelling'. There is, too, the added danger of placing a client in a setting where he will only learn more about the local drug scene. Unfortunately, referral of this type of client to a drug clinic is likely to come about more as a means of dealing with a worker's own anxieties than of helping clients with their problems. It is often an attempt to 'do something to help' which turns out to be totally counterproductive, if not harmful.

Anyone who is referred to a clinic must be advised to attend because the clinic is able to offer a service that the referring worker or agency cannot provide. The continuous pressure on clinics to respond first and foremost to the physically dependent opiate user means that the casual user will be regarded as a low priority case even though he seems to merit urgent attention on preventative grounds.

It is almost impossible to say who is going to do well in drug clinics and who will fail. From a research study carried out with heroin addicts attending London clinics in 1969 it was found that 33–37 per cent had stopped using opiates by 1977 and had not changed over to other drugs in any significant way. Half the addicts were still attending clinics while a few others were still using opiates but managing on their own. The people still coming back to the clinics tended to fall into two groups: those who slowly reduced their drugs of their own volition and retained contact with the clinic on a long-term basis, and those who were chaotic and crashed in and out of crises, suddenly stopping after one such episode. The role of treatment in their drug taking patterns seemed to be very hazy. There was no leading identifiable therapeutic agent. 'Expertise' may not have meant much. Long-term contact with someone at an agency, not necessarily a clinic, seemed to be most relevant to the client's progress and most change occurred during the first few years of control. This research identified very few factors that would predict who was more likely to come off drugs. Those who are successful were a little younger and had been using drugs for a shorter period of time. This suggests that treatment may be best channelled towards younger clients with a shorter drug history. Age apart, though, many workers and, indeed, ex-addicts would argue that, like the problem drinker, drug addicts need to reach 'rock bottom' before they are able to make a decision to change their drug taking pattern.

As I have mentioned, the services described in this chapter operate primarily on an out-patient basis. But sometimes drug takers need to consider spending some time in a specialist residential setting, especially if they have failed to remain drug-free after completing detoxification in the community – with or without the help of a drug clinic.

CHAPTER TEN

Residential rehabilitation services

Some drug takers will need to spend a period of time in one of the specialist drug-free rehabilitation houses, designed to enable the recovering addict to develop a drug-free lifestyle. Rehabilitation projects range from intensive therapeutic communities (concept houses) to supportive half-way house models offering communal living with minimal direct social work intervention. The majority exist as independent charities obtaining their funding from charitable trusts, central and local government, some depending on local authorities for an individual resident's fees. The majority of staff tend to have a social work orientation, with skills in individual counselling and group work. Staff sometimes include ex-addicts, particularly in the concept houses where at least 50 per cent of the staff are traditionally ex-addicts who have had personal experience as clients in a similar community.

What is meant by 'rehabilitation'?
Rehabilitation suggests certain conditions and expectations. So far as the client is concerned he should choose to go into a rehabilitation programme because he wants to get better. To do this he needs to be in a situation where he has support that continually reinforces his decision to make a radical change in his lifestyle and where he will develop confidence and ability to handle the emotional and practical problems of life when he returns to the wider community. To achieve these ends these conditions and expectations are desirable:

– There should be a commitment to abstinence by all residents. The houses are for people who have made a decision to stop using drugs and are prepared to abide by the major rule that no drugs, unless medically prescribed, are allowed in the house.
– Clients must accept the need for a residential experience.

This may be the only way in which the individual is going to free himself from drug use.

– A clear choice is made to remove oneself from an unfavourable environment, for a fairly lengthy period of time, perhaps over a year. This means being prepared to live away from friends, immediate family and the community that is linked with a drug using lifestyle. Being away from family and relationship pressures may be essential for clients if they are to be enabled to handle their lives without relying on the support of drugs.

– Being a resident means accepting the need to belong to a community that offers twenty-four hour support which cannot be offered on a fieldwork basis. Clients must be prepared to live and work with other ex-addicts, and be prepared to learn from and help each other.

It is easier for social workers than for addicts to appreciate how helpful the experience in a rehabilitation house might be for their clients and it is understandable that the social worker should want to persuade them to make a decision to apply for a place. It is important to be clear whose needs are going to be satisfied – the client's or the worker's. It is so easy to project onto others our own desire to see real changes take place. The client must have a degree of motivation, wanting to change the way things are. When applying, he is likely to be competing with several others for one vacancy. He may well be required to convince staff and residents at the house both in writing and at interviews that he has a wish to change and has some awareness that change is a process he has to be involved in and not something that will be done to him.

Many clients need more than one attempt before completing a programme. The first admission may cause people to question their need for drugs and become more aware of the psychological aspect of drug taking. But many find the restrictions, the abstinence and the self-knowledge too much to handle and decide to leave prematurely. Some are able to make a more realistic attempt the next time when they will have a clearer picture of what is involved in entering a rehabilitation programme and may be able to participate more fully with the worker in deciding on the right project for their needs (which may be different to their previous choice). Different projects suit different people, and staff need to develop skills in assessing, along with their clients, which project will be best suited to which individuals.

There are several crucial points to be considered before embarking on the process of trying to find a suitable place for someone who, it is thought, would benefit from a period of residential rehabilitation.

Assessment

It may be difficult to assess at which point rehabilitation should be considered. For example, an addict may be so desperate for a way out of his current crisis that he is prepared to go anywhere without thinking it through and ignoring the difficulties that might arise; or he might be asking for somewhere so unstructured and so tolerant that all he really wants is a roof over his head.

How do our own attitudes to rehabilitation schemes affect the addict's decision? Staff have a habit of talking about 'good' and 'bad' projects. Some of their criticisms may be valid if they relate to the overall security of the project, but not if they are based on subjective factors such as: 'I dislike concept houses because I wouldn't like to go there myself', or 'I prefer a more homely kind of place' – in other words an alternative to city life. Workers are not in the business of finding somewhere for a convalescent rest. Most clients need somewhere where they will be active participants, encouraged to understand their drug problems, and learn new practical and additional skills to cope with a drug-free life.

Instead of seeing projects as 'good' or 'bad', it is more helpful to see them as having strengths and weaknesses. Projects go through good and bad phases and the common allegation, 'They have drugs in there', is probably true of all residential projects at some time or other. What really matters is how those situations are dealt with by the project for the security of the residents.

It is important to understand what addicts are hoping for when they say that they, 'want rehabilitation'. Are they saying that life has been so hectic or chaotic that they need a long period away from the outside world before they can work out what to do next? Or that they feel so out of control that they need a lot of structure to contain them, other goals that they can achieve and perhaps some meaning to life?

For many clients it is misleading to talk about 'rehabilitation'. It may be more accurate to think of 'habilitation', as there may have been little opportunity in life for drug users to develop even minimal skills and confidence. It may be necessary to explore what addicts mean by learning to 'live a normal life'. Does this mean getting back to regular employment and being able to make and sustain relationships? Or are their objectives really to overcome certain difficulties, to seek relief from feelings of depression or to work through feelings of anger that intrude into their everyday life or frighten them? Having weighed these possibilities it may then be possible to work out the contribution, if any, that the different houses can make to these aspirations.

An individual's commitment to certain goals and his willingness to compromise in order to obtain a place is important. Addicts may need to be prepared to accept experiences not immediately attractive to them, such as groups, being told what to do by peers, and restrictions on liberty, all in order to achieve certain long-term goals. For most people rehabilitation is a compromise between what they want and what they are prepared to accept. For example, clients with responsibilities for children may have to be prepared to make sacrifices and suffer considerable conflict in deciding whether to enter a rehabilitation project (see also Chapter 14 on Pregnancy and Child Care). They have to weigh up the risks to their child if they decide not to come off drugs against the disadvantages of separation for a long period of time. There are a number homes that will accept children, while some will arrange for parents to have their offspring for weekends when they have been in rehabilitation long enough to cope with the pressures. The fieldworker may need to remain closely involved with the children and their caretakers, and assist in arranging for the children to visit their parents.

Finally, there is one important point for staff who have been working intensively with clients before their entry to a rehabilitation house. While retaining an interest in their progress, they must be prepared for a diminishing level of involvement with the client. They should also be ready to resume support if the client so wishes when he has completed the programme or if the attempt proves unsuccessful.

It is essential that both worker and client view the process of rehabilitation with a long-term perspective, prepare for it carefully and weigh up critically its advantages and disadvantages. It is not a process that will bring about overnight changes. These may appear to happen occasionally, almost like a sudden conversion, but they rarely endure.

Method of referral
In order to be accepted by a project the client must be off drugs. Ideally detoxification should be planned to happen immediately before admission to a house, otherwise the client is likely to relapse and the process may have to start all over again. If there is a delay in admission the worker will need to arrange temporary support.

Before referring a person to a project it is crucial that workers have up-to-date information about that project so that they do not make inappropriate recommendations to their client. Many problem drug takers have long experience of insecurity and an instinctive mistrust of adults and authority figures who 'let you down'. Referral to an unstable project will only serve to disillusion them further. Many houses operate a waiting list which means that clients preferring to wait for a vacancy in a particular house have to plan their application and detoxification to coincide with a possible place. Most houses have lengthy assessment and interview procedures which prevent impulsive, hasty admissions taking place.

Methods of referral to a house vary. Referrals can be made by the social worker or, in the majority of cases, by the client himself. Many come about as the result of a court appearance or drug related crisis. Some houses insist on potential residents making initial contact themselves as a sign of their motivation. The referrer should check with individual houses. Do they require a written application from the client? Are interviews at the house, the referral agency or wherever the client is living? Does the house require any further information such as a social history or a medical report? The social worker may also be required to submit an application to the local authority requesting that they undertake financial responsibility for the client during his stay at the rehabilitation project.

Current rehabilitation services

Rehabilitation houses tend to fall into three major groups with variations within each category. They can be divided into Concept Houses, Christian Houses, and Community (social work-based) Houses, each with different styles of rehabilitation programme. There are several invaluable guides which provide details of these projects, in particular the SCODA referral guide for *Residential Rehabilitation Projects for Drug Dependents* and the *Drug Resource Pack* published by City Roads (Crisis Intervention) Ltd. Check with SCODA (see Useful Addresses on page 201) or direct with the projects themselves for the most up-to-date information, because changes in practice do take place.

Concept Houses
(sometimes known as Therapeutic Communities)
These are based on the Phoenix House model as developed in the United States, incorporating the concept of self-help by ex-addicts who, on graduating through the system, sometimes return as staff members. The largest is the London branch of

Phoenix House which can take over sixty residents. All these houses are partially staffed by ex-addicts, many being ex-residents ('graduates') of that particular house. Each house has a highly structured programme designed to help residents learn to cope with emotional, work and social situations and conflicts. There is a strong emphasis on house management and self-help activities. Responsibility for running the house is strictly hierarchical. A new resident starts at the bottom level doing the most menial tasks in his work group and moves upwards in the hierarchy as he demonstrates progress and an ability to handle more responsibility. People are moved up and down the various levels according to their progress and ability to remain drug-free. The day-to-day responsibility for running the houses rests with the most senior residents, who are accountable to the staff for the smooth operation of the establishment. As residents succeed at each level they move upwards in seniority, gaining more responsibility and privileges. Irresponsibility leads to loss of privileges for a short period of time. Therapeutic methods include group and individual therapy, gestalt, psycho-drama, and regular encounter groups in which people are encouraged to express their feelings and to accept responsibility for themselves.

These are excellent places for those who see themselves as having a major problem, particularly those who go from crisis to crisis. They are also appropriate for people who have attempted to stay off drugs in the past but failed because their life lacked structure and meaning without drugs, and for those who have realised that they have reached the end of the road, and recognise that they need to start learning basic skills to cope with life. Concept houses also suit people who fit the classic 'junkie' stereotypes and who are good at playing manipulative games, because the staff, being ex-addicts, are particularly skilled at countering such manoeuvres.

These houses have a very direct approach which, while beneficial for some clients, may be counter-productive for others. The houses are not suitable for the psychiatrically disturbed or for those liable to become clinically depressed. Nor are they appropriate for those who need a more sensitive, non-direct approach and who would find it difficult to handle such features as encounter groups and the highly pressurised daily routine.

The programmes are idiosyncratic and very demanding. However, many ex-residents claim that the houses provided them with the only method possible to start doing something constructive with their lives. The programmes are very effective in helping talented residents realise their potential, and in enabling them to acquire basic skills and to prepare for professional training.

Christian Houses

These tend to fall into two groups; those that expect a commitment to worship and those that do not. With the latter group the Christian influence comes from the personal philosophy of the staff and the atmosphere they create in the house rather than from the programme itself. The first group places a deliberate emphasis on helping people to change their lives through conversion, making a commitment to Christ. These houses offer dignity, a caring, supportive atmosphere and a meaning to life which many addicts are seeking. Some of them insist on participation in regular Bible study and church attendance, while there is a strong emphasis on individual and group counselling, using some of the techniques and structure employed by the concept house.

The Coke Hole Trust is probably the best known Christian House in the second group. Situated in Andover in Hampshire, the Coke Hole provides a supportive, caring, family type atmosphere and offers people a chance to break away from a drug taking lifestyle in the peace of the countryside. Residents are expected to participate in the general running of the house and the community which includes helping with the animals and the gardening. There is little in the way of formal group or individual counselling, nor is there a structured programme. There is, however, a lot of informal support. The basic rules include restrictions on freedom for the first few months. This type of programme gives people a break and a chance to grow up away from the temptations of the city. It is suitable for the person who is not in need of intensive psychotherapeutic help and who would not be suitable for a confrontational-style programme. Unfortunately, it may be only too attractive for the person who wishes to avoid uncomfortable truths and prefers to sit back and avoid changing.

Community (social work-based) approaches

These projects are less clear in their ideology and invariably less structured. They are all different and would not necessarily see themselves as belonging to the same group. Some, such as the Cranstoun Houses, are small communities of approximately ten to fourteen residents, marked by a strong emphasis on compulsory participation in groups but with a less structured approach to the rest of the programme, which is geared to suit the individual needs of the residents. These might include doing household chores and cooking or, at a later stage, obtaining part-time employment locally. Their programme, to some extent, is not dissimilar to that of some concept houses, but is unusual in that it also aims to help residents learn to cope with alcohol use during their stay.

A community with a rather different emphasis and structure is Elizabeth House, situated in the Earls Court district of London. This community offers bed-sitting room accommodation to about eight ex-users, aged over twenty-one, and to a similar number of other residents who form a support-group to help create a stable atmosphere away from the drug sub-culture. The house offers regular communal meals, and a caring atmosphere with a sense of security to enable the ex-user to develop. Although there are staff employed to provide general social work, there are no structured group or individual counselling sessions. The majority of residents are encouraged to seek employment or to develop educational and career interests. This community is suitable for the person who does not need to go into a more structured therapeutic community but wishes to spend some time in a supportive setting before trying to cope socially and emotionally alone.

These are less 'ideological' projects, able to accept people who cannot make a commitment to a definite programme. They are able to adapt more to the mood of the moment, are more reflective in their approach and less confrontational.

Clinical settings

A small number of psychiatric hospitals still offer a therapeutic ward-based programme following detoxification in the unit. There are a few special units for drug problems in the London area and in other parts of the country. Some clients may, for example, need a more therapeutic approach, but be unsuitable for a concept house, and may benefit from participating in a programme run by a psychiatrically trained multidisciplinary team. Others may still need support from a half-way house or one of the houses mentioned earlier, after a period in a special unit. Hospitalisation might also be more appropriate for the addict who is prepared to spend a period undergoing detoxification and consolidating that with a few weeks' stay in hospital, rather than making a commitment to go somewhere else for a year. Hospital in this respect may well be more suitable for the client who is in permanent employment or a full-time student needing something longer than two weeks' detoxification in a general ward.

Private clinics

Chapter 7 on Planning detoxification referred to a number of privately run (Charitable Trust) clinics that offer a combined detoxification and rehabilitation programme for people with drug and/or alcohol problems. Most of these houses are currently in the South of England and are not funded by central or local government. Although most residents are expected to pay the fees themselves a number are able to obtain assisted places to some of the houses. A structured rehabilitation programme including individual and group counselling based on the Minnesota model is offered, usually lasting for eight weeks. Patients are expected to continue attending NA regularly on discharge and avail themselves of any after-care support offered.

Re-entry

A number of the residential rehabilitation houses, particularly the concept houses, have a re-entry or half-way house for residents to move into as part of the final stage in the programme. This is designed to help them adapt gradually to the everyday pressures of life in the community. In the half-way house they have more independence but are able to retain some contact with the staff who may need to assist them in finding employment, voluntary work, new interests or openings in further education. Some will need advice and assistance in finding permanent accommodation, perhaps by applying to the local authority or housing associations.

Where else?

This section has dealt with the organisations that specialise in providing rehabilitation for those with serious drug problems. There are a few other projects that offer help for a wide range of problems associated with mental health or criminality. Indeed, even prison can be said to be a form of rehabilitation for some people if they are able to make positive use of their time. Unfortunately, the majority are not and are likely to resume drug use at the end of their prison sentence.

When making referrals to non-specialist agencies it is important to emphasise the client's wider problems and his needs as a person so as to put the drug problem in its proper perspective; in the context of life as a whole.

So far I have been discussing 'clients' as an undifferentiated group, which to some extent they are, in that drug takers share many common problems. However, in recent years, one sub-group has emerged as worthy of special attention, if only for the reason that it appears to be growing in numbers. It is, of course, adolescents, who are, incidentally, less well catered for in terms of residential rehabilitation services.

CHAPTER ELEVEN

Drug use and adolescents

Public concern over the rapid increase in heroin use over the past few years has centred around the assumption that adolescents are the most vulnerable group. Most media coverage and government-sponsored prevention and advertising campaigns have also led the general public to believe that heroin use is likely to be more prevalent among adolescents than adults. However, recent research indicates that, while young people have shown a renewed interest in using a wide range of substances, heroin use and heroin-related problems among adolescents in their mid-teens do not appear to be all that common. Undoubtedly, heroin use has risen significantly among adolescents in a number of towns and cities in certain parts of the United Kingdom, notably The Wirral, Merseyside and Glasgow. However, for most of the country, other freely-available drugs are more popular than heroin. Solvents, amphetamines, cannabis, tranquillisers, 'magic mushrooms' and, of course, alcohol are probably more accessible. When heroin is involved it is more likely to be used on a recreational or intermittent basis. If it is used daily, it is often only for a few weeks. The majority of drug users coming forward for help are still, as in the mid-1970s, likely to be in their mid-twenties.

Not that adolescents do not use drugs. The majority of adolescent drug takers, however, are more likely to be experimental or recreational than problematic users. For many, drug use is a normal part of adolescent experience, alongside pop music, clothes and sex. The preferred drug varies according to fashion, availability and local trends. A growing proportion of adolescents are likely to regard smoking cannabis as normal behaviour. Some have ready access to amphetamines, others prefer alcohol, and a minority will acquire heroin. In some parts of the country solvent inhalation is still regarded as the prime management problem facing youth leaders, teachers and social workers. Solvents are sometimes used before puberty by young children who have acquired the habit from older brothers and sisters. Most lose interest in solvents by their mid-teens and transfer allegiance to alcohol, while a minority turn to other drugs for a different and perhaps less intoxicating effect. The next chapter looks specifically at how to deal with solvent inhalation, but, broadly-speaking, methods of intervention, particularly when dealing with adolescents, are similar, whatever the substance being abused.

The dilemma for many parents and workers having to decide whether to respond to or ignore the signs of drug use in the young are summed up like this by Dr Martyn Gay, a child and adolescent psychiatrist:

'The occasional use of drugs is rarely associated with difficulties. For adolescents, to be bombed out of their minds, to be stupid or crazy and ridiculous, is all part of adolescent experimentation. It allows them to explore themselves. There is, however, the problem of accidental dangers – trying to fly off a car park, or walking across the middle of the M4, believing that they are invisible, and being hit by a car. Accidental difficulties are the principal problem of the adolescents who use, as opposed to abuse, drugs.'

The experimental and recreational nature of drug taking during adolescence means that over-reaction needs to be avoided, as does the sometimes automatic response of referring on to a drug clinic, where most of the clients are physically dependent heroin users. As with other adolescents who indulge in other self-destructive activities the drug user's habit is often symbolic of the need to challenge parental authority and attitudes, and to be accepted by peers. While a minority of users need intensive specialist help, the majority benefit from precisely the same sort of help required by other adolescents who have difficulty handling the transition from childhood, through adolescence, to adulthood.

For many youngsters, drug and solvent use appear to offer instant excitement and short-term relief from boredom, unpleasant feelings, anxieties, unwanted responsibilities, authority, fears and pressures from parents and friends. They enable the young person to cope with self-consciousness, shyness, lack of confidence, the problems of school work and finding a job. They can fill a gap when the prospect of long-term unemployment engenders feelings of hopelessness, powerlessness and a lack of purpose to life.

Most of the principles described in the earlier chapters on

assessment and planning individual work apply equally to adolescent drug takers. However, at times, you may find when working with this age group that a slightly different strategy is appropriate, for several reasons:

1 The user's behaviour is often regarded as part of adolescent risk taking or a way of responding to pressures common to all youngsters.

2 Most people are likely to be still living with their parents and as such are still their legal responsibility. This means that methods of intervention may need to include the family.

3 The worker may be concerned about drug use among a group of youngsters. Effective intervention may mean working with the group rather than individuals, or offering a mixture of individual and group methods.

4 There may already be a number of agencies such as youth or education welfare services in contact with the user. You have to establish some agreement over the complementary roles of the different workers and agencies. Some will have to adopt a lower profile to allow any constructive work to proceed. Otherwise, the client will feel totally overwhelmed by the army of helpers or succeed in playing them all off against each other and his parents. Neither consequence is likely to be of much help to anyone in the long run.

With adult users, experimental and recreational use is unlikely to be seen as an immediate cause for concern. But when the user is under eighteen and still the legal responsibility of his parents (or the local authority social services department), some direct intervention is often contemplated by workers or demanded by parents. When drug use occurs as a passing phase in relatively stable youngsters with no history of social or emotional deprivation, and with an apparent 'normal' relationship with their parents, there is little reason to intervene. However, when an assessment interview and previous contact indicate a troubled adolescent, perhaps with difficult family relationships or a history of unresolved personal difficulties that are likely to resurface, then the use of drugs or solvents should rightly be viewed as possible warning signs for future trouble. Here, intervention should be planned with sensitivity and tact, with a view to channelling the user's interest into other stimulating but less harmful activities.

Assessing the nature of adolescent drug use
Faced with an adolescent drug or solvent user you have several issues to consider when making an initial assessment:

1 How problematic is the use? Is this an experimental or casual user, or has drug use become a dominant, controlling factor in his life?

2 Has the adult concerned (i.e. parent or worker) found out by accident and is he in danger of over-reacting to what may be 'normal' adolescent curiosity?

3 What does the young person see as the problem? Does his drug use concern him? Or is it only worrying to parents or other adults?

4 If the user denies having a drug related problem, does the fact that he has been found out suggest that he has been hoping his drug use would be discovered. Had he started to get frightened of the risks? Is this his way of asking for help?

5 Do users have a reasonable relationship with their parents or a teacher, youth worker or social worker that can be used in looking at their drug taking behaviour in relation to other problems?

6 How stable are they? Is their drug use an expression of adolescent confusion or rebelliousness, etc.? Are there obvious family tensions that might provoke increased drug use and thus increased psychological dependence on the effects of drugs or solvents? That is: are you primarily dealing with a problem of adolescence with drug taking as the symptom, or are you dealing with a drug problem that is further complicated by the needs and frustrations of normal adolescence?

Involving the family – help or hindrance?
Ideally, the parents of the young person should be included in any treatment plans. The family needs to be assessed on its ability to help the adolescent. You have to ascertain whether the home environment is likely to be concerned and supportive. Are the children able to discuss drugs, sex and other problems of growing up with their parents? Have there been any other problems with adolescent children, perhaps resulting in their leaving home prematurely? Is the family likely to co-operate in any work initiated by the worker or another agency, or might they sabotage any such initiatives because they want quick results and cannot accept that 'help' is not necessarily going to result in the young person stopping drug use immediately? Perhaps the family is unwilling to acknowledge that their child's use may result from family tensions or relationship problems such as marital discord or father's heavy drinking. This factor may be of added importance if there are

younger brothers and sisters who are also at risk. Even if the drug user is helped, parents in a disturbed family might shift the problem to another sibling rather than face up to their own underlying difficulties.

Generally though, parents are co-operative. Indeed, the majority would be very upset if they thought that their child had a drug problem that they knew nothing about or did nothing to alleviate. Despite the inevitable initial shock and guilt many parents are happy to work with professionals in order to help a child overcome his or her difficulties.

Sometimes children do not want to involve their parents, and there may be very good reasons. When working with adolescents you have to be able to honour confidentiality in order to win the trust and confidence of a young person. He will only confide in you about personal problems as long as he believes that the information will not automatically be passed on to teachers or parents. This can create a painful dilemma for workers anxious to have a young person's trust and respect in order to do any effective work.

Workers can play a key role in acting as a bridge between the young drug user and his parents, facilitating a full discussion of the young person's difficulties. You should also ensure that parents are provided with adequate information about drugs and specialist resources available, as well as with any help needed to deal with related family problems. Unfortunately, sometimes as with the doctor considering prescribing the contraceptive pill to under-age girls, informing parents does not always generate support for the child. It may even provoke rejection, anger and a family crisis resulting in the child running away from home or escaping further into the company of drug taking friends.

As I discussed in Chapter 4 on Assessing the problem, the decision as to whether or not to proceed with some form of intervention depends on your initial assessment, whether the solvent sniffer or drug user is assessed as 'experimental', 'casual' or 'problematic'. The options for intervention for each category may be something along these lines.

Dealing with the experimental or occasional user
Provided that the youngster has no other difficulties that justify professional intervention, the only appropriate help is likely to be that of providing information for both the drug user and his parents. Written and verbal information describing the effects of drugs and some of the possible complications may be of value. Discussing with the youngster why his parents are worried can be extremely helpful.

Try to use the opportunity to get the youngster to be more knowledgeable about the possible risks of drug taking. Urge him to think for himself and to resist pressure from friends. Discussion might turn on themes such as: what the user likes or dislikes about the experience; what can happen to the regular user; why some people get into difficulties; why the youngster believes these cannot happen to him; whether the experience of drug taking matches up to what the user was led to expect from drug education classes at school or from the media, and if not, why not?

If the referral was made by worried parents the worker can also help them to get the matter into some perspective and be better equipped to discuss it calmly with their children, and not to over-react and panic. Such a reaction is likely to provoke an angry or hurt response from their child who may become even more secretive about his activities. Invariably, talking separately to child and parents can help each party see more clearly why the other is reacting in the way they are. You can facilitate better communication by helping the parents to share with the child their feeling of responsibility without wishing to interfere too much. The child may be helped to explain to his parents that he tried drugs because everyone else did, but this does not mean that he is now addicted. In most instances, just one session may be sufficient. If, however, the worker suspects that the panic over drugs is symptomatic of some profound conflicts between the parent(s) and child, then referral to a youth counselling facility (or, if unavailable, to social services or child guidance) may be advisable.

If you feel that drug use might increase and become more problematic, you should suggest that the youngster could return for a talk with you at a later stage, thus leaving the door open for continued contact. Clearly, this is easier to arrange if a worker has a good relationship and regular contact with the youngster.

Casual (intermittent or recreational) drug use

This is undoubtedly the most difficult pattern of drug use to deal with. How does a worker determine the 'right' response, when there is no foolproof way of telling whether the drug use is going to cease after several weeks or months (which it most likely will), or whether it may escalate to more dependent or problematic use? The most vulnerable youngsters are those whose personal needs are increasingly being met by psycho-active substances, particularly those who live in areas where drugs are easily available. Young people who have experienced social or emotional deprivation are also at risk, but they can be helped. Young people from the most socially deprived backgrounds can discontinue drug use and avoid becoming totally drug centred.

Your options for intervention are similar to those for dealing with the experimental user. That is, you should do nothing, except provide the user with information and an opportunity for discussion, trying to get him to realise that he may not always be totally in control of his drug use. Keep your fingers crossed that his interest in drugs will pass without any major crises. If the youngster expresses anxiety over possible risks, or if he has had a bad experience such as overdosing or feeling afraid when out of control, supportive counselling will help prevent longer-term harm and enable you to assess other ways of intervening. These could include:

1 Providing family support or counselling, directed at improving family relationships, thereby reducing the youngster's need to invest too much time and energy in drug use.

2 Exploring increased use of youth work facilities by linking up with the local detached or club based youth worker.

3 Trying to make the user's school programme (if he is still at school) more attractive or relevant to his needs. Is there an interested teacher or school counsellor who would be able to provide support?

4 Helping the user to develop other interests or hobbies that provide alternative and socially acceptable highs. This might lead the user to develop friendships that are less drug orientated.

5 Referring to a voluntary Intermediate Treatment programme (if available locally) – or formal IT if in trouble with the law.

6 Exploring ways of helping an unemployed youngster to get work experience, paid or voluntary, or training that may divert him from relieving boredom through drugs.

Among the various substances with which youngsters experiment are the volatile solvents, found in glues and other freely available household products. So prevalent has 'glue sniffing' become that it has thrown up a special set of management and intervention problems for social workers and many other professionals. These are discussed in the next chapter.

CHAPTER TWELVE

Solvent inhalation

You can only work effectively with anyone who uses solvents if you understand what the user gets out of the experience. One way of doing this is to talk with the youngster about what it means to him and how he feels when he doesn't sniff. Another way is to recall your own experience of getting pleasantly intoxicated. As a child, you too perhaps were fascinated by the smell of chemicals such as glues or nail varnishes. You may even have been tempted to continue enjoying the smell because it made you feel good. Presumably, though, none of your friends told you that, if you kept doing it, you would forget your worries and perhaps even see strange things. It is also unlikely that you would have seen newspaper reports warning you of the dangers while at the same time furnishing you with a list of products that could make you high.

Remember, too, that some of the feelings induced by solvents are not dissimilar to those produced by games that young children play. Even perfectly harmless activities such as *Ring a ring o' roses* demonstrate what fun it is to get giddy, while many of the attractions at the funfair are designed to encourage similar heady sensations. One reason why solvent use might be so attractive to the thirteen or fourteen-year-old is that it combines childish games with behaviour that mimics that of adults: a mixture of getting excited and dizzy, and getting drunk. Youngsters get a thrill from finding out how much they can take before losing control, and, of course, joining in an activity that is approved of by friends. Peer group approval is also more important than that of parents who suddenly seem old-fashioned people whose authority must be challenged. Thus, solvent inhalation fits neatly into the well documented phenomenon of 'teenage rebellion'.

Many adults, and indeed some social workers, have difficulty in accepting that children may wish to alter the way they feel by the use of chemicals. What is acceptable for adults is not for children. If you are to establish some contact with the young sniffer you have to throw away this rather hypocritical attitude. That is not to say that the worker has to approve of the methods the child is using. You can still point out the risks and why they give you cause for concern.

Solvent inhalation attracts the adolescent looking for a relatively cheap, readily available guaranteed means of getting drunk. The other main attraction of solvents is that they allow the user to experience hallucinations. Many sniffers may not use that term initially but describe their experiences as 'dreams' or 'images'. Only about 50 per cent of sniffers experience these. Those who do not may claim that, like their friends, they too can see imaginary figures, presumably because they do not want to admit that theirs is an inferior experience. For many youngsters, these changes in perception seem to be a substitute for normal childish fantasy and provide excitement in a drab, unstimulating and often unhappy environment. Some children organise their sniffing sessions in a structured way in the hope that, given the right setting, they will re-experience the same hallucinations, like looking forward to the re-run of an old film. Sometimes they hope to impress peers and even adults with tales about their experiences, and so achieve a measure of status and social identity. Some of these hallucinations are pleasurable, others are very frightening. Their most worrying feature is that they endow users with a sense of power, such as being able to see things that others cannot, or sadly, believing that they can perform impossible feats such as flying off tall buildings or, in one tragic case, walking along the railway tracks and stopping oncoming trains.

Sensational press reports about hallucinations add to the drama for the potential sniffer and frighten adults into over-reaction and panic. When planning intervention you have to recognise the role of these experiences in a child's life, particularly when his creative abilities are not being encouraged and when school seems irrelevant. The feelings of power these experiences can produce for the emotionally or socially deprived youngster are illustrated by the case of Joe, a boy who was sent to a community home. When Joe sniffed he saw soldiers rising out of the ground in front of him. When he put out his hand and placed it on top of their heads the soldiers disappeared back into the ground. The phenomenon of seeing people rising from the ground is fairly common among young sniffers.

Unfortunately, any attempt to stop children from obtaining

what, to them, are exciting experiences may only result in increased interest. The conforming child who is reluctant to rebel and risk parental disapproval, or the child who has plenty of creative interests are not likely to become sniffers, and certainly not to the extent that it threatens their destruction.

In order to deal with solvent misuse you have to understand why a particular child or group finds sniffing so attractive. Attempts to stop it by merely banning it on the premises may be effective in 'removing the problem'. But this may also have the unfortunate result of driving the sniffers to more secretive places where they can inhale in peace. Should they overdose, they might remain undetected until it is too late. One goal might be to reduce the risks of harm from solvent use while trying, in the longer term, to introduce sniffers to other activities which provide sufficient excitement.

While many teachers and youth workers are prepared to teach about the safe use of medical drugs and alcohol, many prefer not to discuss safer ways of sniffing glue, such as warning against inhaling with polythene bags over the head. Many children do not realise that this can cause suffocation anyway, irrespective of the presence of solvents. Such advice, difficult though it may be for some to offer, could actually save lives. Therefore, it is important for workers to find a way of putting across such information during informal discussion or as part of a counselling session. Advice on not sniffing in secluded places is another useful preventative measure. In fact, some children do observe these precautions, also making sure that they do not sniff alone in case they should pass out. Adopting a down-to-earth unshockable attitude can undercut the bravado some youngsters exhibit about their sniffing in order to test you out.

The majority of children who centre their daily life around sniffing solvents are likely to have long-standing social and emotional problems that existed before the sniffing started. Solvent abuse in their case is just another symptom of underlying difficulties. As when dealing with other forms of problem drug taking, a realistic goal might be to reduce the frequency of sniffing (perhaps by asking the sniffer to keep a daily diary recording frequency of use) while working with the youngster on the related problems. Change may not come about immediately, so try to adopt a long-term perspective. Occasionally, though, a youngster does suddenly lose all interest in sniffing once other friends, interests and rewards have been found, and where the sniffer's confidence has been boosted. This has been known to happen when a parent has started taking his son to football matches with him or on fishing trips. Helping youngsters to discover activities that have an element of risk and excitement, such as roller- or ice-skating or horse riding, have also proved successful.

Many of the approaches suggested in the previous chapter are equally applicable with the solvent sniffer, especially the use of Intermediate Treatment and youth work facilities. Working closely with parents is also important, of course (see also Chapter 13 on A family affair). Some parents may wish to join local self-help groups or become involved in helping to run alternative community based activities for their children. Unfortunately, for many of the more problematic solvent sniffers who come to the attention of social services departments or the police, parental involvement is often minimal or non-existent. Sniffing may be in reaction to a deprived environment, providing a substitute for parental affection.

A very small number of children may need to be admitted to a special community-based unit that provides a break from outside family pressures, and offers opportunities for developing life skills, without resorting to chemicals for support. Unfortunately, adolescent units prepared to take sniffers are very few because of fear of the habit spreading to other residents. It may be impossible to find a placement even if a suitable adolescent unit is available in your region.

Responding to solvent misuse in a residential child care and youth work setting

It is crucial to agree on a policy for managing solvent use in a residential establishment or youth club. Staff team work is essential. Without it, youngsters can play members of staff off against each other, adjusting their behaviour according to the reactions they have come to expect from different staff members. Staff need to be consistent, able to work in an informal manner, and able to accept that sniffing forms part of adolescent experience. At the same time workers must provide safe boundaries within which youngsters can avoid taking unnecessary risks. Staff need to consider how to respond both as individuals and as a team when confronted with solvent use, whether the consumer is only mildly intoxicated, very intoxicated, or in danger of losing control. There is no absolute right or wrong way to react when someone is sniffing in your presence. Over-reaction on the part of staff and passers-by can be provocative and succeed only in alienating the worker from the group, pushing users into finding places to sniff where they will be undetected.

Management of intoxicated behaviour

Management of youngsters under the influence of solvents depends on the quality of the relationship you have with the individual concerned. If you have a relationship of trust you will be able to take control of events. If worker and child get on badly (if, say, the worker approaches the user in an aggressive manner) the chances are that the situation will not be kept under control. Ideally, the member of staff who has the best relationship with the child is best placed to deal with stoned behaviour. However, there are workers who only seem to want to be around when everything is nice and calm. They have also got to be prepared to deal with the unpleasant effects of a person's behaviour. This sort of involvement can gain the worker more respect from youngsters in the long run.

When dealing with youngsters who are stoned, treat them as if they were drunk from alcohol. Unless you feel that medical help is needed, do not go along with their desire to be 'sick'. There is a strong element of theatrical attention seeking in their wish to have the doctor called. Open the windows. Get as much fresh air into the room as possible. Be reassuring, calm and assertive. Provide a warm drink such as black coffee. Do not try to reason with the sniffer, nor should you argue or be confrontative. This only makes things more difficult. The sniffer wanted to be out of control, he is frightened now that he is out of control. He therefore needs to feel safe and wanted.

When the youngster has come round, put him to bed to sleep it off, ensuring that he is kept under observation and that someone is able to talk with him about the incident when he wakes up. You could alternatively take him home to his parents and persuade them to let the child sleep it off (again, under observation). Stay and talk with them about the incident. See if any further help can be offered if they are not already in contact with a worker.

Try not to get drawn into the 'angry parent' role. This is counter-productive and may invite violence from the user. Sometimes sniffers become 'punch-drunk' and violently aggressive as if under the effects of alcohol or sedatives. If this happens, stay with the youngster; be reassuring, and remove other youngsters or on-lookers from the scene. Lots of people trying to calm a frightened sniffer who is out of control can provoke even more violence.

General management on a day to day basis

Staff need to create an atmosphere of communication and support so that adolescents will feel able to talk about their worries and fears. These may seem minor problems to some adults. To adolescents they are very important. They need to see that they are not the only ones who are shy, unhappy or lonely.

It is upsetting for staff and the parents of adolescents to see them in a distressed, messy state, clearly demonstrating their unhappiness. But often it also makes the onlookers angry and frightened as well as upset. As with adults who are drunk, part of us feels sympathetic and another part angry because they have embarrassed us by drawing attention to their personal distress. Workers should say something like, 'I care about you, but it upsets me to see you like this. I don't like what you are doing because . . .'

If someone has been sniffing and is even mildly intoxicated the worker should immediately separate the sniffer from the company of the others, where he can be given sufficient attention. If one worker can concentrate on dealing with the intoxicated youngster, either in the office or in the child's bedroom, the colleague can ensure that the non-sniffers are not neglected. Otherwise, the other children are often tempted to try to gain more attention and status by getting intoxicated on solvents as well, especially if that seems to bring added personal attention from the staff. Some workers find that it can help to devise incentives, such as outings, as rewards for staying off glue, both for the non-sniffers and those trying to stop.

Youngsters often justify their sniffing on the grounds of boredom. Try to find out what that much used word really means. A youngster may have nothing stimulating or exciting to do. He may be short of ideas or be bad at organising his time. Or he may be depressed. If so, he needs to be helped to gain positive experiences by participating in other exciting, but safer, activities. Come on duty prepared with strategies for combating boredom; perhaps physical activities such as swimming, riding or skating; outings and excursions that provide engaging group experiences with an equal, but different, pay-off to sniffing. Many youngsters have difficulty learning how to get high naturally. Some need to have their access to pocket money limited while trying to control their sniffing activities.

There are inevitably rough periods. Try to ride them out, adopting a philosophical attitude. Do not allow them to affect all staff and residents and totally dominate the daily routine. Most sniffers want to be stopped. It is the way this is done that is important. One question that is often asked is, 'What do we do with the bags and solution?' At one children's home the staff had a policy of putting holes in all polythene bags around the place. It may not always be a good idea to dispose of the 'glue bags' on the premises. Staff can always take them home with them and put them out with their own rubbish, as long as they do not mind what the refuse collector thinks!

Long-term work

The ultimate objective for both the adolescent sniffer and the worker is usually the same – the reduction of sniffing and, finally, complete abstinence. Things may go well for a while. There may be a reduction in regular compulsive sniffing. Some may stop altogether, then relapse. As with other forms of substance abuse, this is normal. It may only be a short lapse. Do not let the user become defeatist. He may well react by saying, 'Oh well, as I didn't succeed then, it means I can't give up, I *need* it.' Explain that it is a case of want, rather than need; that the user has an emotional desire to be stoned in order to avoid normal feelings. When the user is sober you can help him examine some of the reasons why he might have slipped back. Together you may be able to find a way of preventing things from getting out of control. Some youngsters try to conceal their lapses because they fear that they have let you down or that they will be punished. Encourage them away from such attitudes.

Many chronic sniffers who appear to be out of control to their youth worker or social worker, respond well to a secure residential setting, providing that this offers them intensive therapeutic and practical help. They respond well because they do not have to cope with a stressful family setting; they feel safe and cared for. Unfortunately, problems often reappear if the young person is returned to his family and the home situation remains unsatisfactory. In some instances a long-term placement, such as family placement or fostering or a community home may be more desirable and less damaging for the youngster in the long run.

Coping with the reactions of the local community

One problem for residential staff and youth workers is the reaction of neighbours. You may think things are under control and feel that you have a satisfactory strategy for containing or controlling solvent inhalation. Other outside agencies or the community at large may not. Over the past ten years a few children's homes have been subjected to unpleasantness from local people who disapprove of the kids, especially if they think the staff allow them to sniff glue or smoke pot. They blame the staff for infecting their children when sometimes the 'blame' should be the other way round. If you are concerned about this, ask for help from the local beat policeman. Explain the home's policy and ask him to bring home any child found intoxicated just as the police would take any other child home to its parents. But ask the police not to deal with the incident. Explain that this is your job.

Use any contacts gleaned from living in the community to discuss the problems with neighbours who have children. Help them to talk about their own fears that their own children might be tempted to use drugs or solvents. Try and gain the interest and support of local residents' groups. Talk to local councillors if you are approached by angry residents. Make sure that your line managers are aware of your problems and do not over-react to sudden pressure from the media, social services committee or the police.

You may find it helpful in the long run if you can liaise with local residents when you are all confronted with common parental problems. Share your concern and some of your expertise by helping to point out why the kids may be sniffing or experimenting with drugs, and look at some of the possible answers. You can always take the initiative and persuade local shop-keepers to be more vigilant over the sale of solvent-based products. Think, too, of organising a seminar or evening discussion about drugs and solvents and adolescents for local parents. In fact you should always bear in mind the need to consult, where possible, the families of drug or solvent users. When a person is living at home, this automatically becomes a 'family affair'.

CHAPTER THIRTEEN

A family affair
– working with the families
of drug users

Until recently, the specific needs of the families of problem drug takers have been given scant attention. This is partly because the majority of drug users are in their mid-twenties or over by the time they come forward for help, and either live away from their parents or claim to have minimal contact with them. Many do not wish to involve their families, primarily because they just do not want parents to know about their drug problem or do not want to involve them further. They do not want to totally disillusion, frighten, or anger them. Some genuinely fear that the shock would only cause suffering and even the premature death of a parent.

Specialist drugs workers may to some extent have colluded with clients wanting to keep their parents or partner out of the treatment setting, because they were primarily interested in working with the drug taker, and not with his family. Some workers feel that engaging the client in treatment demands a therapeutic relationship of trust and confidentiality that is threatened if the family is brought into the picture. Clearly, if the client is over eighteen years of age, living independently from his parents and does not want them contacted, you should not involve them.

However, the past five years have seen a major growth in parents' groups all over the United Kingdom; the establishment of Families Anonymous as a major resource for relatives; and increased willingness to offer a service to parents, both for their own needs and for those of the client. In some parts of the country pressure to extend and refine services for people with drug problems has come from parents tired of waiting for the statutory health and social service departments to provide help. While some of these groups help drug takers directly, the majority concentrate on other parents whose children are newly involved in drug taking.

The emphasis on the need to work with the whole family

and not just the client varies from agency to agency and, to some extent, from professional to professional. Some now place a higher emphasis on working with the client's family, especially when the drug user is still living at home and his history suggests a need to deal with the unresolved family conflicts and communication problems that may have preceded drug use.

What sort of help do families need?

Many parents ask for help either when they suspect their child is taking drugs or when they need information to hand should their youngster begin to experiment with drugs. Those who suspect drug use may ask for help in broaching the subject with their child, as well as to reduce their anxiety and feelings of inadequacy because they are unsure whether they have any cause for concern. Many will want help in finding out whether their child is using drugs. They may have little cause for panic. Their child may be behaving like any normal adolescent, opposing parental values and seeking the company of friends rather than wanting to spend leisure time with the family. Publicity offering advice to parents about drugs or solvent use among young people may only serve to add fuel to the anxieties of those parents finding it difficult to let go of their adolescent children.

Many parents ask for help, either alone or by bringing their child with them, when the drug use is still experimental or casual. The user probably does not see himself as having a drug problem. The parent does. As far as the child is concerned it is the parents, not him, who have the problem, because they do not understand drugs.

Some parents will seek help because their child has an unmistakable drug problem. It may have suddenly come to light because a drug crisis, such as an overdose or withdrawal symptoms, occurred and the child failed to conceal it. Alternatively, there may have been a visit from the police concerning a drug offence which reveals the true extent of an offspring's drug habit. Parents under these circumstances are often frightened, angry and guilty. They want immediate help from an 'expert'. They may then discover that their child is already known to a local drug agency, in which case they may either be relieved, or even more upset at discovering that a professional knew but did not tell them. They need to be persuaded to accept that effective treatment takes time and depends a good deal on their child's willingness to accept help and to take some responsibility for his drug problem. 'Treatment' is not something that can be 'done' to the user.

Nor should parents believe that they must sacrifice their life to their child, spending their savings or re-mortgaging the house to finance an expensive private clinic or rehabilitation centre.

Before looking in more detail at the sort of assistance that might be offered to parents I want to consider some of their particular anxieties and fears, together with the sort of information they may find valuable.

Some common anxieties for parents

Being the parent of an adolescent is a daunting task. There is no real training for parenting, except by learning from mistakes made with the older children. There is no absolutely right or wrong way to bring up children. Success ultimately depends on the quality of the relationships between parents and child; the parents' personal security; their ability to care, yet not to want to control and possess too much. Even the best adjusted parents cannot be sure that their children will not experiment and become hooked on drugs. However, if they discuss the subject rationally at home, there is less risk of harmful drug use developing.

Many parents do not understand drugs, or are frightened of them. They have no personal experience of using illicit drugs or solvents. Unlike alcohol, and sometimes tranquillisers, drugs are substances that they regard as unsafe. Indeed, some would be happier if their child was drinking alcohol regularly. Some are afraid that their child will die if he or she is not stopped immediately.

Some parents may have difficulty, generally, in coping with their adolescent children. They may be too strict or too ambitious for them, wanting them to have everything they did not have themselves such as a good education, proper qualifications and so on. Or they may be too liberal, having resolved not to raise their children in the way they were brought up, without the freedom to make their own decisions and mistakes.

Some will need help in getting some of the age-old myths into perspective, the usual one being the 'escalation' or 'slippery slope' theory. That is, one smoke of cannabis is followed inevitably by experiments with heroin, onward to an early death. Most young people do not automatically progress to the use of other drugs after smoking cannabis nor become a 'glue addict' after one sniff of glue. Parents may need to be reminded that they do not automatically assume their child is going to become an alcoholic by drinking a glass of wine with the family or at a party.

Many parents are worried about the illicit nature of drug use. Could they be held responsible for any drugs found in their home? The facts are these. They can indeed be arrested for allowing their premises to be used for cannabis smoking or the consumption of other illicit drugs. If they discover drugs at home and want to dispose of them they have two options: either to get them destroyed or to hand them over to the police. As the majority of parents are reluctant to bring the police into the picture for fear that their child will acquire a criminal record or be imprisoned (which is unlikely for a first offence, unless the youngster has also been dealing), the first option may be preferable. Parents do not, in law, have to tell the police if they suspect or know their child is taking drugs.

Some parents are extremely embarrassed at having to present themselves at a local drugs agency where neighbours might recognise them. Some would prefer to go to an agency in another town to retain some anonymity. Most of us prefer to keep our personal family traumas to ourselves and not have them advertised by malicious gossip. It can be even more difficult if the parents are well-known people with some local recognition and status, such as headmaster or local councillor. While it may occasionally be possible to refer such parents to an agency in another town, this is unlikely for the majority. As the worker, you will have to discuss with them their fears of gossip hurting their family.

Ways of offering help to parents
A variety of strategies is available for helping the relatives of drug takers, whether they approach you initially for help, or whether you decide that they should be included in the treatment process. The options are:

1 To provide information about drugs and solvents.

2 To encourage relatives to attend a parent's group. This may be run by a professional or Families Anonymous, or it may be a self-help parents' support group.

3 To provide individual support, counselling or casework to the relatives.

4 To work with the family which may include the use of family therapy techniques.

Earlier I outlined the three stages at which parents may be when they need help. I want now to deal with each of these stages and look at ways of implementing the methods outlined above.

1 *Parents suspect child is using drugs*

Parents need to know that there is somewhere where they can go for help and advice when they suspect their child of drug use. This must be somewhere they can talk in confidence to someone who listens to them. It is your job as the worker to offer reassurance as well as finding out whether their suspicions are, in fact, justified. Your personal response matters a good deal. Avoid passing parents on to yet another agency. Some will have already sought help elsewhere, perhaps from local doctors, so do not get caught up in the all-too-familiar pattern of 'passing the buck' elsewhere. If, during the course of providing information and a supportive chat, you detect signs of more complex problems that require longer-term intervention than your agency can provide, you may need to act as an intermediary. But do not just give them the telephone number or the address – contact the agency and arrange an appointment there and then.

There are a variety of leaflets and books available designed to help parents understand illicit drug use, and the reasons why drugs can appear so attractive to young people. (Some may be obtainable from your Health Education Officer.) Keep a supply of leaflets to hand together with up-to-date information on specialist resources. Offer parents the leaflets first, suggesting that they read them at home, then return for further discussion if needed. With some parents it may be necessary to go through the leaflets to clarify terminology and problems.

For some parents, just one discussion may be sufficient. On the strength of it they may feel able to go home to talk with their child. Others, though, need two or three sessions before they have the confidence to confront their child. You can suggest ways in which they might do this, helping them to remain rational, avoiding tearful histrionics. Statements such as, 'Your behaviour leads me to believe that you might be using something', or, 'I love you very much, but I don't like your behaviour or what happens to you when you are under the influence of heroin/glue and so on', can quickly break down barriers. As one experienced drug worker reflects, 'Children need most love when they're at their most unlovable'.

There are few hard and fast rules as to how parents should respond when they finally discover that their child is using drugs, except that they should try hard not to panic. They should try approaches such as, 'I'm concerned, because from the way you have been talking it sounds as if it may be getting out of control. I would like you to talk with someone about what is happening.' Threats such as, 'You know these drugs will kill you!', only reinforce a user's belief that parents do not understand, especially when he has friends who are long-standing users and yet seem perfectly fit and well. Parents should also avoid recriminations, such as, 'We've spent all this money on your education/video/computer, and look how you repay us.' This may only reinforce his belief that his parents feel they can buy his affection and that they do not love him for himself. Or he may infer that that they are only interested in his fulfilling some of their own lost ambitions, with little concern for him as an individual in his own right.

2 *Helping a parent to respond to casual drug use*
(See also Chapter 11 on Drug use and adolescents and Chapter 12 on Solvent inhalation.)

If the child is a casual user, information and a chance to chat about the problem as the parents see it are, again, useful. So, too, would be a visit to a relatives support group so that they can talk with other parents who are going through similar experiences. If there is no group available, perhaps you should contemplate setting one up with other colleagues. It need not be too ambitious. You just need a place where a small group of parents can meet to share some of their anger and fear, while looking at ways of coping better the next time. The group can also be a forum for learning more about the subject and for sorting out some of the myths about drugs from the reality.

At this stage parents often feel they are walking a tight rope; aware that the young person is taking risks, but at a loss to know how to prevent him from harming himself. Parents need to accept that adolescence is a time for taking risks, pushing out the boundaries and becoming independent from parents. Adolescents deal with this phase in a variety of ways. Taking drugs is one for a minority. The majority prefer safer and more socially acceptable activities.

Parents have to sort out in their own minds – and make it clear to the drug user – how tolerant they are prepared to be when drug taking begins to affect family life, especially if there is evidence of difficult intoxicated behaviour. One useful piece of advice from one parent is that if a child is behaving in an aggressive or violent manner, he should be dealt with as if he is another parent's child. In that way a parent is less involved emotionally and more likely to bring the crisis under control.

3 *Family involvement with problem drug takers*
When assessing the desirability for family work the following factors need to be considered:

– Agency policy regarding work with families.
– Will the client allow partners or family members to be involved in the treatment plan?
– Are the relatives willing to participate in treatment, or are they likely to sabotage initiatives?
– The worker's (and colleagues') skills and training in working with families.
– Whether the client is still living at home with parents. If so, then family work to help reinforce change may be essential.

Parents, partners, brothers, sisters and sometimes even grandparents may need advice, support and an opportunity to attend relatives' groups. They may sometimes need therapeutic help themselves, both to help the client change and to help them cope with having a problem drug taker in the family. Sometimes, as noted in Chapters 5 and 6, the full assessment and early counselling sessions with clients may suggest that their problems are inextricably intertwined with long-term unresolved relationships with one or more family members. If the client is eventually to move towards a drug-free lifestyle, he probably needs to sort out these relationships, or at least come to accept the significance of early unhappy experiences that drugs seemed to alleviate.

Some parents and relatives benefit from individual sessions with a professional. Others benefit from family meetings. These can help the family unit to co-exist with the user, and still continue with their own lives. While in some families the drug user may be causing enormous stress and suffering, threatening the stability of the whole family, particularly the parents' marriage, in others the client's problems may be interpreted as a symptom of long-standing family difficulties that preceded and may have contributed to the client's dependence on drugs. (See also Chapters 3, 5, 6, 11.)

Some parents are tempted to offer help to their offspring that amounts to collusion with the drug user. They pander to his desire to avoid the need for change and to take some responsibility for that change. It is almost as if the parent tries to come off drugs for the child, a trap that even the professionals can fall into. Common examples of this are: paying fines when he has committed an offence; failing to confront a child when money or valuables have gone missing; giving money so that a youngster can buy drugs to prevent withdrawals. Families Anonymous use the expression 'Tough Love' to describe the approach parents need to adopt to be of most value to their child. This concept, along with that of 'letting go' is explored in considerable depth and insight in Liz

Cutland's book, written with parents in mind, *Kick Heroin*. It makes helpful further reading and details can be found in the Bibliography on page 202.

Some clients need help to grow less dependent on their parents, to stop being the child of the family and to learn to take responsibility for themselves, especially if they are in their twenties or thirties. Some would benefit from a stay in a drug rehabilitation community in order to achieve this, preferably one that offers a graded re-entry programme and family meetings.

In this chapter I have focused on drug taking children. In the next, I turn to the drug using parent, or rather parent-to-be, with a look at the special problems of drug taking in pregnancy.

CHAPTER FOURTEEN

Pregnancy and child care

Drug takers who become pregnant are invariably a source of concern not only for professionals but also for their relatives, friends and neighbours. Health visitors and social workers, too, worry about the ability of the mother (or both parents if the father is also addicted) to provide adequately for the child's physical and emotional needs. As a result, most problem drug takers, on discovering that they are pregnant are afraid to come forward for the normal obstetric and ante-natal care, believing that the new-born baby will be taken away from them.

There are several key management and assessment issues that need to be addressed. This chapter examines ways of helping a drug-taking mother (especially those physically dependent on opioids) to cope with the pregnancy and to retain the long-term care of her child.

Despite the fact that many of these pregnancies are unplanned, clients often do want to have the baby. They frequently believe that motherhood provides an incentive to give up drugs. Unfortunately, this does not always happen. On the other hand, staff in drug clinics in London and other major cities have experience of clients who have demonstrably been able to cope with the responsibility of parenthood, while continuing on a long-term maintenance prescription and gradually stopping drug use altogether after several years. Fear that the local authority might remove their children forces them to work hard to present themselves as 'perfect parents' and to keep their drug use under control. Many rightly say, 'I can care perfectly well for my children when I've got heroin. It's when I'm without it that I can't cope.'

Sadly, the parents who suddenly want to stop drug use and avail themselves of residential treatment and rehabilitation facilities often have to hand over the care of the child temporarily to either a close relative or the local authority. This is primarily because there are few facilities at present which enable the mother to detoxify while retaining direct responsibility for her children. A small number of new initiatives are under way in the London area. These include the Day Programme at University College Hospital Drug Clinic; a mother and child unit at City Roads due to open during 1987; and an extension to Phoenix House to offer facilities for families. These steps will help the drug taker anxious to provide a secure future for their children.

Some drug takers, on the other hand, find it difficult to look after their children while undergoing intensive therapy. All their emotional energy is channelled into coping without drugs. If both parents are addicts undergoing detoxification at the same time, they also have to cope with adjusting to each other in a non-drug relationship. This is difficult enough without the added responsibility of children. When a mother feels she cannot complete her treatment while coping with her child, a compromise may be the only option. The mother participates in a treatment programme while the child is cared for by a close relative, or placed with a sensitive foster parent able to reassure the child that the parent still cares. Clearly, frequent visits should be arranged so that the child feels he has not been abandoned. Inevitably, both parent and child are in a 'no win' situation. If the mother continues to use drugs, the child may be at risk. If the mother is separated from the child in order to become permanently drug-free both will suffer. The latter may, in the end, be preferable, provided that it is agreed that both parties maintain as much contact as possible.

Management of the pregnancy: should the mother detoxify?

Providing that the mother realises that she is pregnant during the first four months, she may be able to detoxify successfully either as an in- or out-patient during the first six months of pregnancy. If she does this the baby has a reasonable chance of being born drug-free. If the mother fails to admit to drug use, continuing, say, to use opiates throughout the last three months of pregnancy, the baby may need to be treated for withdrawal symptoms within a special care baby unit. Unfortunately, many drug takers do not realise that they are pregnant until well into the second trimester (fourth to sixth months). Many assume that they are infertile while taking heroin and other opioids, particularly as their periods are often irregular. By the time they realise what has happened it may be too late for a safe termination.

136

If your client is pregnant she should be seen as soon as possible by the obstetrician, who will probably liaise with the local drug clinic to discuss the detoxification programme. The regime varies according to the individual consultant's preferences. Some prefer all mothers to undergo complete detoxification before the last three months of pregnancy. Others reduce the daily opioid consumption and stabilise the mother on a small daily dosage of methadone until after the baby's birth. Although this usually results in the baby being born in withdrawals some paediatricians feel that is something they can treat reasonably successfully. It is preferable to the mother relapsing from emotional stress during the last three months, thereby risking foetal damage or death. This can also occur if a mother decides that the way to prevent her baby from being born 'addicted' is to stop all drugs completely; 'cold turkey'. You must warn clients of the dangers of doing this. It can cause miscarriage. Whether the client is encouraged to stabilise or detoxify, reduction should be very gradual, and by not more than $2\frac{1}{2}$ mgm per week of methadone mixture.

If a woman comes for help early in her pregnancy a supervised hospital admission with counselling may be the most effective way for her to achieve abstinence. Use this approach with those clients who are fairly stable and well-motivated to remain drug-free for the remainder of the pregnancy.

The mother-to-be should be encouraged to be totally honest about the amount and range of all the drugs she is taking, because only then can the appropriate level of methadone be estimated for her withdrawal regime. Failure to be honest at this stage may create problems for her and the baby. When looking at the possible effects of the mother's drug use on the baby remember that a baby can suffer withdrawals from a range of drugs, not just the opioids, but also like tranquillisers, barbiturates and alcohol.

Preparation of mother for the birth:
ante-natal care

The client must be aware that all the professionals around her are working together to help her cope with her difficulties, and to enable her to have as normal a pregnancy as possible. Sort out who is going to provide counselling designed to help the parents prepare for the new responsibilities they are about to undertake. If drug treatment is being provided by the local drug clinic they need to keep in touch with the obstetric and paediatric teams to let them know precisely what is happening with their 'patient'.

Many drug takers hope that by proving they can be good parents they will regain self-esteem and be seen as responsible members of society, not irresponsible junkies. At the same time, many mothers fear that their drug taking may have harmed the child or that they will not be capable of motherhood. Close relatives, such as grandparents, who can provide support and occasional practical help, can be of enormous help to parents in preparing for the birth and coping with the pressures during the first few months. You may find that the mother wants to involve the grandparents or other close relatives and to share her pleasure with them, but that they know nothing of her drug problem. If she can be persuaded to discuss the situation with them, she is likely to find that they have long suspected anyway that she was using drugs. Usually, once the initial shock is over, they are willing to help.

If the mother fails to keep ante-natal appointments she may need to be visited at home regularly by the community midwife and health visitor. The health visitor has a particularly important role in providing advice and health care after the birth, so any rapport developed at this stage will be invaluable.

Should a pre-birth case conference be called?

A decision to call a case conference implies that the baby is thought to be at risk. If the baby is likely to be born in withdrawals, or if you feel concerned about the mother's ability to cope with the care of the baby, you should hold a preliminary case conference six weeks prior to the delivery, to allow for the possibility of premature delivery. This should ensure that hurried decisions do not get taken after the birth, when people begin to get anxious about the baby being at risk. This can happen if a mother has not been honest about her drug use and the child is unexpectedly born in withdrawals. American studies suggest that the risks for the infant are reduced if the mother has only a short history of drug misuse, refers herself to a drug clinic for help, and expresses concern about the risks to the foetus. A stable relationship with a man who is not addicted is also helpful.

The case conference should include social workers, nurses, paediatricians, obstetricians and legal representatives. The aim is to assess the mother's progress, her attitude towards drugs, how she is using the support offered, and how regular her attendance is at ante-natal classes and clinics. Other topics include the level of support and social circumstances she will be discharged to, taking particular note of any practical needs, such as housing or baby clothes and pram. Even if the mother-to-be has managed to abstain in the latter stages of pregnancy, she will be more vulnerable after the birth with the added stress caused by a new-born infant.

Most parents are extremely anxious about case conferences and need reassurance about the prime objective: to ensure that their baby receives the maximum help. If the baby is likely to be born in withdrawals the parents should meet with the paediatrician to discuss the method of treatment. Often parents feel defensive and guilty about putting their child at risk. Try if you can to make them see that everyone around them wants to help them and the baby.

If there is a strong likelihood that the child will have to be placed on the 'at risk' register at birth, this should be explained to the parents-to-be and not left until after the birth. Emphasise to them that 'at risk' does not automatically mean that their child will be removed from their care, but that it does mean that a local authority social worker will be allocated to them to give them as much help as possible, to prevent their child having to come into care. A word of warning. Many are initially likely to interpret this information in a hostile manner. You have to be sensitive in counselling parents so that they come to see the intervention of a social worker as a preventative measure, designed primarily to protect their child, and not to punish them.

In deciding whether to place the baby on the 'at risk' register each case should be considered on its individual merits, relying on the recognised child care assessment criteria as a guide for such decisions, plus an assessment of the effect of the parent's drug taking on their general stability and coping skills. If there does not appear to be undue cause for alarm the child should not automatically be placed on the register.

Management of labour

It is often difficult for obstetricians to pin-point the delivery date because of the mother's erratic menstrual cycle, and because many have no idea of even the approximate date of conception. Other than the risk of the baby being born prematurely, many mothers have no special problems during labour. Because drug users are often tolerant to pain-relieving drugs, some obstetricians prefer patients to have their baby by epidural injections instead of administering opioids.

Management of the neonate (new born baby)

If the baby is born prematurely and/or in withdrawals it is

usually transferred to the special care baby unit until treatment has been completed. There are certain characteristics of the withdrawal syndrome in the neonate. These include a high pitched cry, inability to establish a sleep pattern, fast heart rate, sweating, fever, yawning, sneezing and, particularly dangerous, seizures. Other symptoms include poor sucking ability, vomiting, and diarrhoea which is especially difficult to control because of a risk of dehydration and electrolyte imbalance. Babies with the withdrawal syndrome are often extremely irritable and tense, over-reacting to external stimuli such as noise and light.

The withdrawal syndrome can start any time shortly after delivery up to two weeks later. The average is seventy-two hours after delivery. The symptoms can take up to two or three months to disappear. Methadone causes a moderate to severe withdrawal state, while barbiturates also have a prolonged withdrawal phase, starting later and carrying a higher mortality risk. The commonly used drug for treating neonates in the United Kingdom is chlorpromazine (2.8 mg per kg in four divided doses) although some paediatricians prefer to use paregoric. In the new born, the symptoms are controlled within hours of a dose being given. The main side-effect is drowsiness which can easily be eliminated by decreasing the dosage. When symptoms are under control doctors will try reducing medication every three or four days. Diazepam may be used for barbiturate withdrawal at 3–6 mg per kg daily in three divided doses.

The baby may need to be vaccinated against hepatitis B, particularly if the antibody is not detected in the mother who should be tested late in pregnancy. The growing incidence of HIV virus infection (the AIDS virus) among injecting addicts has of course increased the risk of an unborn child being born with the AIDS virus, although it is not until he is six to eight months old that doctors can determine whether he will develop the AIDS syndrome. There is a one in four chance of the AIDS virus developing, and a 50 per cent chance of contracting the disease, which currently has an extremely high mortality rate.

When a baby is being treated for the withdrawal syndrome, parents need to be offered counselling. This is an extremely stressful time for them. As one paediatrician comments, 'They have to stare their habit full in the face and see how it affects others'.

Breast-feeding does not appear to carry any undue risk for the baby unless the mother is HIV positive, when it is contra-indicated. No significant amount of a drug taken by the mother is passed through her milk. There is then no need to discourage a practice which greatly aids the mother–child bonding process and which can be disrupted if the baby has to remain in hospital until the treatment is completed, with mother returning home and visiting daily. Difficulty in maintaining daily visits invariably means that, for the majority of mothers, breast-feeding tends to be unsuccessful. Unfortunately few hospitals appear to have a room available to enable the mother to stay near her child.

Preventing long-term harm

Mothers who are relatively stable before and after giving birth and who have a solid relationship with a partner who does not use drugs, or good support from relatives, need the usual services of the health visitor. But these must be supplemented by counselling from their key drug worker. These sessions can be reduced in frequency in the usual manner as the drug-free period increases. Make sure, though, that the client feels able to resume contact if things get difficult.

There is a need to balance understandable concern for the well-being of the child with a recognition of the mother's feelings of guilt and inadequacy. She is likely to be scared stiff that, if she fails to perform as a perfect mother, she will lose the child. Some parents see the baby as solving many of their future problems. They invariably have a strong investment in the baby and have high expectations for their offspring. Babies, however do not tend to reduce problems. On the contrary, they create further problems, especially in the context of unstable relationships, financial, housing and legal problems. At times of crisis the social worker may need to arrange for temporary family aide assistance in order to avoid the child being removed to a foster placement. Other options to be considered might be referral to a local family centre and the use of day nurseries.

If the child is placed on the 'at risk' register, it is important to clarify who is doing what to avoid confusion. Because the social services social worker has to put the child's needs first, it is usually wiser to ensure that the parents have a separate worker whose primary concern is to help them deal with their drug related problems. Research into drug taking parents suggests that a significant proportion of their children are at risk, not so much from child abuse, but from neglect and the effects of a chaotic lifestyle. Some studies suggest that as the children grow older they are more likely to become separated from their mothers – some permanently – and are likely to spend time temporarily in care or being looked after by relatives while their parents struggle to become drug-free.

When assessing the ability of the parents to care for their children, it is important to look at each family situation individually, and not to assume automatically that drug use necessarily indicates poor child care. The quality of care may well be excellent as was noted earlier. If you have serious concerns, be honest with the client about them; she may prefer to be able to talk about the issues frankly, especially if you can agree a realistic strategy together. Above all, recognise your own feelings and anxieties, and share them with colleagues or a supervisor.

Drug taking parents are not the only clients who create specific problems for both specialist and non-specialist staff. While many of the difficulties posed by problem drug takers have already been covered in earlier chapters, there are a few that merit more detailed discussion.

CHAPTER FIFTEEN

Some common problems

Many of the problems workers experience in dealing with drug users are shared with other client groups: problem drinkers, delinquents, the mentally ill and so on. In this chapter I want to concentrate on those difficulties specific to drug takers.

Lack of motivation

Most workers express frustration at some time or other over problem drug takers, whom they describe as 'lacking motivation'. These are clients who do not appear to have any interest in trying to change, or in using the help the worker is offering. Bearing in mind that most drug takers are ambivalent about changing their lifestyle, it is not surprising that they also suffer from very mixed motivation. Sometimes a client appears to be one hundred per cent motivated to change, and at other times virtually ninety-nine per cent unmotivated.

Poor motivation is common following a pre-trial period when clients are often full of good intentions and express a willingness to change. After the court case, however, the good intentions disappear. So too does the motivation to change. Many are afraid of change. Their self-image is so low that they feel they can never be any different. Often people do not really know what they want. They are just aware that they are 'doing themselves in' and then are scared. They are unlikely to be able honestly and confidently to say that they 'want' to attend for therapy or go to a rehabilitation house. They are likely to be aware that things are out of control, yet they remain very reluctant to develop the inner controls they need, especially if this involves abandoning the only method they have known to achieve some measure of happiness, however short-term. This applies especially to the more chaotic, multiple drug user.

Like the rest of us when confronted with difficult decisions over personal problems, drug users are unlikely to be totally willing or motivated to change their lifestyle. This is particularly true if they are still getting some pleasure, status or friendship from their drug use. Many drug users do not know what 'normality' is. Reality for many who try to lead a so-called 'normal' drug-free life is a depressing and hopeless existence with severe limitations.

Motivation is not a static quality that clients either have or do not have. It varies according to the client's interpretation of his current circumstances. People tend to slip backwards and forwards in their motivation. Workers may have to accept that while some 'parts' of the person want to change other parts are still resistant. You should concentrate on working on those parts that are still positive.

It is part of the worker's task to encourage motivation by creating a suitable climate. Miller's work on motivational interviewing with problem drinkers suggests that motivation can be viewed as a see-saw. The therapist's responsibility is to enhance or to facilitate those influences which will tip the balance towards the client making a positive resolution to abstain or to reduce drug intake. This means that developing motivation is a joint therapist–client venture.

Nevertheless, if someone is clearly totally unmotivated to change and repeatedly indicates as much by his or her behaviour then it is probably not worth putting a lot of energy into that individual's case until there is a glimmer of interest in change. Your time is better spent on others who are at least partly motivated.

Intoxicated behaviour

If a client is stoned and incapable of participating in a coherent interview, no attempt at either assessment or recommendations should be made. It is a waste of time if the client is in no state to hear what you are saying or to participate in any discussion about his problems. It may be necessary to call an ambulance if the intoxication increases, and to keep in touch with the hospital accident and emergency department. Arrangements can be made to see such clients when they recover. As they may well forget any verbal instructions, it is advisable to write them down so that they will know the time and date of the next appointment.

When this comes round the client may again turn up stoned. Indeed clients may continue to repeat the same behaviour pattern hoping they will be taken care of when they overdose. If this does happen, make it clear that you are unavailable but that you are willing to spend time with the drug user when it is possible to engage in a sensible conversation. Be firm while still showing concern. There is little, if anything, that can be done with someone when he is intoxicated, least of all persuade him that it is time to give up drugs. This is certainly not the moment to counsel somebody about the risks they are taking. They will simply not remember anything you have said.

Talking about drugs

It is easy to get inveigled into discussions about drugs that are irrelevant to the interview. Inexperienced workers may find it fascinating initially to talk with clients about different kinds of drugs and their effects. It builds up the worker's store of information, but this is of no help to clients. In fact it may only reinforce their suspicion that the only thing that is interesting about them is their drug use. They will leap at an opportunity to avoid discussing their drug related problems by romanticising about drugs and reminiscing about 'the good old days'.

Some discussion of drugs and the drug sub-culture is inevitable. Most new clients need it as a preliminary to treatment, whether seeing someone individually or participating in a group. It can be part of the process of preparing to lose part of their life, as well as being a way of avoiding discussion about the future. But if constant talk about drugs continues well beyond the normal settling-in period, you must try to bring the person back to the task in hand, encouraging him to talk about his current situation, perhaps pointing out that generalised drug talk is a way of avoiding any real work. Insisting on talking about drugs, using all the sub-culture jargon, is an effective way of playing on an inexperienced worker's feelings of inadequacy and lack of knowledge.

Jargon or slang

Some clients will use jargon as a way of keeping the inexperienced worker at a distance. Therefore it helps to know some. You should know what clients are talking about. But the argot of the drug user changes over the years and there are regional variations. A client in Yorkshire might, for example, talk about 'cranking up' when describing injecting rather than 'fixing', which is standard terminology in the South. If you do not understand what clients mean by a certain expression, ask for an explanation. Avoid using jargon initially unless you are obviously very much at home with it. Even then it is not necessary to talk like a 'junkie' in order to communicate. Your ability to indicate that you understand

145

the client's predicament is of more importance than your mastery of his specialised language.

Denial – or telling lies

Many experienced professionals are frustrated by the drug taker's apparent inability to tell the truth. Clients constantly deny any sense of guilt in order to deceive. Denial is part of a behaviour pattern that builds up over a long period of time. It stems from the lifestyle of the illicit drug user who finds it necessary to deceive the authorities, employers, close relatives, friends and even oneself in order to avoid rejection, confrontation, prosecution or failure. Relatives and friends may, over the years, put pressure on the drug taker to stop. For the sake of peace and quiet he may try and deceive them into believing that he has done so. Probation officers with the power to prosecute someone for breach of probation, or drug clinic workers who can withhold prescriptions are also likely to be subjected to regular denial or lies.

One reason for denying drug use may of course be to avoid being reminded of the need to change. If clients refuse to tell you that they are using drugs it may be constructive not to confront them directly with doing so but to focus attention instead on other related problems. Constant probing can increase the client's wariness of the worker. If trust and respect develop, your client will undoubtedly discuss his drug use more honestly later on. Sometimes it helps if the worker spells out what he sees the drug user trying to do, acknowledging that it is difficult to be totally honest. People may feel forced into the position of telling lies if the worker insists on absolute truth. They may be frightened of such demands because it reveals their weakness. They then retreat into drugs and oblivion.

There are exceptions, though. An occasional well-timed confrontation by a worker may just be what the client needs or wants to hear. It is sometimes worth pointing out to the client that he may find it difficult to be honest with the worker, or indeed himself, about what is happening in his life. You might occasionally say something along the lines of, 'I am prepared to see you weekly for an hour or thirty minutes, and we can start doing some work together on the problems you have identified. If you choose to tell me lies from time to time, because you can't cope with the truth, you won't be wasting my time – but yours.' There is no fool proof way by which you know when to confront clients. It is a case of old-fashioned intuition, timing and experience.

Fear that clients might die

Any concerned worker worries about clients killing themselves. What should be done about such fears? Drug users are probably far more aware of the risks they run than anyone else. They are, for example, likely to have friends who have died. Strange though it may seem to those who do not use drugs, this experience often fails to frighten some drug takers. The worker is in danger of revealing his naïvety by warning of the dangers; most drug takers know only too well the risks they are running. For some, flirting with death may be a valid risk.

Many accidental deaths could be prevented. Reminding people who have been detoxifying or who have been drug-free for a time (such as those coming out of prison) of the dangers of using sedatives and opioids again when their tolerance is low can help to avoid disaster. So, too, can informing people that heavily adulterated and possibly toxic drugs are being sold on the street. Likewise advice about not using dirty or shared needles is clearly valuable if clients are to avoid hepatitis B or AIDS. Solvent sniffers need to be told about the dangers of using butane gas or aerosols which can cause sudden death and warned against the use of large polythene bags that might lead to suffocation. Working out how you offer such advice without increasing adolescent curiosity is not easy. It is usually best dealt with informally as part of an ongoing discussion by a worker whom the client respects and with whom he already has a good relationship.

Coping with the death of a client

Most adults find the death of a close friend or relative difficult to cope with. For many workers, too, the death of a client is a considerable blow. Although this can come as no great surprise if it happens to someone who is seriously ill or who has a pattern of overdoses or self-destructive behaviour, it can also occur quite suddenly and unexpectedly. Death may strike clients who were thought to be fairly stable or who, when last seen, were actually drug-free. The latter group is particularly vulnerable. If an addict, having been off drugs for some time (perhaps because of imprisonment or residing in a drug rehabilitation house) uses drugs suddenly and forgets that his tolerance is reduced, accidental death can occur. Such circumstances could be avoided if the user had used a much smaller quantity.

Any worker who decides to work with drug takers has to be prepared to cope with his own reactions to a client's death. You may be lucky and never have to face such a situation. Or you may find that you have to cope with several deaths within a few weeks of each other. Facing death is an inevitable part of working with drug takers, as it is when working with the mentally ill, particularly depressed and suicidal patients. It can be extremely difficult, especially when working with younger people, to accept that clients cannot be totally prevented from taking risks and killing themselves. Try, if you can, to avoid developing a self-protective layer of total cynicism. At the same time, try not to become too distraught at the loss of a client, particularly when you have known him for a long period of time. Death nearly always comes as a shock, however hard a worker tries to disguise his or her reactions to colleagues, the client's relatives and other drug users.

Death creates feelings of loss, failure, guilt, anger and, sometimes, relief in both relatives and professionals. While workers may need to give support to relatives, they themselves also need support from their colleagues and line manager, team leader or senior. They need time to mourn, to reflect and talk about the client in much the same way as when a close friend has died. Some workers feel guilty about having strong reactions to sudden death, believing that they should be seen as being 'able to cope' and able to handle such crises. This can result in workers blocking out their reactions by appearing to deny any feelings. Although it is desirable for you to appear in control when dealing with other clients, ensure that you have some time and space to talk to your senior or a colleague about what has happened. In this way you do not feel so overwhelmed with feelings of failure that the rest of your work is affected. Avoid falling into the trap of vowing, 'I will never work with another addict – they let you down'. This is a sign that a worker is becoming over-committed emotionally to helping people to give up drugs.

A client's death invariably engenders feelings of hopelessness and powerlessness in workers, often mirroring the very feelings of their clients. There may be a feeling of, 'Why bother, I can only cope with so much pain in other human beings'. Staff support groups can help individual workers talk through these feelings and gain support from colleagues to help handle them. If a client dies in unexpected circumstances the support of a caring staff group can be the most constructive way of helping staff to get over the initial shock and not transfer their feelings to other clients or personal situations. None of us is superhuman. None of us should pretend that we are unaffected by our clients' failures. Try to see the client who has died as an individual and not representative of all other clients. There is no point in rushing around trying to prevent other clients from killing themselves.

Confidentiality

Virtually every client using illegal or illegally acquired drugs is breaking the law. While most drug takers learn to live with this complication and develop survival tactics to cope with the inherent risks, many professionals, new to working with problem drug takers, find they are walking a tightrope. They are trying to safeguard the confidential nature of their relationship with the clients but worry lest they should be seen to be refusing to co-operate with the police in their attempt to 'stamp out drugs'. Most police officers, however keen they may be to arrest the dealers, accept that drug workers have to maintain a code of confidentiality, otherwise clients would not come for help. So, although local police might like to know who is currently attending for treatment, they would not expect to be told, although some would be grateful if you could pass on information about local dealing centres (pubs, etc.). They are likely to know of these anyway – and drug takers are certainly not going to tell you who they are buying drugs from!

Very occasionally, it may be necessary to break confidentiality – and your client may at times actually want you to do so, if for example they confess to being involved in a serious crime such as murder. If this happens they may need help in finding a way of going to the police themselves and obtaining legal advice.

Likewise, issues around 'children at risk' mean that some social workers and others may feel that they have no option but to report evidence of a neglected or abused child to the responsible local agency. Most local authority social workers make it clear to the client that although they respect confidentiality they would have to break it in such circumstances. It is generally wiser to be honest with clients than to studiously avoid such conflicts. They may not like it but are more likely to respect you for being straight with them.

Confidentiality can also become an issue when it comes to inter-agency liaison, when, for example, there are two or more professionals involved in dealing with a client's problems, child abuse being a good example. It is difficult to help clients properly if you don't have all the relevant information. Again this needs to be explained to clients who may have a vested interest in keeping everyone apart. Total confidentiality may not be possible or helpful for them in the long run. It is clearly important, as with all social and medical problems, that workers understand each other's need to share some information but also to respect the confidential nature of the disclosure.

Measuring success

When people start working with drug users there is a tendency to see success only in terms of people stopping drug use completely. I have learnt from hard experience not to use the word 'cure', and have instead talked about someone being 'drug-free'. Many who were once happy to refer to themselves as 'ex-addicts', now prefer the term 'recovered addict' (or 'recovering'), used by Narcotics Anonymous, to indicate that recovery is a life-long process.

Success has to be defined in a variety of ways, according to the progress made by individual clients in the light of their previous situation. So far as City Roads, the crisis intervention unit, is concerned, success must be seen in terms of keeping people alive, and helping them to develop more control over their drug use; and being ultimately able to make informed choices about alternatives to drugs. Success can also include users taking adequate precautions with their injecting practices (not using dirty or shared needles), preferably stopping injecting altogether, in order to avoid being infected with the AIDS virus. In practice, users will only be more hygienic in their injecting practices if drug clinics are prepared to supply them with clean needles, a controversial issue, currently under discussion.

Each drug-free period can be viewed as a success. The periods of abstinence and successful attempts to build a drug-free lifestyle can lengthen each time until, suddenly, drug taking feels like it was something to do with the past and not the present. When this happens, it usually takes years, not months.

Throughout this book I have been looking at ways of helping drug takers within the context of existing services and facilities. But if you develop a special interest in drug problems you may be asked to assist in planning services yourself at a local level. How should you respond? This is the topic of the next chapter.

CHAPTER SIXTEEN

Developing a community response

The Advisory Council on the Misuse of Drugs in its 1982 report on treatment and rehabilitation recommended that each District Health Authority should have its own drug advisory committee. Most districts now have their own co-ordinating committee with members drawn from a wide range of agencies, both statutory, non-statutory, voluntary and local self-help groups. The report further recommended that key functions of the committee should include monitoring the prevalence of drug use, assessing proposals for improvements in services, promoting liaison between the various agencies and professions, including the generic services, and assessing the need for training and information on problem drug taking. Anyone who has joined a similar committee recently, and who has not read the report, would be well advised to do so, in particular Chapter 6, 'A Framework of Services for the Future'. (See Bibliography on page 202 for publication details.)

Some committees have concentrated on identifying local patterns of drug use and assessing service needs in their own area. A number have applied directly or indirectly for money from the DHSS central funding initiative to establish new locally based services. Most regional health authorities have also established similar committees to assess the overall needs of the region in relation to individual district needs. For example, while most districts might identify the need for a specialist drugs worker or a small community drug team, it is unlikely that they will require an in-patient drug unit or a drug rehabilitation house, but there may be a need for one per region and for some inter-district facilities.

What is meant by 'community'?
In 1975, a United Nations travelling seminar on community involvement in the prevention of drug abuse, used the following working definitions:

– *National community*: central and local government departments all play a key role in the provision of services with the
help of our taxes and rate contributions.
– *The local community of agencies*, both statutory and non-
statutory, whose staff are employed to provide locally based
services.
– *The local community of residents*: peer groups, tenants' groups
and other local community groups which represent different
interests.

When drug specialists and other professionals address the
theme of 'community responses' they usually focus on either
the second or third definition, and occasionally on joint
responses from both groups, although this is rarer and more
difficult to achieve.

Concerned local residents are unlikely to have a formal
background in social work or a related discipline. Their
interest is more likely to stem from having a friend or a family
member who has become seriously involved with drugs, or
from having suffered personal tragedies from the drug related
death of a child.

The development of self-help and parents' support groups
has been one of the most striking new initiatives to develop in
response to the latest wave of heroin use in the United
Kingdom. Most groups have started with the basic aim of
seeking to provide members with emotional and practical
support, though some have also acted as pressure groups to
persuade local politicians and statutory agencies to provide
more resources. Others have sought to provide a service
themselves for families and the drug taker – a development
that has created conflict among many professionals who have
had to rethink their assumptions about who is best qualified to
offer a service to problem drug takers.

While some statutory agencies were trying to decide
whether dealing with drug problems was their responsibility
(when many had little, if any, direct experience or interest in
the problem), many parents of drug taking youngsters, angry
about the lack of concern and local resources came together to
find their own solutions. Some went so far as to reject any
initiative that came from the local services, and the advice of
professionals, unless they had some credibility with local
users and their families, was spurned.

Identifying the need for a specialist service
One of the major decisions that has to be taken by an
interdisciplinary group is whether or not drug problems can

adequately be dealt with by the services available or if it would be better to establish a specialist facility. Ideally, most clients benefit from having access to the expertise and resources of both specialist and generic services. However, money is severely limited, and for many areas the drug problem still only affects a small number of people compared with those clients needing help with other pressing health and social problems. If this is the case, it may be more cost- effective to concentrate on developing the skills and knowledge of staff in the existing agencies, rather then setting up new, but inadequately staffed services. If a specialist facility is established, it is important to clarify whether this is to meet the needs of the majority of problem drug takers, or whether it should be designed to act as a sort of intermediary service. The latter would offer direct help to selected clients, while liaising closely with the regional drug problem team and the primary health care and social work services, encouraging the latter to play a major role in service delivery.

Justifying the need for a specialist service: the use of prevalence studies

Deciding whether or not to establish a special service for drug problems has to depend on the approximate number of problem drug takers likely to be in need of help in a local area, both now and in the foreseeable future. Anyone requiring guidance on setting up a prevalence study to acquire in-depth knowledge of local needs should obtain the publications produced by the Drug Indicators Project (DIP), based at Birkbeck College, London University. (The address can be found in Useful Addresses on page 201.)

DIP has developed a valuable set of guidelines specifically for 'administrators and managers who are concerned with planning or providing services for drug takers and who require guidelines for assessing the nature and extent of local drug problems'. It recommends that information on drug use needs to come from as broad a range of sources as possible. These include:

– Routine statistics obtainable from the Home Office and the police, and from hospital in-patients, drug related deaths and hepatitis statistics.
– Information obtained directly from agencies. These should include general practitioners, probation officers, local or regional drug clinic, police, voluntary agencies and social services.
– Information from the local community including drug takers if at all possible.

Developing the role of the statutory agencies

If an assessment suggests that only a very small number of problem drug takers seem to be causing concern, it may be wiser for each agency to improve the expertise of their staff so that clients with drug problems can be offered direct help. This may mean improving the knowledge and sharpening the confidence of those staff likely to come into contact with problem drug takers. Multidisciplinary training courses can provide a forum for shared learning and a unique opportunity to develop a broader based response.

A number of staff in certain agencies will also need in-depth, practice-orientated training so that they can offer both short-and longer-term help as the key worker. These might be probation officers, local authority fieldwork and hospital social workers, general practitioners, community psychiatric nurses, and counsellors in youth counselling and alcohol counselling centres. If there is a local counselling centre for alcohol problems it may be worth exploring the possibility of including drug problems in their brief, providing that the centre is adequately staffed. Similarly, a youth counselling centre can be an effective base from which to provide direct help for the younger casual or problematic user. Such a centre may be more cost-effective if it can respond to the needs of a wide range of young people, rather than a minority whose numbers will fluctuate according to fashion.

There needs to be inter-departmental agreement that staff from the statutory agencies will undertake work with drug users, not just with those who are seen because of statutory duties (eg child care), and that a multidisciplinary approach will be encouraged. Agencies also need to find a way of letting problem drug takers and their families know that the local services are willing to offer help.

Most social services departments, for example, offer some scope for specialism among fieldwork staff. It may be worth encouraging one or two staff in each area office to take a special interest in drug problems. If they can build up sufficient expertise by working directly with clients, they will increase the credibility of that office in the eyes of local drug users who will then come to realise that there are sympathetic staff available who 'understand about drugs'. Ultimately, so far as referrals are concerned, the local grapevine is generally far more effective than posters.

If a similar approach is adopted by the local probation office, health centre and community psychiatric nursing service, those staff allowed to specialise can begin to develop an inter-agency response without undue extra expense. If the problem continues to grow and there seems to be a need for a full-time specialist resource their expertise and local knowledge will be invaluable in determining the most suitable facility – or they could form a community drug team, or a CADET (Community Alcohol and Drug Education Team).

What sort of specialist facility?

A specialist service needs to take into account:

– Who is it going to serve? eg What age group? Type of drug use?
– What is it going to offer?
– How is it going to operate?
– Where is it going to be sited so that it is easily accessible?

The question of who manages a new service needs to be considered carefully. Is it to be a joint initiative with each key agency contributing towards the funding? Or is one agency going to act as the host agency, with staff seconded from other agencies? Some areas have decided to set up a new non-statutory agency, while others have arranged for a locally recognised and well-established non-statutory agency to assume responsibility for the day-to-day management. In a number of areas two non-statutory agencies have collaborated in establishing a service after discussions with local committees.

There has been an extremely wide range of services established in the United Kingdom since 1983. However, there are a number of models that are typical examples of the initiatives that have been taken in different parts of the country. These include:

– drug advice and counselling centres (some with detached youth work);
– community drug teams (often known as CDT);
– community and alcohol drug education teams (also known as CADET);
– telephone advice and information lines (often staffed by volunteers);
– a specialist adviser employed by the local authority (likely to be based with social services) to co-ordinate local response and provide consultative advice and training to other professionals;
– no specialist resource, but better use of health and social services.

Community drug teams

A community drug team is a multidisciplinary team of two or three (or more) professionals, with at least one member drawn from a psychiatric nursing background and one with social work expertise. Some include a health visitor while others may employ someone with detached youth work experience able to undertake outreach work. Some teams may have formal links with a local general practitioner, psychiatrist, health centre or drug clinic. The style of working varies. Some devote most of their time to providing a specialist service for individual clients and their families, while others divide their time between carrying a limited case-load and providing support and training to local statutory and non-statutory agencies. This appears to be the model adopted by most teams in the North West Regional Health Authority where there has been an impressive growth in this type of resource since 1984, resulting from collaboration between health and social services and the local specialist non-statutory drugs agency, Lifeline, based in Manchester.

Individual team members are invariably employed by different authorities according to their professional background. For example, a nurse is usually employed by the health authority, while the social worker is likely to be accountable to the social services department. It is easy to see how problems can occur at a management level when there is no one overall employer. Most teams try to overcome this by developing a structure whereby the team members' line managers meet together on a regular basis as a 'management' or 'advisory' team to discuss inter-agency issues and mutual concerns of practical and financial responsibility.

There is considerable overlap between a CDT, a CADET and some advice and counselling centres. Most CDTs require a base from which to see clients. Some advice centres also provide support and training opportunities for other professionals. Irrespective of the specific orientation of the agency, ideally staff need to be based in suitably equipped community premises that are easily accessible to clients. Although it is sometimes possible to see clients in their own homes it is not always desirable. An office base with interviewing rooms provides privacy for individual work and neutral ground away from family pressures. It also provides a base to develop other initiatives such as group work and a drugs information service.

Community Alcohol and Drug Education Team

Alternatively it is possible to set up a CADET – a community alcohol and drug education team – without necessarily needing a specific office base for team members. Its primary role (as developed, for example, in Newcastle-upon-Tyne) is to offer advice and support to all non-specialist staff who are in contact with alcohol, drug and solvent problems. It is, theoretically, possible to work to this model without requiring extra money to create new posts, thus making it an attractive option for some areas. It can be a multiple agency team of staff whose members work full-time for a range of statutory and non-statutory agencies, such as social services, probation, health service (health visitor and community psychiatric nurse), general practice and alcohol counselling service. While still continuing in their chosen area of work, each member also agrees to provide on-call cover on a rota basis to other professionals on matters related to drug abuse. While some of them may be working as drug specialists others may not, although each team member needs to have some specialist expertise and an ability to support other professionals.

The team established in the last year or so in Newcastle-upon-Tyne emphasises its liaison, consultancy and training role in its publicity:

'The CADET is *not* a specialist agency which takes direct referrals, but is designed as a multiple agency on-call service of specialist workers, operating on a rota basis, and providing a continuous source of training, advice and support to all non-specialist workers in the CITY OF NEWCASTLE, who encounter alcohol, drugs, solvent and tranquilliser problems on their patient/caseloads. It should be emphasised therefore, that the Team does *not* take formal clinical or casework responsibility, but restricts itself to offering advice and support to the enquiring primary worker.'

Volunteer services
While CDTs and CADETs are staffed by paid professionals, other set-ups depend wholly or partly on volunteers to provide a service. The use of volunteers in dealing with drug problems is not new but it remains a contentious issue for many professionals. It is important to be specific about the roles and tasks expected of volunteers, especially those without any formal training in counselling or casework. Unfortunately, volunteers are invariably an option considered when authorities are trying to provide a service on the cheap, or when the statutory agencies are unwilling to shoulder the responsibility themselves. In dealing with a client group, who need, and are entitled to, the skills of experienced professionals, it is clearly irresponsible to pass that responsibility over to unpaid and initially untrained volunteers.

If a deliberate decision is made to recruit volunteer staff it is essential that appropriate training in drug problems, basic advice and counselling skills and resources is provided. Such training needs to be linked to the tasks they will be expected to undertake. This can include telephone advice and counselling for clients and relatives, helping to refer on to more specialist help, making initial assessments, befriending, and helping recovering addicts to develop new interests and hobbies. As a general rule it should not include responsibility for longer-term counselling or casework, or psychotherapy, unless the volunteer is suitably trained. As with paid professionals, volunteers also need regular support and supervision to avoid over-involvement and burn-out, to help clarify objectives and boundaries, and to share experiences with other workers.

Local involvement

Any local initiative is best developed with the support and interest of the local community, ideally working in liaison with existing self-help and parents' groups to ensure that the services are complementary and are not competing for each other's clients.

Some areas may decide to establish a residential facility for drug takers. Such initiatives really do put to the test the question 'does the community care?' It is one thing to pay your rates and hope the council trains teachers and social workers to deal with the drugs problem, but quite another to find that they have approved the opening of a drugs hostel or therapeutic community on your doorstep. There have been a number of examples of local hostility towards such ventures. In the Midlands, a hostel planned for ex-addicts caught fire and arson was suspected. Setting up a residential facility can take several years of careful planning, which must include consultation with local residents and community groups, aimed at reassuring them that the new initiative (if properly staffed and managed) will not add to the local drug problem, but could actually help those youngsters most at risk to find alternatives to drug use. Once positive local interest is aroused it can be harnessed to provide long-term support for the project, which is of benefit to all.

The long-term objective of many projects, as well as of the government's 'Just Say No' and other campaigns, is prevention. It is frequently said that 'prevention is better than cure'. Drug problems are no exception. But we know more about actually treating drug dependence and its related difficulties than we do about stopping it developing in our communities. What then are the prospects for prevention? The last chapter discusses this important question.

CHAPTER SEVENTEEN

What about prevention?

Preventing drug use is an attractive and desirable goal, but how realistic is it? Whose responsibility is it? Is it something that all agencies should be doing, even those heavily committed to providing treatment and rehabilitation services, or is it really the responsibility of staff dealing with primary health care and those responsible for the social and emotional development of children and young people? Or is prevention really a parental responsibility? With any amount of preventative work, is it possible to stop drug use increasing once a source of supply has become available in an area? If not, then should central government concentrate on controlling suppliers, and so take the pressure off teachers to come up with answers to stop children experimenting with drugs?

The majority of staff in social work, probation, medical and counselling agencies are more likely to see clients once drug use has become a controlling factor in their lives, not before they start using drugs. There are, though, a few staff who are in contact with young people and adults when they may not have started experimenting or when they are still intermittent users. Whether or not staff are in contact with clients prior to drug use many are under the impression that they should be doing something about preventing drug use, either by stopping it from becoming an attractive option for members of the community, or by stopping it from progressing from experimental or casual use to more problematic use. In reality this is probably one of the most challenging aspects of dealing with the drug problem. It is also one that demands very long-term strategies by central government, society, parents and professionals – not short-term shock tactics.

Defining prevention
Prevention has traditionally been subdivided into three separate categories – primary, secondary and tertiary.

Primary prevention is the term commonly used to describe strategies to prevent drug use ever starting. It is often described as 'education'.

Secondary prevention describes strategies aimed at reducing the number of people dependent, or at risk of becoming dependent on drugs. This assumes that they have already started using drugs but are still intermittent or casual users. This kind of prevention is often referred to as 'early intervention'.

Tertiary prevention aims to alleviate the effects of harmful drug use, usually through treatment and rehabilitation. It is concerned with preventing people who have had a drug problem from returning to drug use by developing intervention strategies to prevent relapse.

The Advisory Council on the Misuse of Drugs made a detailed study of the subject, published their findings and recommendations in a 1984 report called 'Prevention'. The Council found these three definitions somewhat restricting when looking at elements of prevention policy, and decided to base their discussion and recommendations on two basic criteria: reducing the risk of an individual engaging in drug misuse and reducing the harm associated with drug misuse.

The 'reduction of harm' strategy is not an approach that is happily accepted by some, who view it as a form of collusion with the user and condonation of drug taking, because it does not appear to encourage the person to *stop* taking drugs. Harm-reduction strategies directed at dealing with solvent sniffing were greeted with derision by the popular press and by some politicians when they were first discussed in the early 1980s. However, the tragic reality of AIDS as a major life threatening risk for injecting drug users finally underlines the urgent need for harm reduction strategies to help opioid users avoid unnecessary risks and to take greater control of their drug use. Most people would support strategies that help to reduce harm from excessive alcohol consumption and smoking, so why not illicit drugs or solvents? It is the old problem of double standards. My drug is OK but yours is not because it is illegal and therefore not socially acceptable.

The main recommendations of the 'Prevention' report emphasise the role of education in three main areas:

1 The community in general

2 Specific groups who may be vulnerable

3 Training for professionals who are likely to come into contact with drug misuse at an early stage so that they can

respond appropriately. The training of some groups of health professionals should take into account the need to educate the general public on the proper use of medicines.

The report also recommended that the Home Secretary should assume responsibility for the overall co-ordination of prevention policy at a national level. It also advised Ministers that the District Drug Advisory Committees should extend their role and membership in order to consider suitable local prevention strategies. It stated the need for research into different prevention strategies, including an evaluation of the broad aims of health and social education programmes and ways of reducing harm associated with drug misuse.

The broad recommendations, including those concerning the Home Secretary and the wider role of the local advisory committees were accepted and adopted by the government. Since then, a number of initiatives have taken place with the help of additional funding in the form of £2 million to help with pump priming for a maximum of three years. To date, the majority of these initiatives have centred on 'reducing the risk of an individual engaging in drug misuse' rather than reducing harm, although a number of initiatives are directed at improving the expertise of professionals who come into contact with problem drug takers.

Although the government was happy to endorse the majority of the recommendations it clearly did not go along with the Council's view that 'national campaigns to reduce the incidence should not be attempted'. The Council felt that current evidence suggested that knowledge itself does not usually change attitudes, far less alter behaviour; and that however attractive it might be to assume that the success of anti-smoking campaigns could be repeated with similar issues, there was no guarantee that similar techniques were appropriate to trying to prevent drug misuse. It believed there might even be a greater risk of stimulating interest where none previously existed. The government-backed advertising campaigns in newspapers and on television indicate that such advice was not heeded. The government felt that a suitably low key informative campaign alerting young people to the dangers of heroin use was necessary. The effectiveness of this approach is currently being evaluated.

The government response

The report *Tackling Drug Misuse: a summary of the government's strategy*, published in 1986, outlines four main responses that have been implemented since the 'Prevention' report was published.

1 Prevention through health education

This has been one of the key elements of the current prevention strategy. It has consisted of an education and information campaign to discourage drug misuse, including advertising on television and in the press, and providing a series of leaflets for parents and professionals containing basic information about drugs and designed to allay some anxieties. Other initiatives included the production of two video training packages, one for professionals *Working with drug users* and the other for twelve to fifteen-year-olds for use in schools, with an emphasis on encouraging young people to make healthy and positive choices about their lifestyle.

2 Action in the education service

A proportion of the £2 million has been allocated to the education authorities in England to enable them to appoint or second a member of staff to work as a Drug Education Co-ordinator. He or she is expected to be able to offer advice, support and training for teachers and youth workers to enable them to respond more effectively and immediately to drug misuse among young people, and to help them initiate drug education in the classroom. Most of these appointments have been made for a two-year period, hence the advantage of secondment.

Other initiatives include providing booklets for teachers, and funding the production and testing of teaching materials aimed at curriculum development and teacher training. Similar initiatives have been developed in Scotland and Wales.

3 Prevention through training

Following some of the key recommendations of the 'Prevention' report a number of initiatives have been funded which are aimed at providing more opportunities for in-service training for health and social work professionals. This has largely taken the form of several regional or similar (e.g. London-wide) Drug Training Units in England and Scotland and a number of specialist Training Officer posts attached to local authorities or to non-statutory drug agencies. These initiatives aim to meet the training and development needs of staff in both the specialist drug agencies and non-specialist (generic) statutory and voluntary agencies. The Advisory Council on the Misuse of Drugs has also set up a working group to review the training of professionals who work with drug misusers.

4 Co-ordination and community action

The government's booklet also emphasises the role of the District Drug Advisory Committees in sharing the responsibility for local education and training needs. Some committees have already established a sub-committee with a special responsibility to explore possible prevention initiatives that could be developed both between agencies and in the wider community. *Tackling Drug Misuse* also welcomes the more localised community response symbolised by the development of self-help groups for drug takers and their families.

Further steps

It is important to remember that reducing the availability of drugs is also an important aspect of prevention policy. The Government has sought to do this by improving the staffing levels and surveillance techniques of Customs and Excise Officers and the police, as well as by increasing the penalties for those dealing in drugs. Some observers feel that greater emphasis should be placed on reducing the availability of both legal and illegal drugs, rather than ploughing money into education strategies that have yet to demonstrate that it is possible to deter young people from wanting to experiment with drugs.

While there is considerable doubt about the effectiveness of recent advertising campaigns aimed at young people, few professionals would argue with the need to find ways of educating the general public to adopt a more responsible attitude towards the use of all psycho-active substances, not just illicit drugs. Prevention is still a relatively new strategy that demands imaginative thinking about why people take drugs and what influences people to change their behaviour. It includes looking at innovative ways of working with the media, local community groups, employers, trade unions, and local authorities.

Meanwhile, it is equally important for professionals already in contact with drug takers, whether they are concerned with primary health care, or work in a specialist drug agency, to look at ways of reducing drug related harm by helping people to avoid taking unnecessary risks and to take greater control of their drug use, while developing skills in helping users to explore alternatives to drug use. Those working with young people in a youth work, Intermediate Treatment or residential care setting are uniquely placed to develop secondary prevention strategies, providing that they as workers receive adequate training and support and do not set themselves unrealistic goals such as stopping all drug use ever happening.

APPENDIX ONE

Action and effects of drugs

1 *Sedatives and tranquillisers* – barbiturates, alcohol, minor tranquillisers

2 *Stimulants* – amphetamines, cocaine, caffeine, tobacco

3 *Opiates* – natural and synthetic derivatives of the opium poppy – morphine, heroin, methadone, pethidine (also described as opioids)

4 *Volatile solvents* – glues, aerosols, dry-cleaning fluid

5 *Hallucinogenic (psychedelic) drugs* – lysergic acid (LSD), mescalin, cannabis

Major tranquillisers and anti-depressants are not generally liable to abuse – they will be mentioned in connection with groups (1) and (2). Where appropriate both the non-proprietary (scientific) name, and the common trade (or proprietary) name is given for drugs. The latter are shown in italics.

Sedatives and tranquillisers

Sedatives and tranquillisers make up the largest group of psychoactive drugs prescribed in the United Kingdom. They are also likely to be used by non-medical drug users, particularly multiple drug users. Barbiturates, the best known and historically most used and abused drug in this group, were introduced as barbituric acid in 1903. Over the last twenty-five years many other sedative drugs have been produced, some of which have advantages – such as being less dangerous in terms of the likelihood of lethal suicidal overdoses and possibly, but not necessarily, a lower dependency risk. The best known and most widely prescribed are the benzodiazepines (for example, *Valium* and *Mogadon*).

Legal status: All sedatives and tranquillisers are only available on prescription under the Medicines Act. From 1 January 1985 all the barbiturates are included in Class B of the Misuse of Drugs Act (M.D.A.) – this means that doctors are still able to prescribe them but only a patient for whom they are prescribed is legally entitled to possess them. (Therefore possession other than on a legal prescription is a criminal offence.) From 1 April 1986, thirty-three of the benzodiazepines are included in class C of the M.D.A., the class with the lowest maximum penalties.

Barbiturates

These were originally prescribed as hypnotics (sleep inducers) and as day-time tranquillisers and sedatives until the advent of the minor tranquillisers. Barbiturates are now rarely used for treating anxiety,

The symbol above is used to facilitate reference to this section stress or insomnia in general practice, except in intractable cases. Chaotic and invariably crisis-ridden behaviour associated with their use by drug takers in the 1970s (including deliberate and suicidal overdoses) led to increased pressure to reduce their availability by less prescribing (eg the CURB campaign) and to control under the Misuse of Drugs Act. However, despite the marked reduction in prescriptions for these drugs, committed drug takers can still obtain illicit supplies from sources such as chemist break-ins or thefts in transit between the factory and pharmacist's counter. Some may still be able to persuade the occasional GP to prescribe small amounts. Most problem drug takers who preferred barbiturates have transferred to other drugs, including minor tranquillisers.

Commonly used barbiturates (often referred to as barbs, downers, sleepers)

Tuinal	quinalbarbitone and amylobarbitone
Nembutal	pentobarbitone
Soneryl	butobarbitone
Sodium amytal	amylobarbitone sodium
Seconal	quinalbarbitone
Pentothal	thiopentone (short acting intra-venous anaesthetic)
Phenobarbitone	(a long-acting drug and rarely abused, used to treat barbiturate withdrawal states)

Medical uses
– suppression or epileptic fits (especially phenobarbitone)
– short-acting anaesthetic (*Pentothal*)
– as sedatives and hypnotics, but rarely now as first drug of choice

Method and administration
– swallowed as pills, capsules or elixirs
– injected by some non-medical drug users (see *Complications*)

Effects
– small doses (eg one or two pills) cause relaxation and reduce anxiety, similar to one or two drinks
– larger doses induce sleep
– if the consumer stays awake, larger doses will produce an effect of drunkenness which may include slurred speech and incoordination (e.g. unsteady gait) which can result in accidental injury (if, for example driving or operating machines). Even in therapeutic use, when a patient awakes suddenly, this is known to be associated with an increased risk of accidental injury.
– much larger doses cause unconsciousness, circulatory and respiratory failure and death
– blackouts, ie periods for which the user has no memory but during which apparently purposeful behaviour continues (amnesic episodes), may occur. This is similar to the phenomena of blackouts associated with heavy alcohol consumption.
– aggressive behaviour. Often seen with people using these drugs (and alcohol), it is due to the higher inhibiting centres of the brain being suppressed first, thus lessening normal social controls. It may be seen as an exaggeration of the socially desired effect. The user may appear to be suddenly impatient, abusive, aggressive and violent.

Long-term effects
– dependence. This can occur with long-term regular use, although with therapeutic doses it is usually only manifest in difficulties with sleeping if the drug is stopped.
– tolerance occurs and more of the drug is required to produce the desired effect
– withdrawal syndrome. If the drug is stopped suddenly after regular high dose use, a serious medical condition can occur which requires management by slow withdrawal of the drug with gradually reducing doses. Abrupt withdrawal leads to progressive restlessness, anxiety and irritability, possibly to delirium, epileptic convulsions and even death (see notes below).
– depression following habitual use can occur
– no known permanent physical damage occurs

A minority of multiple drug users (of both opiates and non-opiates) still prefer to inject barbiturates. This produces an immediate feeling of pleasurable warmth and drowsiness, and must be one of the most self-destructive and potentially dangerous forms of drug misuse.

Complications of injecting barbiturates
– abscesses can occur at injecting sites due to the irritant nature of the drug. These can become secondarily infected, and if neglected, can prove serious.
– accidental injection into arteries can produce severe danger to the limb supplied by the artery, including gangrene
– complications of poor injection techniques, such as septicaemia (blood poisoning) and serum hepatitis (jaundice) if needles or syringes are shared.

Other risks
Heavy users are liable to:
– bronchitis and pneumonia because the cough reflex is depressed
– accidents (especially burns)
– hypothermia, because the peripheral blood vessels dilate but the drug blocks normal responses to cold
– repeated accidental overdoses due to mental confusion and tolerance effects. (Heavy users often take excessive doses.)
– possible brain damage from overdoses

Signs and symptoms of drug induced state (leading to overdose or withdrawal)
– client is disorientated, appears drunk, and speech is thick and slurred
– walk is unsteady, as if drunk
– breathing slower
– if injecting, will have signs of track marks, possibly ulcers, abscesses
– overdose – ie increased drowsiness leading to a coma. Breathing becomes slower and irregular or laboured. Face and lips turn blue, skin is cold and clammy. Pin-point pupils.
– signs of withdrawal fits: client very anxious and irritable, with fine tremor of hands. Pulse may be 100 per minute.

Management of overdose
– EMERGENCY – dial 999 and call an ambulance. Meanwhile:

– check airways are clear, remove dentures, vomit and mucus
– prevent tongue from falling back into throat by laying patient on side, tilting head back, chin straight up and pulling the tongue forward
– if breathing ceases start mouth-to-mouth resuscitation

Management of withdrawal
– get medical help; if no doctor available, call 999 and ambulance
– if fitting, lay patient on side, loosen clothing

Abstinence (withdrawal) syndrome
This occurs as a result of sudden withdrawal of the drug, particularly when non-therapeutic doses have been consumed. As the amount of drugs in the body falls there is first an improvement as signs of intoxication abate; then as levels fall further the withdrawal syndrome develops. The common symptoms are – anxiety, involuntary twitching, tremor of hands, progressive weakness, dizziness, distortion of visual perception, sleeplessness and falling blood pressure. If untreated, a confused mental state with hallucinations, identical to the delirium tremens associated with alcohol withdrawal and/or major epileptic convulsions, may occur. This presents a more severe medical problem than that of opiate withdrawal and can prove fatal. The medical management requires the administration of drugs from this group (eg phenobarbitone) with progressive but carefully supervised diminishing doses. This supervision can only be achieved on an out-patient basis with the most co-operative and stable patient. Therefore it is advisable to use short-term hospital admission (or City Roads in Greater London) whenever possible.

Pregnancy
The prolonged use of sedative hypnotics in the later stages of pregnancy can result in withdrawal symptoms in new-born babies.

Non-barbiturate sedatives
Other drugs have been introduced as substitutes for barbiturates, in the hope that they would not produce dependence. However, tolerance and dependence can develop with these drugs and some have become liable to serious misuse by multiple drug users. Hazards of accidental overdose and interaction with other central nervous system depressants are similar to those of barbiturates although the safety margin is somewhat higher. Thus the caution advised for the use of barbiturates also applies to other sedative hypnotics.

Drugs in this group include:

Doriden glutethamide – 'Cibas'
Heminevrin chlormethiazole – 'Hem', 'Heminev'
Chloral hydrate – 'Knockout drops', 'Mickey Finn' 'Chloral'
Welldorm dichloralphenzone
Qualude methaqualone – 'Ludes'
Mandrax methaqualone with dyphenhydramine – 'Mandies'
Benzodiazepine hypnotics – see below under *Minor tranquillisers.*

Heminevrin may present particular problems of withdrawal. If abused, withdrawals can induce a severe confused state which may last for over a week. It is sometimes used in the treatment of alcohol problems and obtained by drug users, illicitly or on prescription, claiming that they are being treated for alcoholism. It is advisable not to prescribe this drug to drug users or alcoholics on an out-patient basis.

Minor tranquillisers

These have increasingly been prescribed since 1960 as alternatives to the barbiturates and daytime sedatives. Although the hazards involved in their long-term usage are fewer than with the barbiturates, they do create problems of psychological dependence and there is evidence of physical withdrawal occurring if the supply is suddenly stopped. They should not be confused with the major tranquillisers (see below) used in the treatment of particular psychiatric illnesses. There has been increased criticism of liberal prescribing for minor complaints to all sections of the population – especially women – when many of the presenting and related problems would be better helped by practical social work, counselling, psychotherapeutic or psychological intervention (eg relaxation techniques) and community work responses. Partly because of this and increased awareness of the problems associated with psychological, and sometimes physical dependence, there has been growing recognition by medical practitioners of the need to reduce prescribing levels and to encourage patients to seek non-medical help, including joining self-help groups. There is currently no evidence of illicit manufacture but some prescribed or stolen supplies find their way onto the black market. In some parts of the country drug users may refer to them as 'barbs', so check what people think they are using when making an assessment.

Drugs in this group include:

The benzodiazepines	most commonly prescribed minor tranquillisers (all controlled under class C of the M.D.A.):
Valium diazepam *Librium* chlordiazepoxide *Ativan* lorazepam *Serenid* oxazepam	mainly prescribed to relieve anxiety and tension
Mogadon nitrazepam *Dalmane* flurazepam *Euphynos* temazepam *Halcion* triazolam	for night sedation
Non-benzodiazepines	
Equinal Miltown meprobamate	rarely prescribed, being less effective than benzodiazepines

168

Medical use
– treatment of anxiety, tension and also insomnia
– used in the management of some forms of epilepsy
– may be used in the treatment of withdrawal symptoms of alcohol and barbiturate dependence
– have been recommended for muscular disorders (eg back pain)
– tend to be used as a general panacea for all forms of nervous upset including bereavement, tension and depression. These drugs have been known to make people more depressed.

Method of administration
Usually swallowed as pills or capsules, but sometimes injected (dentistry)

Effects
– normal doses usually provide relaxation, a distancing of problems, a feeling of well-being and perhaps some loss of inhibition. The effects of diazepam last for approximately three to six hours, longer in the elderly; and long-acting drugs prescribed for night sedation can last into the day.
– moderate to high doses can cause a general depression of nervous, muscular and several other bodily functions
– side-effects include drowsiness, increased sensitivity to alcohol, lethargy and skin rashes
– excessive use can lead to disorientation, confusion, and other symptoms similar to drunkenness
– driving is particularly likely to be impaired with high doses

Long-term effects
– tolerance develops to the effects and the dose may need to be increased in order to obtain the desired effect. It has been suggested that after continuous use over some weeks benzodiazepines tend to lose their pharmacological effectiveness as sleeping pills and, while effective in the short-term management of anxiety, they do not offer a long-term cure.
– development of psychological and physiological dependence, similar to alcohol and the barbiturates, and common with those previously dependent on those drugs. The strong psychological dependence is primarily related to over-reliance on 'pills' to cope with situational or psychological problems. Severe panic or anxiety may develop if the drug is temporarily unavailable.
– the abstinence syndrome may follow abrupt withdrawal, especially after large doses. Mild withdrawal symptoms can occur also in a small minority of patients after several years of treatment with normal therapeutic doses, and in the majority after six to eight years.

Withdrawal syndrome
The withdrawal syndrome in some patients can resemble the original complaint, and it is therefore quite possible for both the patient and doctor to fail to recognise the significance of the symptoms, and instead to be tempted to continue with the treatment.

Withdrawal effects after suddenly stopping medication may take several days to appear and last two to three weeks or longer. They include anxiety, insomnia, perceptual hypersensitivity, tremor, irritability, nausea and vomiting, and after unusually high doses, may include convulsions and mental confusion. These are not as serious or common as with the barbiturates, but can be extremely distressing.

Signs and symptoms of drug-induced state
– client feels relaxed, happy and euphoric with mild to moderate dose
– increased use will lead to drowsiness/sleep, uncoordinated drunken behaviour, confusion, slurred speech, dizziness and weakness
– with heavy doses collapse or unconsciousness may occur
– withdrawal symptoms are described above, perhaps preceded by alertness, irritability and restlessness – and depression, a further possible symptom of prolonged use of a depressant drug

Pregnancy
There is some medical evidence to suggest that taking a high dose of diazepam during the latter part of pregnancy can sometimes lead to withdrawal effects in the new-born baby. As a result the use of minor tranquillisers in pregnancy is viewed with caution.

Major tranquillisers
The first of this group, *Largactil* (chlorpromazine) was introduced for the management of severely disturbed psychotic patients, usually diagnosed as schizophrenic or manic. A range of other major tranquillisers have been developed including *Stelazine* and *Modicate* (long-acting drug give by injection). *Largactil* was available prior to the introduction of minor tranquillisers and perhaps has some limited usefulness in the treatment of anxiety. There is no cross-tolerance with the drugs described above – indeed *Largactil* has been known to increase the risk of epileptic convulsions in drug withdrawal. Their consumption does not produce euphoria or a reduction of social inhibitions, so there is a negligible risk of hedonistic misuse. They can however be fatal if taken as an overdose.

Alcohol
This is society's most commonly legally approved and socially sanctioned non-prescription drug (other than caffeine based beverages). It is probably the most commonly used central nervous system depressant and can produce psychological and physical dependence.

Effects and side-effects
Broadly the same as the other groups previously described in ths section. Alcohol withdrawal provides the model which has subsequently been described with the other drugs.

Additional side-effects
– gastric irritation which may lead to gastritis and peptic ulcers
– liver damage, causing cirrhosis which can lead to liver failure and/or varicose veins in the oesophagus and rectum (can lead to fatal bleeding)
– pancreatitis, hypertension, peripheral nerve disorders

– brain damage ranging from deterioration in mental state to full blown dementia
– sudden withdrawal when someone is physically dependent can lead to a confusional state known as delirium tremens (the DTs) requiring hospitalisation
– vitamin deficiencies resulting from the often inadequate diet of the alcoholic. These may in part be responsible for some of the effects listed above.

nb: Cross-tolerance and cross-dependence occur between all the drugs described in this section – that is between sedatives, tranquillisers and alcohol. Taken in combination the effects of these drugs are heightened and the serious effects of large doses are exaggerated. They may well lead to a potentially fatal overdose or disturbed and dangerous behaviour.

Stimulants

This group includes a wide range of substances that have a stimulant effect on the central nervous system. There are similarities between the actions of all the drugs, but amphetamine and cocaine will be the main drugs described. The actions of amphetamine and related drugs have a similarity to the naturally occurring neuro-transmitter and hormone, adrenalin (called epinephrine in the USA), and thus provide an artificially induced form of perceived energy for the user. The slang term 'speed' is often used to describe these drugs – and a person may be described as being 'speedy' when behaving in an overactive manner due to the effects of amphetamine.

Historically many different groups of people in society have used stimulants; to avoid sleep when studying for exams or driving, or to stay awake at parties are a few examples. Others include the improvement of athletic performance and to increase work input. Some may use them to counteract the effect of depressant drugs. The heroin addict of the 1960s took cocaine as well – whether it was to counteract the sedative effects of heroin or as an additional or alternative euphoriant is debatable. Some drug users may take amphetamines in the daytime to counteract the depressant 'hangover' effect of sleeping pills consumed the previous evening. The enormous popularity of *Drinamyl* (known as 'purple hearts' in the 1960s) was largely due to the euphoric effect produced by its combination of stimulants (dexamphetamine) and depressants (amylobarbitone). These tablets are no longer being manufactured for pharmaceutical purposes in Britain.

Drugs in this group include:

Amphetamines	– *Dexedrine* (dexamphetamine) – 'dexes', 'blues'
	– *Durophet* (combination of dexamphetamine and amphetamine sulphate) – 'black bombers'
	– *Methedrine* also *Pervitin* (methylamphetamine) – disappeared from the illicit market

171

	– Amphetamine Sulphate – manufactured illicitly, probably main source of supply for regular 'sulphate' amphetamine users
Related drugs	– *Ritalin* (methylphenidate) – *Preludin* (phenmetrazine) – *Tenuate Dospan* (diethylpropion) – *Apisate* – both the latter used as short-term appetite suppressants in obesity
Cocaine	– 'Coke', 'Snow'
Caffeine	– Contained in coffee, tea, cocoa, soft drinks (eg Coca-Cola)
Nicotine	– Tobacco, cigarettes, snuff
Ephedrine and pseudo-ephedrine	– Both common stimulants found in many medicines, can be obtained from chemists.

Amphetamine

Amphetamines were introduced into medical practice in the mid-1930s and were mainly prescribed as appetite suppressants and as treatment for some forms of depression. Their use over a prolonged period of time has been increasingly questioned, because of their detrimental physical and psychological side-effects. In neurotic states, where depression is combined with lack of energy, the patient often demanded ever-increasing doses. In severe depression (endogenous or psychotic) anti-depressant drugs of the tricyclic or similar groups are both more effective and also non-addictive (see later).

Legal status

Amphetamines and related drugs such as *Ritalin* have been controlled under the Misuse of Drugs Act since the early 1970s, under Class B, but if prepared for injection then the increased penalties of Class A apply. Minor amphetamine substances are included in Class C, recent additions being *Tenuate Dospan* and *Apisate*.

Medical use

Now rarely advocated as suitable medication for slimming or depression.
– treatment of narcolepsy, a condition in which an individual suddenly drops off to sleep several times a day
– occasionally used with some hyper-active children. They have a paradoxical effect and seem to reduce restlessness

Method of administration

Prescribed drugs usually intended for oral use. Non-medical use of amphetamine sulphate may include sniffing or injecting, while some prefer to obtain *Ritalin* for injectable purposes.

Main effects and side-effects

– central nervous system stimulants give a feeling of alertness and energy

– reduce the appetite
– the adrenalin-like effects lead to increased heart rate, dilated pupils, increased blood pressure, faster breathing, restlessness, excited, enthusiastic and over-talkative reactions
– in larger doses anxiety reactions and panic states may occur
– amphetamine psychosis: the development of a paranoid illness is almost inevitable when larger doses are consumed over a period of time. It may even occur with a small dose with certain users, depending on their susceptibility. It resembles paranoid schizophrenia with delusions of persecution and hallucinations where sensory stimuli are imagined or misinterpreted, often as threatening. Some may experience tactile hallucinations, believing that there are bugs under the skin. Many users, particularly with higher doses, experience auditory hallucinations (hearing voices).
– obsessive and compulsive behaviour may occur

Long-term effects
These are mainly an exaggeration of short-term effects. With a continued high dose the ill-effects are almost inevitable and chronic weight loss, for example, is often apparent.
– dependence occurs. A compelling psychological need to continue taking the drug.
– if amphetamine use is stopped suddenly the heavy user may develop depression, irritability, long but disturbed sleep, fatigue and hunger
– later, episodes of violent action may occur. These disturbances can be temporarily reversed by taking the drug again.
– chronic weight loss and dietary deficiencies
– amphetamine psychosis (as with short term use)
– violence. Because of a distortion of perception and paranoid interpretation of reality some users may become aggressive and violent.
– may be occasional risk to blood vessels and of heart failure because amphetamine raises the blood pressure and increases heart rate

Signs and symptoms of amphetamine induced state
Client appears restless and talkative and over-active. There may be signs of anxiety and irritability with a low frustration threshold. Paranoid symptoms may range from suspicious reactions to definite paranoid delusions, according to the frequency and intensity of use. Loss of weight. Fine tremor sometimes occurs.

Management of toxic state
Try and reassure client that nothing terrible is going to happen. This can be a very lengthy and tiring process according to the nature of the client's reactions to the drug. In acute toxic states, especially those resembling a paranoid psychosis, seek medical help. Short-term admission to a psychiatric unit may need to be considered or a residential detoxification facility (eg drug crisis centre). Client will be very tired and exhausted and extremely hungry. Psychotic symptoms may take a week to wear off as drug is excreted and depression may be evident for some time.

Cocaine

Cocaine has returned to popularity in the past decade, particularly amongst the well-off, primarily as a form of recreational drug use. In contrast to the 1960s – when most available cocaine was obtainable on prescription (mainly by heroin addicts) – today's supplies are illicit, originating from South America. There the leaves of the Andean coca shrub may be chewed or infused as a beverage and in these circumstances use is controllable and socialised as with tea and coffee. The leaves may be used by the natives to help them cope with arduous or extra work. The cocaine sold on the black market in Britain has been extracted from the coca leaf and made into a white powder ('snow').

Cocaine was first extracted in 1855 and became a popular stimulant and tonic. A coca-based tonic wine was enjoyed by nineteenth-century popes and royalty, while, until 1904, Coca-Cola, formulated by a chemist as a tonic, contained a significant quantity of cocaine – now replaced by caffeine. Historically it has tended to be seen in this country as a rich man's drug with perhaps equal status to champagne, although there is evidence that its use is spreading to other groups.

Legal status

Stringently controlled under the Misuse of Drugs Act carrying the highest penalties. Class A drug. Only licensed doctors are able to prescribe to addicts although cocaine has rarely been prescribed for self-administration since 1970.

Medical use

Used as a local anaesthetic in eye and throat surgery. May be included in a euphoriant mixture in the management of terminal illness.

Administration

Most recreational users sniff cocaine up the nose through a tube (e.g. a £5 note rolled up) so that it is absorbed into the blood supply through the nasal membranes. Some may inject it and/or mix it with heroin.

Effects

These are similar to short acting amphetamines. Therefore these notes should be read in conjunction with the previous notes on amphetamines.

Short-term use

– produces feelings of exhilaration, well-being, of possessing great physical strength and mental capacity
– reduces hunger and gives a marked indifference to pain and fatigue
– when sniffed, the psychological effects tend to peak after fifteen to thirty minutes and then subside. The user may repeat the dose every twenty minutes to maintain the effect.
– sometimes the desired effects are replaced by anxiety and panic
– larger doses can lead to extreme anxiety, agitation, paranoia and possibly hallucinations – similar to amphetamine psychosis

After-effects

– can include fatigue, sleeplessness and depression although less noticeable than the corresponding effects of amphetamine use

– excessive doses can cause sudden death brought about by respiratory or heart failure, although this is rare
– cocaine may also be adulterated with other substances which can be harmful when injected

Long-term use
– no significant withdrawal symptoms or tolerance, even for repeated doses
– strong psychological dependence may develop to the grandiose feelings of physical and mental well-being. The user may be tempted to increase the dose to counteract the increased after-effects of fatigue, sleeplessness and depression.

Chronic frequent use
– produces an increase in the unpleasant symptoms. The euphoria is replaced by an uncomfortable state of restlessness, hyper-excitability, nausea, insomnia and loss of weight.
– may make user chronically nervous, excitable and paranoid
– paranoid psychosis (cocaine psychosis) may develop. This can include tactile hallucinations causing the sufferer to scratch at imaginary bugs under the skin.
– these unpleasant side effects generally clear up once use is discontinued
– repeated sniffing damages the membranes lining the nose and can also damage the septum (structure separating the nostrils)
– long term injecting can lead to abscesses and generally expose the user to the special risks of this method of administration.

Crack
An extremely potent smokable form of cocaine derived from cocaine hydrochloride powder. It is therefore 'free-base' cocaine produced by an easier method. Despite extensive publicity stemming from its use in the United States, there is little evidence of its availability in the UK.

Caffeine
Caffeine is to be found in the most commonly used beverages, tea and coffee, soft drinks such as Coca-Cola and in over-the-counter analgesics and a range of proprietary stimulant medicines. In the latter context caffeine itself is a white powder used as a mild stimulant in preparations. It is not subject to any legal controls on its manufacture, sale, distribution, or possession. Taken in moderation in tea or coffee the drug allays drowsiness and fatigue, helping to prevent boredom and tiredness interfering with performance on manual and intellectual tasks. Very heavy consumption, particularly of black coffee, can produce over-stimulation with symptoms similar to that of an anxiety state. Abrupt withdrawal from heavy use has been known to produce irritability and migraine-type headaches. Each cup of instant coffee contains about 65 mg of caffeine (although this varies from brand to brand), brewed coffee (drip method) about 115 mg, percolated about 80 mg. Tea and cola drinks contain on average 60 mg a cup or glass.

Nicotine

Nicotine is a complex drug with a variety of effects. Although clearly not socially perceived as a 'drug' in the same context as others described in this section, it should be noted that it is pharmacologically probably the most commonly consumed dangerous stimulant drug. It is predominantly a mild stimulant producing euphoriant effects and strong psychological dependence, which many consumers spend a long time trying to overcome. It is a major factor in consideration of chronic medical problems including bronchitis, hypertension, coronary disease, lung and other cancers which account for large numbers of premature deaths in middle age and early old age.

Anti-depressants

Anti-depressants are effective in the treatment of severe depression. They are not attractive to the patient (consumer) because of their unpleasant side-effects such as dry mouth, tiredness and blurred vision. They do not produce an immediate stimulation of mood. Their effect tends to build up over a period of days. The majority have a potential for fatal overdose.

They include:
Tofranil and *Tryptizol* (tricyclic anti-depressants)
Nardil and *Parnate* (monoamine-oxidase inhibitors) act somewhat differently by potentiating sympathetic amines (amphetamines, adrenalin, etc). Users need to avoid eating certain contra-indicated foods, for example cheese and chocolate and drinks such as *Marmite* and *Bovril*. This group of drugs have some stimulant action and they can dramatically increase the physical effects of amphetamines causing severe and potentially fatal reactions.

Opiates

also referred to as natural and synthetic opiates or narcotics

This group can be subdivided into two main groups. First, the natural opiates – those substances derived from the opium poppy such as morphine and heroin – and the synthetic opiates, strictly referred to an 'non-opiate major analgesics', and including drugs such as methadone and *Diconal*. The principal constituent of opium is morphine with some natural codeine although most derivatives (including medicinal codeine) are derived by chemical modification of morphine. Heroin is readily produced by heating morphine with acetic acid. Historically, many of these substances have been produced to provide a safer and less addictive remedy for physical pain. Many of the synthetic 'opiates' were produced in attempts to develop an analgesic (pain-killer) without addictive properties. All these drugs are capable of producing both physical and psychological dependence.

The principal opiate drugs include:

Opium, morphine, codeine, heroin (diacetylmorphine, diamorphine)
Slang terms – smack, junk, H, horse.

Heroin

Has usually been the preferred drug of choice for most opioid users. This is probably because of its quick action and the relative absence of undesirable side-effects associated with some of the other opioids (eg nausea, vomiting, constipation). Its potency makes the smuggling of small amounts more profitable. Most of the heroin available today is illegal – street heroin. It is likely to be adulterated (ie not 100 per cent pure) with a variety of powders such as talc, glucose, chalk dust, caffeine, quinine and flour. Although it was possible to obtain pharmaceutical heroin on prescription until the early 1970s, it is now rarely given to new patients, or to long-term patients obtaining a maintenance prescription from a treatment centre, the majority having been transferred to methadone mixture or linctus.

The opioid drugs include:

Pethidine (*Pethilorfan, Pamergan*), methadone (*Physeptone*), dipipanone (*Diconal*), dextromoramide (*Palfium*), dihydrocodeine (*DF118*), dextropropoxyphene (*Distalgesic*)

Over-the-counter remedies

There is a range of opiate-based preparations that can be purchased from the chemists' shops. Some drug users may prefer these because of their easy availability and legal status, while others with a preference for stronger opiates will resort to their use when cash, heroin or other alternatives are unobtainable. These products are subject to regular scrutiny because of their misuse potential. They include *Actifed*, *Phensydyl* and *codeine linctus* (all codeine based), *Gee's linctus* and *Collis Browne's mixture* (opium based), and *Kaolin and Morphine* mixture (morphine based).

Misuse of these products by daily consumption of several bottles of the preferred medicine can result in physical dependence, necessitating gradual withdrawal on, for example, methadone mixture as with the opioid drugs. For example, 1.4% opium in 100 ml *Dr Collis Browne* is equivalent to 10 mgm methadone.

Legal status

All opioids, except for over-the-counter preparations, are controlled by the Misuse of Drugs Act.

They are classified as follows:

Class A: Heroin, morphine, opium, methadone, dipipanone, pethidine
Class B: Codeine and dyhydrocodeine (*DF118*) – unless prepared for injection when it counts as Class A
Class C: Dextropropoxyphene (*Distalgesic*)

Only licensed doctors are allowed to prescribe heroin, cocaine and dipipanone to addicts. Strictly speaking, general practitioners can still prescribe these drugs for genuine physical conditions.

Medical uses

– acute physical pain, especially heart attacks
– post-operative pain
– chronic pain – usually only given for terminal illness, eg cancer

– cough suppression and symptomatic treatment of diarrhoea.

Method of administration
Medical use – usually orally or intra-muscular or intra-venous injection. When heroin is used non-medically it is likely to be used in a variety of ways. Initially it may be either sniffed (also called 'snorted') up the nose, or smoked. If the latter method is used the heroin powder is heated (in silver paper) and the fumes usually inhaled through a small tube. This practice is known as 'chasing the dragon'.

Heroin powder may also be dissolved in water and injected. Although sniffing and smoking heroin has become more fashionable since the late 1970s, the committed opiate user is still likely to transfer to injecting in order to obtain maximum effect of the drug. Some opioids are specifically prepared for injectable purposes – eg methadone freeze-dried ampoules. Others are not intended for injection, eg *Diconal*; misuse of this drug can cause unpleasant physical side-effects. Methadone, the synthetic opiate prescribed by drug clinics in the treatment of physical dependence is dispensed in both injectable and oral form. It is the latter, either as methadone mixture or linctus preparation that is primarily prescribed to opiate addicts.

Main effects and side-effects
In a therapeutic (medical) setting opioids are used to relieve physical pain, while effectively distancing the person from pain. In fact, the pain may still be perceived but the reaction to it is weakened. A state of contentment is achieved as the drugs bring detachment from concern and freedom from distressing emotion. It is the latter effect that non-therapeutic drug users are seeking.

The effects can be subdivided into four groups:

– depressant action – producing pain relief, respiratory depression and reduction of cough reflex
– mood change – produces a detached euphoric effect and tendency to withdraw
– stimulant actions – vomiting, pin-point pupils, dilation of blood vessels (giving feeling of warmth)
– direct action on the gut – depresses bowel activity causing constipation

Short-term effects
This means those effects that appear rapidly after a single dose and disappear within a few hours. The non-therapeutic user seeks an immediate surge of pleasure (a 'rush'), then a fixed state of gratification into which hunger, pain and stress do not intrude.

First use of heroin is invariably accompanied by nausea and vomiting. Some experimenters will be deterred by this, while others will be encouraged by the effect of the euphoria and reassurance from others that if they continue they will find that the unpleasant reactions quickly disappear with repeated doses.

Injection into the veins intensifies the effect, while injection into the muscle or under the skin ('skin-popping') produces a slower and less intensive effect. Sniffing heroin gives a less intensive effect than intravenous use. Smoking heroin produces a rapid effect, but with less intensity than in intravenous use as the available dose is used over a period of time rather than injected all at once. Unlike barbiturates, there is little interference with sensation, motor skills or intellect even when in a euphoriant state. With high doses the user become increasingly sedated, drowsy and contented. Excessive doses produce stupor and coma.

Long-term effects
These are the effects provoked by use over a long period of time.

The two primary effects are:

– a marked development of tolerance and need to increase the dosage
– development of physical and psychological dependence with occurrence of withdrawal syndrome if supply is suddenly stopped

Other long-term effects include:

– physical self-neglect due to the satiating effect of the drug
– marked social withdrawal may occur
– no long-term physical damage occurs directly due to the drug but physical complications and illnesses can occur that are related to infections caused by unsterile injection techniques, the injection of adulterants and the lifestyle of some regular injectors. The illnesses include HIV infection, serum hepatitis, cellulitis, endocarditis, pulmonary complications, abscesses at injection sites, respiratory complaints and constipation. Female users are likely to develop an irregular menstrual cycle, sometimes resulting in complete cessation of periods for months or years if on continuous high doses.

Signs and symptoms of drug-induced state
Generally, the client is quiet and withdrawn with eyelids partially closed and head nodding periodically as if dropping off to sleep. These signs are more likely to be noticeable with recent or high dosages (this is known as 'gouching out' or 'on the nod'). May have increased pulse rate and, with larger doses, slow respiratory rate.

The eyes have pinpoint pupils which become dilated about eight hours after the last injection. They will not appear pinpointed if opioid drugs are taken with stimulants at the same time (eg with amphetamine or cocaine).

Recent needle marks are usually a fair indication of current use by injection. Opioid drugs cause less irritation to the surrounding tissues than barbiturates, except for *Diconal*, which is highly irritating to the tissues. The tablets are ground up and injected, causing prolonged tissue reactions, even when filtered before injecting.

The withdrawal syndrome (also known as the abstinence syndrome)
This can develop after as little as three days of regular high doses, but more often after three to four weeks of regular high dosage use, if the supply is suddenly stopped. The effects appear or are experienced as similar to a bad bout of flu. They can start from eight to twenty-four hours after the last dose, generally sooner with heroin and later with

methadone which is a longer-acting drug. The withdrawal state reaches peak intensity at about twenty-four to forty-eight hours and subsides spontaneously over seven to ten days.

At the onset of withdrawal the symptoms are yawning, sneezing, water eyes, running nose, perspiration and dilated pupils. The person is tremulous, goose-fleshy, extremely anxious and irritable. There may be nausea, vomiting and diarrhoea which can lead to dehydration. There may be an increase in blood pressure and abdominal and muscle craps. It is unlikely to be fatal in a young adult – the main danger lies in possible unrecognised and additional dependence on barbiturates. It is less dangerous than withdrawal from alcohol or barbiturates. Feelings of weakness and loss of well-being can last for several months.

Historically, this state is known as going 'cold turkey' when someone has to stop using opiates without any medical help. 'Cold turkey' refers to the cold goose-fleshy appearance of the skin – similar to that of a plucked turkey.

Volatile Solvents

There is a wide range of household and industrial products that have been subject to misuse in Britain since the early 1970s, and in America since the 1950s. These products contain volatile hydrocarbons (organic chemicals) which are produced from petrol and natural gases. Because they are volatile and evaporate quickly at room temperature they are regarded as an essential base for fast-drying products such as glues and paints. The inhalation of solvents and similar chemicals is not peculiar to this generation; ether was inhaled in Victorian times and produced effects similar to those of the modern solvents. The principal effect obtained when their vapours are inhaled is one of intoxication, similar to that of alcohol or anaesthetics.

The majority of solvent sniffers are likely to be in their early to mid-teens, although some start much earlier, while some continue beyond adolescence into their twenties. The inhalation of these solvents has always appeared to be a largely experimental or casual (recreational) experience for the majority as with other peer group activities and crazes. A minority of users may continue sniffing on a daily basis for several years and develop a strong psychological dependence. For the consumer the main sought-after effects are a desire to become euphoric and intoxicated and to experience visual hallucinations.

Products likely to be misused
Historically, solvent inhalation has invariably been referred to as 'glue-sniffing' because the glues or adhesives were the most popular and publicised products. The volatile hydro-carbons are to be found in three main groups of products – first, as solvents in glues, paints, dry-cleaning fluids, nail varnish removers, shoe dyes, type-writing fluid, etc; secondly, as fuels in petrol and cigarette-lighter gas (butane); and thirdly, as propellant gases in aerosols. Although the glues continue to be more popular, other products may be used from preference or because of reduced availability of the adhesives. The

possible list of household products with abuse potential is probably unknown. Although there are approximately twenty-three chemicals that have implications for misuse, toluene in adhesives is probably the most common.

The following are some of the commonly abused products and the solvents they contain:

Product	Solvent
Adhesives and glues	Acetone and toluene
Dry-cleaning substances	Trichloroethylene, trichloroethane, tetrachloroethylene, carbon tetrachloride
Dyes	Acetone, methylene chloride
Hair lacquer	Methanol, ethanol
Lighter refills	Butane
Nail polish remover	Acetone and amyl acetate
Aerosols	Fluorocarbon propellants
Petrol	Benzene and other aromatic compounds
Typewriter correction fluid (thinner)	Trichloroethane

Legal status
There are no current legal controls against the use, distribution or possession of solvents. Under Scottish Law it is an offence to 'recklessly' sell solvents to children knowing they intend to inhale them. Scottish social work legislation lists solvent misuse as a possible reason for making compulsory care or supervision orders in respect of children under seventeen years of age. In England, Wales and Northern Ireland it is an offence for a retailer to supply a substance (other than a controlled drug) to under eighteen-year-olds 'If he knows or has reasonable cause to believe that the substance is or its fumes are likely to be inhaled . . . for the purpose of causing intoxication'.

Method of administration
Solvents can be inhaled in a variety of ways – all resulting in the inhalation of the fumes, vapours or gases through the nose or the mouth. The most common method is to pour the glue into a polythene bag, hold it to the nose and mouth, and with deep breaths inhale the fumes from the chemicals.

Other methods include:

– soaking a cloth in the solution and holding it up to the mouth and nose for inhalation
– sniffing from the container, such as the can of glue or bottle filled with dry-cleaning fluid
– sniffing from hankies, cuffs or lapels, etc, soaked in the product (not so apparent to observers)
– sniffing from a large bag (eg bin-liner) placed over the head, or while sniffing from a smaller bag, pulling a larger bag down over the head to exclude oxygen and derive maximum effect from the fumes
– spraying aerosols directly into the mouth

Short-term effects

The effects may last for five minutes to half an hour approximately, and sometimes longer, depending upon the amount used and the length of the sniffing session. With small doses the main feeling derived is one of euphoria and exhilaration, lack of co-ordination, dizziness and disorientation, similar to the early stages of alcohol intoxication; the intensity depending on the concentration of exposure to the fumes.

– solvents act as depressants on the central nervous system. Therefore normal breathing and heart rate are depressed. Increased or repeated use can lead to loss of control, slurred speech and loss of consciousness. If the sniffer remains in contact with the fumes after this (normally the bag should fall away from the face as they lose consciousness thus allowing oxygen to return), there is a risk of increased unconsciousness leading to death.

– larger doses may produce hallucinogenic experiences; approximately 50 per cent of users are said to experience these. Sometimes referred to as 'images' or 'dreams' by the sniffers, they are usually visual and vivid, occasionally auditory, and may be experienced as good or bad.

– in *some* individuals the state of mind can be similar to a psychotic state

– cross-tolerance occurs with other depressant drugs such as alcohol and sedative-tranquillisers

Acute effects and after-effects

Immediate after-effects may include a headache and hangover (similar to alcohol) and sometimes depression. Some may repeat the experience in order to counteract the unpleasant side-effects and risk becoming increasingly intoxicated as a result. *Note* – this is not the same as physical dependence which rarely appears to occur. Those sniffing small amounts on a casual basis may suffer minimal after-effects.

For many, some or all of the following acute effects may be observed:

– asphyxiation, accidents, cardiac sensitivity and tachycarditis
– tinnitus (ringing in the ears), the sign of the start of the hallucinatory experience
– partial or complete amnesia – many users have little recollection of what has happened after the sniffing episode is over, or, more important, cannot remember the advice or counselling of concerned workers/parents
– flushed skin
– bloodshot eyes, dilated pupils
– nausea and vomiting
– electro-encephelograph changes may occur and very occasionally epileptic type seizures

Lingering after-effects
– halitosis (smell of breath)
– bloodshot eyes

– chronic rhinitis – running nose and eyes, sniffing as if sniffer has a cold
– acne-like rash on face, cause by irritant effect of the chemicals when prolonged application of the bag or cloth to the face has occurred. These may appear as a rash or boils and should clear up when the sniffing phase ceases
– lethargy and tiredness
– irritability and depression
– nightmares or sleep disturbances sometimes associated with the hallucinogenic experience
– headache and general hangover

Long-term effects
These occur after prolonged periods of regular sniffing:

– tolerance develops, so that after sniffing for perhaps a year a sniffer may need to inhale several times more, in order to get high, than originally
– repeated hangover effects of tiredness, loss of appetite, amnesia, loss of concentration and general debility can become a recurring daily pattern in reducing ability to function and cope with everyday pressures. There may be weight loss, depression, tremor, interferences with liver and kidney function, and bronchitic disorders caused by the effect of the fumes on the lungs. These seem to clear up once sniffing has stopped.
– extensive research has been carried out to investigate possible long-term effects, ie physical damage, to different parts of the body including the liver, kidneys, brain, bone, lungs and chromosomes. There is some evidence to suggest that very long-term solvent misuse can result in moderate lasting impairment of brain function, affecting especially the control of movement. Chronic misuse of aerosols and cleaning fluids has caused lasting kidney and liver damage. Repeated sniffing of leaded petrol may result in lead poisoning. Despite the evidence that these solvents have the potential for toxicity, there appears to be little evidence of harm to the majority of youngsters, even those who have sniffed over several years. Several surveys suggest that evidence of harm in Britain is limited to an isolated number of cases, while international studies demonstrate that those more at risk are workers employed in industrial settings who have been exposed to the fumes of industrial solvents over a period of ten to twenty years.
– although withdrawal symptoms have been observed, physical dependence is not a recognised problem
– psychological dependence on the effect of the solvents occurs in a minority of committed regular sniffers. These youngsters develop a strong attachment to the sniffing ritual and effects, repeating the experience in order to alleviate stress, boredom, depression and general unhappiness. The majority have an earlier history of social and/or emotional difficulties and generally need more intensive help from professionals.

Risks
– overdose due to excessive inhalation or using a polythene bag over

the head to obtain maximum effect. If undetected this can lead to unconsciousness and death from suffocation or swallowing vomit.

– overdosing or intoxicated behaviour can cause accidents to the sniffer or to others

– bizarre hallucinations can create a false sense of power in the user causing him to believe that he can do things he would not normally attempt, such as flying, jumping off high buildings or into a canal when intoxicated and unable to swim. Some deaths have been attributed to this phenomenon.

– sniffing alone in an isolated place (can result in some of the earlier risks occurring when they could otherwise have been prevented)

– development of psychological dependence on the use of psycho-active substances as compensation for emotional or social discomfort, and thus the development of faulty coping methods in dealing with problems and life in general

– general debility, short-term illnesses and loss of weight (as described in long-term effects). These clear up when sniffing is discontinued

– aerosol gases and cleaning fluids sensitise the heart to the effects of exertion or excitement and can cause heart failure, especially if the sniffer exerts himself at the same time by, for example, running away to escape the wrath or concern of observers. Gases in the form of aerosols or lighter fuel refills squirted into the mouth can cause death through suffocation.

– death, despite all these risks, is a comparatively rare occurrence. However, when it does happen it is more likely to be associated with the inhalation of aerosols or butane gas, or with bags being placed over the head, than the more usual practice of sniffing glue from a small bag or cloth held up to the mouth and nose. It is as likely to happen to the inexperienced (first time) sniffer as to the chronic sniffer because of the former's lack of knowledge.

Signs and symptoms

As with some other drugs, it is difficult to assess accurately whether someone has been sniffing or not. Many so-called symptoms could well be used to describe other forms of adolescent behaviour so caution should be used in describing signs of solvent sniffing, especially in young people. It must also be remembered that many of the immediate effects and after-effects are similar to those of alcohol, and that some sniffers may well have been drinking alcohol while sniffing solvents, and possibly taking other drugs as well.

There are, however, certain more obvious and distinguishing features that can be identified:

– the smell of glue or other products on the person
– signs of glue on the person's clothing, around the nose and mouth
– drunken behaviour, slurred speech, unsteady walk
– rash or boils around the nose and mouth (as described earlier). These could be part of normal adolescence.

Other factors that may be attributed to sniffing, but not always include:

- loss of appetite and weight
- behavioural or mood change, secretiveness
- irritability, tiredness, argumentative, aggressive behaviour
- general debility and tiredness
- a recurrent cough caused by irritation in the lungs

Management of intoxicated or overdosed state

1 *If the sniffer is intoxicated and disorientated:*
- approach in a firm and caring, but not confrontational, manner
- remove the user from the glue environment, or open windows and remove solvent from the room, avoiding getting into an aggressive battle with user who may try and hang on to the product
- stay with him to ensure he will not injure himself
- remain calm and reassuring, offer hot drink such as coffee as he sobers up and, if possible, see that he returns home safely

2 *If breathing is shallow or absent:*
Make sure all airways are clear and then apply artificial respiration techniques. Place a handkerchief or piece of cloth over the sniffer's mouth to prevent the rescuer from inhaling the fumes.

3 *If sniffer is unconscious:*
- remove from the glue environment as above
- turn on the left lateral position to ensure that vomit cannot be inhaled
- phone immediately for an ambulance and transfer to hospital

Halucinogenic (psychedelic) drugs

This group contains a range of drugs that have similar effects in terms of altering mood, sensations, perception and consciousness. This may involve distortion of perception and hallucinations (the perception of phenomena that have no objective reality). Cannabis tends to be linked with this group but its classification is debatable. It is the least potent of the psychedelic drugs, often thought to be primarily a mild intoxicant, similar to alcohol. There is evidence that a high dose of cannabis in some individuals can occasionally produce effects similar to those of the hallucinogens and it is not unusual to find that milder aspects of the hallucinogenic experience occur when cannabis is consumed. Because of the markedly different effects experienced by most low dose, social cannabis users this drug will be considered separately.

Lysergic acid diethylamide – LSD

This can be regarded as a true hallucinogen. It is derived from ergot, a fungus found growing wild on rye and other grasses. It has been the hallucinogenic drug most frequently used in the United Kingdom, particularly during the late 1960s and early 1970s. It has mostly been used as a recreational drug, sometimes associated with cannabis, and historically, in the days of 'flower power', used for mind expansion. Few users are likely to develop dependency problems although some might develop a psychological dependence on the effects. It was isolated in 1938, and was accidentally ingested in 1943 by its discoverer, who underwent the first LSD trip. It is extremely potent and only a few micrograms are needed for effect, say, between 50 and 100 μg for a significant experience.

Legal status
LSD is a Class A drug, controlled under the Misuse of Drugs Act, prohibiting medical and non-medical use, but providing for medical use under special licence.

Medical use
This drug was used therapeutically in the 1950s and 1960s until prescribing ceased in 1968. It was used as an abreactive technique in psychiatry in a controlled setting, to assist in uncovering unconscious and repressed thoughts, memories and feelings during psychotherapy.

Method of administration
– usually taken by mouth. It is a white powder, generally mixed with other substances in the form of tablets or capsules and swallowed.
– it may also be in a solution and absorbed on blotting paper or in sugar cubes.
– it may occasionally be injected.

Short-term effects
A 'trip' normally starts about thirty minutes after ingestion and can last for several hours; it can vary a great deal. On average, it peaks after two to six hours and fades out after twelve hours. The effects experienced depend on dosage, and to a large extent the setting. The same person can have 'good' (pleasant) or 'bad' (frightening) trips on different occasions, even within the same trip. Whilst LSD experience is variable, compared with other drugs it is relatively more open to the user's intentions and the suggestions of others.
– perception of time and space is distorted. Visual effects include intensified colours, distorted shapes and sizes. Hearing is also distorted.
– heightened self-awareness occurs and sometimes mystical or ecstatic experiences. Feelings of dissociation from the body may be reported.
– physical effects include dizziness, increased blood pressure, dilation of the pupils and relaxation of lung muscles
– the underlying mood is exaggerated, so that in an anxious, severely depressed or unstable individual a psychotic episode or suicide may be a risk. If the former occurs this is usually short lived, characterised by paranoia and hallucinations.
– panic reactions may occur in a 'bad trip'.

Long-term effects
– chronic anxiety and psychotic reactions may occur in predisposed individuals
– flashbacks can occur. These are a re-experience for a brief period of a trip and cause variable disturbances. They usually appear after repeated use and can leave the person feeling disorientated, anxious and depressed. They are rarely dangerous.

186

– there is no evidence of brain damage
– there might possibly be risks to the developing foetus but there is less evidence than for cannabis, tobacco, caffeine or alcohol
– no physical dependence, but a minority may develop psychological dependence

Symptoms of drug induced state
– user may appear restless, agitated, euphoric and excited
– may have a sense of observing while participating, see distortions of reality, hallucinations and express feelings of tremendous insight
– may have increased blood pressure and heart rate (pulse). Pupils may be dilated or constricted.
– physically, the user may suffer occasional nausea, sweating, tremors and poor co-ordination
– mentally, he may be in an acute state of distress, frightened or suspicious. Self-destructive or aggressive acts may occur, and the user may feel very anxious, depressed, out of control and fear that he is going mad.

Management of drug induced state
– separate user if possible from others
– provide friendly reassurance if possible in a calm undemanding environment, away from loud music or other noises. Talk quietly.
– make the person physically comfortable
– reassure the person that the effects are caused by the drug and not 'madness'. Try to focus attention on pleasant phenomena rather than the hallucinations.

Risks
– suicides or deaths related to LSD due to false perceptions do occur, although they are very rare. Death due to overdose is unknown.
– driving is contra-indicated

Psilocybin (Hallucinogenic mushrooms)
Also known as 'magic mushrooms', psilocybin is the active halluci-nogenic ingredient in the psilocybe mushroom and some of the other psilocybe and conocybe species. It has attracted attention since the late 1970s because people have discovered that the mushrooms grow wild in this country. They have to some extent been used as a legal and more organic alternative to LSD. A bewildering array of hallucinogenic plants were used by ancient tribes as a means of gaining access to the spirit world. There seem to be a dozen or so hallucinogenic fungi that grow in Britain, most containing psilocybin or psilocin. These were sacred intoxicants used by the Aztecs of Mexico at the time of the Spanish Invasion in the sixteenth century. Psilocybin mushrooms may be eaten fresh, cooked or brewed into a tea. They may also be preserved by drying. The most commonly occurring and used species seems to be the liberty cap, which is also the most consistently potent. It fruits between September and November, as far north as Glasgow. About twenty to thirty liberty caps are required for a full hallucinogenic experience.

Legal status
The drugs themselves are normally illegal classified under Class A of

the Misuse of Drugs Act. But mushrooms are not illegal until they are boiled or crushed to make a 'preparation or other product' containing psilocin or psilocybin. The courts are likely to convict if they are crushed.

Short-term effects
– similar to LSD, although more signs of euphoria and hilarity. Effects start after about half an hour and peak at three hours, lasting for about four to nine hours, longer with higher doses.
– with low doses, eg two to four mushrooms, euphoria and detachment predominate
– at higher doses visual distortions can progress to vivid 'pseudo-hallucinations' of colour and movement
– physically may feel nausea, and suffer from vomiting and stomach pains
– prominent signs of physiological arousal including increased heart rate, blood pressure and pupil size
– inexperienced, depressed or anxious users may experience 'bad trips', see *Risks*

Long-term effects
– tolerance develops rapidly so, for example, the next day it may take twice as many liberty caps to produce the same experience
– no significant withdrawal symptoms, no apparent physical dependence
– psychological dependence may occur with consumers who wish to keep repeating the experience
– currently no substantial evidence of serious lasting effects
– flashbacks and recurrent anxiety attacks may occur

Management of drug induced state
– similar to LSD

Risks
– 'bad trips', characterised by deep fear and anxiety, can, in inexperienced or unhappy users, develop into a psychotic episode
– greatest danger comes from risk that users may pick poisonous amanita species by mistake. These can be mistaken for the liberty cap and can cause death in up to 50 per cent of cases. Fatal poisoning due to mistaken identity has not so far been confirmed in Britain.

Cannabis
Much controversy exists around this drug which, although illegal, is widely used recreationally for relaxation and as a mild intoxicant. It has been, and still is, the subject of continuous scientific studies and political debate internationally to determine objective evidence of harm and its consequent legal status. It is derived from the plant Cannabis Sativa, found wild in most parts of the world and easily cultivated in Britain. The main ingredient that produces the typical effects on mood and perception is called tetrahydrocannabinol (THC). Cannabis can be prepared in three forms:

a *Marijuana*
Also known as grass, pot, weed, smoke. It is made from the leaves and flowers of the plant.

b *Hash or hashish*
This is the commonest form of cannabis in Britain. It is a dried cake resin produced from the tops and leaves of the female plant. It is compressed into blocks, resembling Oxo cubes.

c *Cannabis oil*
Less common in Britain, it is prepared by percolating a solvent through the resin.

Legal status
Controlled under the Misuse of Drugs Act for both medical and non-medical use. Cannabis in herbal form (except for seeds and stalks), cannabis resin, and cannabis oil are controlled under Class B. Active chemical ingredients, 'cannabinoids' that have been separated from the plant, are Class A drugs.

It is illegal to supply, cultivate, produce or possess the drug, except in accordance with a Home Office licence issued for research or other special purposes. It is an offence to allow premises to be used for producing – including cultivating – supplying or smoking cannabis. Allowing the actual use of a drug applies only to cannabis or opium.

Short-term effects
It must be stressed that the effect of this drug depends to a large degree on the expectation, mood and social setting of the user.
– basically acts as a depressant drug on the central nervous system
– tends to exaggerate the underlying mood of the consumer
– causes talkativeness, laughter, heightened sensory perceptions of sound and colour
– interferes with short term memory
– with larger doses, perceptual distortions may occur. In an apprehensive or depressed individual panic reactions may occur.
– effects start within a few minutes of smoking and, depending on the dose, may last for several hours. Some people claim there is no hangover.

Long-term effects
– there is little evidence of definite physical dependence occurring
– a small proportion of users develop a psychological dependence so that it becomes essential to their emotions, thoughts and activities
– heavy regular use, especially by teenagers and young adults, is said to lead to the 'amotivational syndrome' – lack of energy or drive, or motivation to plan activities. All one can say is that some individuals spend a long time smoking and lack motivation and spontaneity; however, there is insufficient evidence to suggest that cannabis is the cause and some of these features may have been present prior to drug use.
– frequent inhalation of cannabis smoke over several years may cause bronchitis and other respiratory disorders (as with tobacco). There may be special risks for users with lung, respiratory or heart disorders.

– people with existing or underlying psychiatric disorders may run risks of adverse reactions. Prolonged heavy use may cause a temporary psychiatric disorder including mental confusion and delusions which should clear up within a few days once the drug is stopped.

Long-term damage
Research continues over possible long-term damage. However, to date, there is no conclusive evidence that long-term cannabis use causes damage to either physical or mental health. There may be some evidence from animal studies of long-term ill effects to the regular user such as reduced fertility, chromosome damage, lowered immunity to certain diseases and damage to the developing foetus. It is dangerous to extrapolate from animal studies to human experience. If true, then it almost certainly relates to regular, heavy users and not the occasional user.

Pregnancy
– frequent cannabis use during pregnancy may cause premature births. Findings are conflicting and cannabis use is likely to be one of a number of factors affecting foetal development.
– very heavy users may give birth to babies who temporarily suffer tremor and distress and are easily startled. There is no evidence that adverse effects continue beyond the first year of life. However, as with most other psycho-active drugs, it is clearly wiser to avoid cannabis use during pregnancy.

Drugs and the law – notification procedure

The 1971 Misuse of Drugs Act has already been referred to in Chapters 2 and 9, as well as the previous Appendix where it was discussed in relation to the classification of particular drug groups. The Act also provides for the notification by doctors to the Chief Medical Officer at the Home Office, of those people who are considered to be, or are suspected of being, addicted to certain drugs. Notifiable drugs are: cocaine, dextromoramide (*Palfium*), diamorphine (heroin), dipipanone (*Diconal*), hydrocodone, hydromorphone, levorphanol, methadone (*Physeptone*), morphine, opium, oxycodone, pethidine, phenazocine and piritramide.

If the assessment interview is being completed by a doctor, or if referral is made to a doctor to assist with the treatment plan, the client may need to be formally notified to the Home Office. This procedure affects those drug takers who are considered to be, or are suspected of being, addicted to the drugs noted above, particularly the opioids described in the previous Appendix. Failure to notify within seven days could result in disciplinary action against the doctor. The doctor has to provide data concerning the user's name, address, sex, date of birth and National Health Service number (if available), together with the date of attendance and the names of the drugs concerned.

Many drug takers are reluctant to ask for help for fear of the possible implications of the notification system, still wrongly described by drug takers, many professionals and the media as being 'registered'. The notifications are compiled in the *Addicts Index* at the Home Office, and provide two important sources of information. First, epidemiological data which contributes to the development of national policies on the management of the drug problem, and secondly, as a way of helping the prescribing doctor to check that the client is not already obtaining prescriptions or treatment from another doctor – sometimes referred to as 'double-scripting'.

The doctor or key worker should explain to the client that they have to comply with the law and notify him or her to the Chief Medical Officer at the Home Office. Most clients realise that this is the inevitable price they pay for admitting their addiction to the authorities and asking for help, especially if they want a prescription. It should be explained to them that this information is dealt with in confidence by the Home Office and is not made available to the police and other law enforcement agencies.

Annual Home Office statistics related to notified addicts
The Home Office publishes annual figures relating to the number of

notified addicts, their sex, ages, the drugs used at time of notification, drugs prescribed in treatment and the sources of notification, such as general practitioner, drug clinic or prison. The statistics are normally published in the summer of the following year. They are obtainable at a cost of approximately £2.50 from the Statistical Department, Home Office, Lunar House, Croydon, Surrey CR0 9yd.

It is generally accepted that these annual figures are best seen as 'the tip of an iceberg', and that the actual number of people using opiates on a regular basis is several times, possibly at least five times, the number notified to the Home Office. At best the figures provide a crude means of estimating recent patterns of problem drug taking in Britain, but they do not tell us about people who are using non-notifiable drugs or those who are not in contact with a doctor. Neither, of course, do they tell us about those who are experimental or casual drug users.

During any one year a proportion of those already notified will be denotified, mainly because they are no longer receiving notifiable drugs in treatment (and may have discontinued treatment), but also because of imprisonment and death. A significant number of those who have been denotified because of stopping treatment or imprisonment will be renotified at some stage, usually indicating that they have resumed regular drug use and have returned for further treatment.

The following table shows the number of narcotic addicts notified to the Home Office during the year, the number no longer recorded as addicts, and the number recorded at 31 December. To estimate the actual total number of addicts known to the Home Office during any one year you need to combine the number known to be receiving drugs at 1 January with the number of new addicts and former addicts. The official figures given out in a press release each year tend to refer only to the number known to be still receiving drugs on 31 December, which excludes those who have stopped receiving notified drugs during the year.

United Kingdom   Number of persons

Narcotic drug addicts notified to the Home Office during the year, numbers no longer recorded as addicts, and number recorded at 31 December

	1976	1977	1978	1979	1980	1981	1982	1983	1984	1985
Addicts recorded as receiving notifiable drugs at 1 January	1,949	1,874	2,016	2,402	2,666	2,846	3,844	4,371	5,079	5,869
Persons notified during the year as addicts by medical practitioners:										
New addicts	984	1,109	1,347	1,597	1,600	2,248	2,793	4,186	5,415	6,409
Former addicts	541	622	753	788	841	1,063	1,325	1,678	1,995	2,410
total notified during the year	1,525	1,731	2,100	2,385	2,441	3,311	4,118	5,864	7,410	8,819
Persons no longer recorded as addicts at 31 December:										
Removed by reason of death	63	40	60	49	73	46	49	80	86	93
Admitted to penal/other institutions	513	442	484	553	429	546	607	782	1,308	1,715
No longer recorded as receiving notifiable drugs	1,024	1,107	1,170	1,519	1,759	1,721	2,935	4,294	5,226	5,828
Total no longer recorded	1,600	1,589	1,714	2,121	2,261	2,313	3,591	5,156	6,620	7,636
Addicts recorded as receiving notifiable drugs at 31 December	1,874	2,016	2,402	2,666	2,846	3,844	4,371	5,079	5,869	7,052

Narcotic addicts known to the Home Office. UK 1975–1985

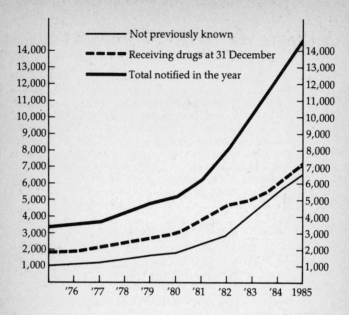

APPENDIX THREE

Sample detoxification regimes

The majority of problem drug takers are likely to detoxify alone without the help of professionals. When opioid addicts want a medically supervised detoxification, the majority are likely to be offered methadone mixture on a reducing prescription, either on an out-patient or in-patient basis. Phenobarbitone is used for withdrawing barbiturate addicts, while those dependent on benzodiazepines (minor tranquillisers) are likely to be withdrawn on reducing doses of diazepam (*Valium*) or equivalent, or perhaps in more severe cases (and preferably as an in-patient) with phenobarbitone.

There are several publications aimed at doctors, which describe detoxification with some sample regimes. These include:

Drug addiction and polydrug abuse: the role of the general practitioner Dr A. Banks and Dr T. A. N. Waller, ISDD 1983.
Guidelines of good clinical practice in the treatment of drug misuse DHSS 1984
Coping with drug misuse in general practice Dr Jackie Chang. Abbot Pharmaceuticals, 1987.

Doctors requiring fuller details to help them plan a detoxification regime should refer to their copy of the DHSS Guidelines and, if they need further advice, contact their local drug dependence clinic. Most experienced doctors suggest that it is generally unwise for a general practitioner to prescribe more than 30 or 40 mgm of methadone mixture to new patients. The length of the detoxification programme should be agreed between doctor and patient, and should be assessed according to the client's drug history, previous attempts to detoxify, current stability, support networks and apparent motivation. In some instances the client's drug of choice may not convert easily into methadone. Table 1 is a rough guide taken from the DHSS guidelines and based on information from City Roads (Crisis Intervention) Limited, London.

Three sample detoxification regimes for opioid users are included to give the reader some idea of the rate and type of reduction currently recommended. Again readers are advised to follow this up with further reading as already suggested.

Two week methadone detoxification

Only suitable for a recently confirmed opioid user, with less than one year's use, and daily use of not more than 40 mg equivalent methadone. Clients need to have stable accommodation and support from family or close friends. 25 mg methadone (25 ml) should be given initially and may follow prior reduction from a higher starting level. If possible the volume of liquid base should be maintained at 25 ml per day, but for safety reasons the actual dose of methadone must be clearly stated on each bottle. A typical course might be: methadone mixture (DTF) 25 mg (three days); 20 mg (three days); 15 mg (three days); 10 mg (three days); and 5 mg (three days).

A four week regime

Meth. mix. (DTF) 30 mg (four days); 25 mg (three days); 20 mg (four days); 15 mg (three days); 10 mg (four days); 6 mg (three days); 3 mg (seven days). The volume of dispensed methadone liquid base should not be less than 20 ml throughout.

A two monthly regime

Meth. mix. (DTF) 40 mg (seven days); 35 mg (seven days); 30 mg (seven days); 25 mg (seven days); 20 mg (seven days); 15 mg (seven days); 10 mg (seven days); 5 mg (seven days). The volume of dispensed methadone base liquid should not be less than 20 ml throughout.

Table 1: Opioid equivalents for prescribing
It is not possible to directly convert the effect, time duration and addictive potential of opioid based drugs to a fixed equivalent of methadone. The following table is a rough guide only*.

Drug		Methadone equivalent
Street heroin	1 gram at £60–80	80 mg (should not be attempted as outpatient)
Street heroin	½ gram at £35	40–60 mg
	¼ gram at approx 2 × £10 'bags'	30–40 mg
Pharmaceutical heroin	10 mg tablet	10 mg
	10 mg freeze dried ampoule	10 mg
	30 mg freeze dried ampoule	25 mg
Methadone	Physeptone ampoule 10 mg	10 mg
	Mixture (1 mg/1ml) 10 ml	10 mg
	linctus (2 mg/5 ml) 10 ml	5 mg
	suppository 50 mg	30–40 mg
	100 mg	80–100 mg (should not be attempted as outpatient)
Morphine	10 mg ampoule	10 mg
Diconal (dipipanone)	10 mg tablet	0–5 mg
DF118 (dihydrocodeine)	30 mg tablet	0–3 mg
Palfium (dextromoramide)	5 mg tablet	5–10 mg
Pethidine	25, 50 mg tablet	3–5 mg
	50 mg ampoule	5 mg

Drug		Methadone equivalent
Temgesic (buprenorphine hydrochloride)	0.2 mg tablet 0.3 mg ampoule	2.5 mg 4 mg
Fortral (pentazocine)	50 mg capsule 25 mg tablet	4 mg 3 mg
Codeine linctus 100 ml Codeine phosphate	300 mg codeine phosphate 15 mg, 30 mg, 60 mg tablets	10 mg 1,2,3 mg
Actifed compound 100 mg	200 mg codeine phosphate	6 mg
Gee's linctus 100 ml	16 mg anhydrous morphine	10 mg
Dr Collis Browne 100 ml	1.4% opium	10 mg

If heroin is smoked, or inhaled ('chasing the dragon'), rather than injected, the methadone equivalent can be reduced by one third.

* Based on information from City Roads project, London (the heroin street prices are those in London 1984).

APPENDIX FOUR

AIDS

Drug takers who self-inject and share needles run a high risk of becoming infected with the HIV virus, and possibly later developing the AIDS disease. This is probably the most daunting and emotionally stressful aspect of dealing with the drug problem in the 1980s. Whether you work in a generic or specialist agency you will need to be able to advise and counsel your drug taking clients about AIDS. Clients need to feel that they can talk about their fears concerning the disease in confidence with their workers. If you work where you may come into contact with contaminated blood or needles you need to take the normal health and safety precautions, as you would when avoiding other infections such as hepatitis.

Some basic facts about AIDS
AIDS is an abbreviation for the *A*quired *I*mmune *D*eficiency *Syn-drome*. It describes an invariably fatal syndrome of diseases resulting from damage to the immune system caused by infection with the HIV virus.

The immune system: body systems responsible for maintaining resistance to disease.

The HIV virus: a human immunodeficiency virus formerly known as the HTLV3 virus. While only a proportion of those with HIV infection will actually develop the AIDS disease (approximately 10 per cent, although the figure may be higher in the long term), a larger proportion will develop less serious non life-threatening illnesses.

HIV antibody: the antibody produced by the body in response to the HIV virus. Tests for HIV infection rely on detecting the presence of this antibody. Absence of this antibody does not necessarily mean that individuals thought to be at risk are clear of infection.

Some people who are infected with the virus stay well and symptom-free, but whether they will continue to do so is uncertain. Although it is difficult to determine who is most likely to develop the actual disease, it is thought that those who manage to stay healthy while infected are likely to be less susceptible to AIDS. This means clients reducing their drug use, eating fresh foods (possibly with vitamin supplements) and sleeping properly.

Some implications for practice
Pre-counselling: that is, providing advice and counselling to help your clients to reduce the risk of infection, and to help them decide whether they want to be tested. There are arguments for and against. Most professionals specialising in this area are against compulsory testing, believing that, whether or not a client is infected, all drug takers need to be counselled on ways of reducing the risk of infection. For

example, stopping injecting altogether would be ideal, but if they cannot they should not share injecting equipment with other drug users, and should always use clean needles. Check to find out whether or not there is a local needle exchange system operating in your area. Drug takers should also follow all the other safeguards advised in the AIDS literature, by restricting their number of sexual partners and always using a condom. While some people may have little difficulty in following this advice, others will find it means being prepared to make a radical behavioural change in their lifestyle.

The majority of drug takers welcome the opportunity to talk about their fears regarding the disease and prefer to take the test, so that they know the worst and at least know where they stand. A number may be too afraid to find out, fearing that if their test is positive there will be nothing to live for. Some may just not be able to cope emotionally with knowing that they may develop AIDS.

Counselling for sero-positive clients

If, after testing, your client is found to be infected with the HIV virus, he or she will need long-term support and counselling, and help in deciding whether they should inform anyone else. While it is important for them to consider what their partner should be told, in some cases it may not be wise for them to inform their family, friends or employer, who may react in a prejudiced and hostile manner. If they need medical or dental treatment, their GP and dentist may need to be informed in strictest confidence, because of the possible contamination from blood or other body fluids.

The staff responsible for carrying out the test are likely to offer short-term counselling automatically but if you know your client well, he will need to know that he can discuss his reactions with you. Typical reactions include: denial (the test must be wrong), guilt, anger, uncertainty (over the diagnosis, the risk to others and the risk of developing AIDS), anxiety about the future, and a sense of powerlessness. 'People feel under control of the virus and not in control of their feelings, emotions or destiny.' (Phoenix House internal strategy paper – *Counselling residents for HTLV3 infection* by Dr Morris Gallagher).

Even if an infected drug user is healthy, he or she can still pass the virus on to others, either by sharing needles or unprotected sexual intercourse. Pregnant women who are infected are particularly at risk of developing the AIDS disease themselves (pregnancy after 20 weeks affects the body's auto-immune system) and of passing the virus on to their baby through the placenta at birth. It is estimated that 50 per cent of the babies infected are likely to develop the disease. For both these reasons, women who are infected are advised against pregnancy. Some will be devastated by this and will need careful counselling.

Other sources of advice and information

This appendix has looked briefly at some of the key issues that concern workers needing to counsel drug takers who may have the HIV virus infection. Many readers will already have detailed information about the disease. Those who have not should check on what is available in their agency or local Health Education department. Some local authorities are establishing specialist posts to help co-ordinate training for professionals and provide support for AIDS patients and their carers. There are several organisations that produce information for professionals and drug takers. They include SCODA, who have a specialist AIDS worker, and the Terrence Higgins Trust (the AIDS charity) which has a drug education officer. They may also be able to advise on support groups for HIV-positive clients in your area. (See *Useful addresses*)

USEFUL ADDRESSES

For further reading, library and bookstall materials and information
Institute for the Study of Drug Dependence (ISDD), 1/4 Hatton Place, Hatton Garden, London EC1 8ND. Telephone: 01–430–1991.
ISDD also publishes DRUGLINK, a journal for professionals dealing with drug problems in Britain.

For advice and information about local services
Standing Conference on Drug Abuse (SCODA), 1/4 Hatton Place, Hatton Garden, London EC1N 8ND. Telephone: 01–430–2341.
SCODA is the national co-ordinating body for voluntary and non-statutory organisations working in the drugs field. They publish a newsletter which deals with issues affecting workers and clients.

Legal and Drug-related advice
Release, 169 Commercial Street, London E1 3BW.
Telephone: 01–377–5905.
Provides advice, information and referral on legal and drug-related problems for users, families and friends. National twenty-four hour EMERGENCY telephone service: 01–603–8654.

For advice and publications concerning drug prevalence studies
Drug Indicators Project, Department of Politics and Sociology, Birkbeck College, University of London, 16 Gower Street, London WC1. Telephone: 01–580–6622, Ext. 2488/2512.

Self-help for drug users
Narcotics Anonymous (NA), PO Box 246, c/o 47 Milman Street, London SW10. Telephone: 01–351–6794 or 351–6066 (24 hours).

Self-help for families and friends of drug users
Families Anonymous (FA), 88 Caledonian Road, London N1. Telephone: 01–278–8805 (24 hours).

For information on counselling and advisory services for young people
National Association of Young People's Counselling and Advisory Services (NAYPCAS), 17/23 Albion Street, Leicester LE1 6GD. Telephone: 0533–558763.
Teachers' Advisory Council on Alcohol and Drug Education (TACADE)
TACADE, 3rd Floor, Furness House, Trafford Road, Salford M5 2XJ. Telephone: 061–848–0351.
TACADE provides educational consultancy, resources centre, and in-service training courses for Local Education Authorities and others concerned with young people and drug education.

Terrence Higgins Trust
BM AIDS, London WC1N 3XX. Telephone: 01–833–2971.

BIBLIOGRAPHY

Books

AUSTIN, G. A. ed. *Perspectives on the history of psycho-active substance abuse.* Research issue, 24 National Institute for Drug Abuse, 1978. Available from NIDA, 5600 Fisher's Lane, Rockville, Maryland, USA.

BANKS, A. and WALLER, T. A. N. *Drug addiction and polydrug abuse* Institute for the Study of Drug Dependency, 1983, op.

BEAN, P. *The social control of drugs* (Law in society) M. Robertson, 1974.

BERRIDGE V. and EDWARDS, G. *Opium and the people: opiate use in nineteenth century England* Allan Lane, 1981.

BLUM, R. H. et al *Society and drugs: social and cultural observations* 2 vols. San Francisco: Jossey-Bass, 1969.

CANADA *Commission of inquiry into the non-medical use of drugs: interim report* Penguin, 1971. op.

CHANG, V. *Coping with drug misuse in general practice* Abbot Laboratories, 1987. Available from Abbot Laboratories Ltd., Queensborough, Kent, ME11 5el)0795 663371).

CUTLAND, L. *Kick heroin* Gateway, 1985.

DEPT HEALTH and SOCIAL SECURITY *Guidelines of good clinical practice in the treatment of drug misuse: report of the Medical Working Group on Dependence* DHSS, 1984. (*See* Useful Addresses).

DEPT HEALTH and SOCIAL SECURITY *Treatment and rehabilitation: report of the Advisory Council on the Misuse of Drugs* HMSO, 1982.

FIELD, T. *Escaping the dragon* Unwin pbk, 1985.

GALLAGHER, M. *Counselling residents for HTLV III infection: a strategy for South Shields* Available from Dr M. Gallagher, Phoenix House, Westoe Drive, South Shields, Tyne and Wear.

HARTNOLL, R. et al *Drug problems: assessing local needs* Drug Indicators Project, 1985. Available from Drug Indicators Project or ISDD (*see* Useful Addresses).

HARTNOLL, R. et al. *Assessing local problems: a short guide* Drug Indicators Project, 1986. Available from Drug Indicators Project (*see* Useful Addresses).

HOME OFFICE *Drug addicts known to the Home Office*, 1985. Statistical bulletin, 40/86 Available from Home Office Statistical Dept, Lunar House, 40 Wellesley Rd, Croydon, Surrey CR0 9yd)01–760 2850).

HOME OFFICE *Prevention: report of the Advisory Council on the Misuse of Drugs* Chairman P. H. Connell. HMSO, 1984.

INSTITUTE FOR THE STUDY OF DRUG DEPENDENCY *Drug abuse briefing* ISDD, 1985. Available from ISDD (*see* Useful Addresses).

INSTITUTE FOR THE STUDY OF DRUG DEPENDENCY *Drugs: What every parent should know* ISDD, 1985. Available from ISDD (see above).

LISHMAN, J. and HOROBIN, G. *Approaches to addiction* (Research highlights in social work, 10) Kogan Page, 1985.

MARLATT, G. A. and GORDON, J. R. eds *Relapse prevention: maintenance and strategies in the treatment of addictive behaviours* Guildford Press, 1985.

MINISTRY OF HEALTH AND SCOTTISH HOME AND HEALTH DEPT.

Drug addiction: the second report of the interdepartmental committee Chairman Lord Brain. HMSO, 1965. op.

MOTT, J. *The social characteristics of non-therapeutic opiate users in the United Kingdom* Home Office Research Unit, 1976. Internal publication.

PEARSON, G., GILMAN, M. and MCIVER, S. *Young people and heroin: an examination of the use of heroin in the north of England* Health Education Council, 1985.

SCHECHTER, A. ed. *Rehabilitation aspects of drug dependence* Cleveland, Ohio: CRC Press, 1977.

STANDING CONFERENCE on DRUG ABUSE *Facts about AIDS for drug workers*, SCODA, 2nd edn, 1986. Available from ISDD (*see* Useful Addresses).

STIMSON, G. V. and OPPENHEIMER, E. *Heroin addiction: treatment and control in Britain* Tavistock, 1982

UNITED NATIONS DIVISION OF SOCIAL AFFAIRS *Community involvement in programmes for the prevention of drug abuse and the social reintegration of users: report of a travelling seminar in Stockholm, Amsterdam and London, 1–20 April, 1975* NY: UN, 1976 (Code SOA/ESDP/1975/1).

UNITED NATIONS FUND FOR DRUG ABUSE CONTROL *The aetiology of psycho-active substance use* C. Fazey. Paris: UNESCO, 1977. op.

WEIL, A. *The natural mind* Cape, 1973; Penguin, 1975. op.

WINICK, C. *Sociological aspects of drug dependence* Cleveland, Ohio: CRC Press, 1974. op.

YOUNG, J. *The drug takers* Paladin, 1971.

Articles

FRASER, A. C. 'Cause for concern: the pregnant drug addict' *Maternal and Child Health*, November 1983, **8** (11), 461–463.

FRY, A. 'Preparing for a major change: Lothian aims to keep AIDS babies out of institutions' *Community Care*, 10 April 1986, no. 606, 4–5.

GAY, M. 'Drug and solvent abuse in adolescents' *Nursing Times*, 29 January 1986, **82**, 34–45.

LAWSON, M. S. and WILSON, G. S. 'Parenting among women addicted to narcotics' *Child Welfare*, February 1980, **S9** (2), 67–79.

MALINOWSKI, A. 'No free lunches' *Drug Link*, September–October 1986, **1** (3), 14. Available from ISDD (*see* Useful Addresses).

MILLER, W. R. 'Motivational interviewing with problem drinkers' *Behavioural Psychotherapy*, April 1983, **11** (2), 147–172.

SALMON, R. and SALMON, S. 'The causes of heroin addiction: a review of the literature, parts I and II' *International Journal of Addiction* 1977, **12** (5), 679–96; **12** (7), 937–51.

STIMSON, G. V., OPPENHEIMER, E. and THORLEY, A. 'Seven-year follow-up of heroin addicts: drug use and outcome' *British Medical Journal*, 6 May 1978, **i**, 1190.

STRANG, J. 'Changing the image of the drug taker' *Health and Social Service Journal*, 11 October 1984, **93** (4918), 1202–1204.

WILLIAMS, M. J. H. 'Cause for concern: the problems of children born of drug addicts' *Maternal and Child Health*, June 1983, **8** (6), 258–263.

'Arson setback for the Midlands' *Turning Point News*, 6 May 1986 (2).

Resources

Drug resource pack City Roads (Crisis Intervention) Limited, 1984. Available from City Roads, 358 City Road, London EC1 (01–837 2772).

INDEX

Acknowledgement is due to the following, whose permission is required for multiple reproduction:

CONTROLLER OF HER MAJESTY'S STATIONERY OFFICE for the table 'Statistical report on the numbers of narcotic drug addicts; the prose taken from *Treatment and rehabilitation report – advisory council on the misuse of drugs*, the table and prose taken from *Guidelines of good clinical practice in the treatment of drug misuse – 1984*; INSTITUTE FOR THE STUDY OF DRUG DEPENDENCE for the prose taken from *Drug Link Nov/Dec 1986* and the graph taken from *Drug Link May/June 1986*; MACMILLAN PUBLISHERS LIMITED for the literary material by J Strang from *Health and Social Services Journal, 11 Oct 1984*.
AUTHOR for literary material by Martyn Gay.